INCLUSIVE EDUCATION
Through the Creative Arts
in the Early Years

INCLUSIVE EDUCATION
Through the Creative Arts in the Early Years

EDITED BY
**AMANDA NILAND, LAURA HUHTINEN-HILDÉN &
KATHY COLOGON**

 Sage

S Sage

1 Oliver's Yard
55 City Road
London EC1Y 1SP

2455 Teller Road
Thousand Oaks
California 91320

Unit No 323-333, Third Floor, F-Block
International Trade Tower
Nehru Place, New Delhi 110 019

8 Marina View Suite 43-053
Asia Square Tower 1
Singapore 018960

Editor: Delayna Spencer
Editorial Assistant: Harry Dixon
Production Editor: Neelu Sahu
Cover Design: Sheila Tong
Typeset by: TNQ Tech Pvt. Ltd.
Indexer: TNQ Tech Pvt. Ltd.
Printed in the UK

Library of Congress Control Number: 2023951526

British Library Cataloguing in Publication data

A catalogue record for this book is available from the British Library

ISBN 978-1-5297-3492-8
ISBN 978-1-5297-3491-1 (pbk)

We would like to express our deep gratitude to all the children and families who have shared their journeys with us, as we built our understanding of inclusion and the power of the arts.
Laura wishes to thank the Association of Finnish Nonfiction Writers for their funding support for her work on this book.

Contents

About the Authors

Dr Amanda Niland (PhD) is a Senior Lecturer in early childhood at the University of Sydney and Programme Director of the Master of Teaching Early Childhood. Amanda has extensive experience as an early childhood teacher, music specialist and early childhood intervention teacher. Her research interests are in the creative arts, particularly music and children's literature, with a focus on their potential for supporting a positive sense of identity and belonging for all children. Amanda has published more than 30 peer-reviewed journal articles, book chapters and monographs, and is an editorial committee member for the *International Journal of Music Education*, *International Journal of Music in Early Childhood* and *Journal of Early Childhood Literacy*. She enjoys singing, playing the piano and ukulele and writing songs and stories for children, and is the author of two picture books.

Dr Laura Huhtinen-Hildén (PhD MMus) is a Principal Lecturer and Researcher at Metropolia University of Applied Sciences (music education and creativity, arts, health and wellbeing) and head of the Master's degree programme Creativity and Arts in Social and Health fields. She also leads the Cultural Wellbeing, Research and Education Centre (CuWeRE) in Finland. Laura developed and served as the Chair for the BA programme in Early Childhood Music Education and Community Music (2007–2022). Her research interests include pedagogically sensitive music education, developing professional knowledge and narrative as well as advancing well-being and health in and through creativity and arts-related practices. Laura has served on the board of the European network for Music Educators and Researchers of Young Children and is currently a board member of the early childhood music education commission of the International Society for Music Education.

Dr Kathy Cologon (PhD) is Principal Consultant at *Toward Equity, Diversity, and Inclusion*, and Honorary Senior Lecturer in Inclusive Education at Macquarie University, Sydney. Kathy is privileged to work with children, families, educators, allied professionals, services and organisations. Driven by a belief in the value of human beings in all our wonderful diversities and recognition of the important implications for the early years and beyond, Kathy seeks to contribute to increasing knowledge and understanding to support opportunities for all people to flourish as valued community members. This requires challenging normative and deficit assumptions and engaging with practical issues relating to children's rights and inclusion. With extensive experience in the early years, and 15 years of educating teachers, Kathy has a depth and breadth of understanding of the many facets of inclusive education. Nationally and internationally renowned for her work in Inclusive Education and Disability Studies, Kathy has published more than 50 papers, book chapters and books.

INTRODUCTION

Amanda Niland, Laura Huhtinen-Hildén and Kathy Cologon

Openness to ongoing learning and critical reflection on our experiences, attitudes and values is at the heart of inclusive pedagogy and practice. Our purpose in writing this book is to support this openness to professional learning and reflective thinking and hence the practice as inclusion in early years settings. In the work each of us does with preservice and practising early years practitioners, and with young children and their families, our aim is to share knowledge about, advocate for and practice inclusive education. This book is another way of working towards those aims.

Many conversations took place during our processes of envisioning and writing this book. For example, we shared with each other how arts-related experiences have influenced our own lives and our journeys as inclusive educators. Inevitably, our thoughts went back to our childhoods:

Many of my strongest childhood memories centred around music – singing or dancing along to the piano being played by my aunt or grandfather. So it was music that opened up my love of the arts, and my journey towards being an inclusive educator. Everyone can gain something from music. (Amanda)

I grew up in a really musical household. Music was everywhere. My family's socialisation was all about music – we were always singing something, playing something – and for me it was very natural to engage with children with music. It was also about visual art. My mum loves art and we would always be painting and drawing and sculpting. My grandmother is an artist and I have such vivid memories of watching her paint and of her teaching me to paint as a child. I can still recall the smells and sounds and feeling of painting with Gran, but also every day when I look at the world around, I remember how she taught me to 'really see' the colours and shapes that are there, which are often so different to what I think they will be. (Kathy)

I think it's most clear with music how it creates an environment that accepts everyone. Almost like a large 'lap' you go into. There is this non-verbal thing that is difficult to describe in words, but it means being accepted. It creates this sense of togetherness, this feeling of being here, now, present, accepted and sharing something valuable. (Laura)

While it seemed that, for each of us, music was especially powerful, we also discussed the many ways that all forms of arts can be companions in the ongoing formation process that makes us who we are today:

> The arts are so rich in terms of creating spaces to explore and express identity. I think they create possibilities that go beyond what you have otherwise for being able to share that and even co-construct that, which is so important. (Kathy)

> I've been thinking about life narratives – creating the 'you' you want to be. Identity formation is a constant process of shaping the narrative, and being in contact with your own creativity through the arts opens up possibilities that otherwise wouldn't be possible. (Laura)

> In my early days as a teacher, I assumed differences were a barrier to understanding and working with children. But engaging in the arts with children who had been labelled as 'different' and seen by some as problematic, I quickly realised that all I needed to know was that here was a child who was a valuable person, a child I wanted to connect with, get to know, and support. And the arts gave us time, space and possibilities for understanding each other. (Amanda)

Another important reflective process in the writing of this book involved our use of language. While in no way ignoring the significance of language choices, in this book, we are using child-first language, such as 'a child who experiences disability' or 'a child of Afghani back-ground' rather than identity-first language such as 'a disabled child' or 'an Afghani child'. While changing gradually, person-first language is the currently preferred usage in early years policies in the contexts that we are writing from. In reflecting on language choices, and the complex and deeply emotive beliefs that we may hold about the words we use to describe ourselves and each other, we acknowledge the importance of each person choosing how they define themselves and what language they prefer to be used to and about them. While, as adults writing this book, we may hold strong (and potentially differing) views about this, person-first or identity-first language use is not something that young children are likely to have a fixed idea about, unless this is coming to them externally, as the early childhood years are a time in life for the constant process of exploring who we are and what we might become.

This book has been organised into three parts, so that it can be navigated in various ways, according to need. The first three chapters – Part One – set the scene by focusing on under-standings of inclusion, creativity and the arts that inform the book as a whole. Part Two comprises a chapter on each of the art forms that are commonly part of children's lives and education in the early years. Each art form has unique features to its 'language', and unique qualities and functions for children, thus exploring each art form separately enabled us to provide specific approaches and examples of practice. Part Three weaves together common threads across the arts. We hope that this section will provide support to you in drawing together your reflections from the book and applying them to inclusive early years arts pedagogy within your individual context. Throughout this book there are case studies that provide examples of children's everyday creative arts explorations and play. Some are drawn directly from our research or anecdotal observations as early years practitioners, while others are creative adaptations inspired by our experiences within early years practice over our careers. Thinking points and questions, and suggestions for practice are also offered throughout the book.

Each context, each environment and each person within is unique and ever changing. Thus, to be meaningful and responsive, what exactly inclusive early years arts pedagogy will look like will vary from one setting to another. It is very much our hope that through this book you will be inspired to use music, art, drama, dance, puppetry, books and stories to connect with every child and build creative, inclusive early childhood communities of practice.

INTRODUCTION TO PART I

The explorations of inclusion, inclusive education, diversity and creativity in Part One lay the foundations that underpin this book overall. These chapters present definitions and understandings that provide background and theoretical contexts for the chapters in Parts Two and Three.

The experiences of inclusion and creativity are cornerstones of life, and central to the provision of inclusive early years education and care. All children have the right to experience a sense of belonging in order to flourish. Inclusion is in essence the provision of environments and communities where everyone feels that they belong – that their ways of being and doing are valued. Creativity and the arts allow us to express who we are – our ideas, thoughts and feelings. Artistic expression is inherently a celebration of human diversity. An arts-infused curriculum in early years settings therefore has an important role in inclusive education.

1

TOWARDS INCLUSIVE PEDAGOGY AND PRACTICE IN THE EARLY YEARS

Amanda Niland, Kathy Cologon
and Laura Huhtinen-Hildén

Chapter objectives

This chapter introduces you to these key ideas:

- The need for inclusion
- Defining inclusion
- Inclusion and learning
- Inclusion and communities of practice
- The arts as inclusive practice

INTRODUCTION

This chapter establishes a basis for understanding inclusion and inclusive early years education and care. As inclusion is often misunderstood or misrepresented, it is important to establish the foundational ideas on which this book rests. Thus this chapter offers definitions of key concepts and ideas that respect the rights of all children, and value diversity and belonging in light of the complexities of 21st-century life. The chapter includes some introductory discussion of how the arts offer possibilities for both children and adults to connect, make meaning of their worlds and build inclusive communities of practice.

THE NEED FOR INCLUSION

Joy, feeling one's own value, being appreciated and loved by others, feeling useful and capable of production are all factors of enormous value for the human soul. (Maria Montessori, 1948/1973, p. 87)

The world is a complex and beautiful place, and diversity is part of that beauty. While we share a common humanity, we are also all different – in our life experiences, interests, geographical, political and economic circumstances, ethnicity and language backgrounds, genders, physical features, abilities, opportunities and ways of doing and being. These factors contribute to shaping our lives and identities, strengths and vulnerabilities, and ultimately the realisation of our rights and sense of belonging. Our differences may be experienced as good or bad, depending on the perspectives of others, and often due to circumstances beyond our control.

As global economies expand and people move from country to country for a variety of reasons – positive and negative, by choice or necessity – societies are increasingly diverse. While education and social policies and curricula in many countries incorporate concepts such as multiculturalism and inclusion, the reality is that marginalisation, discrimination and other forms of oppression are still common for many children, families and communities, in education and beyond. Various social and political movements have long been working to draw attention to failures in social justice, and researchers and thinkers, past and present, have pointed to education as a key to changing lives. Today, the ubiquity of social media has further contributed to broadening awareness and discussion of such issues, so that advocating for social justice doesn't just happen in political institutions or mainstream media, but in the everyday digital communications of people's online lives. Personal connections and contributions that challenge unfairness and celebrate everyday individuals across the world are possible with a smartphone and internet access. However, despite the potential of these ways to communicate and connect regardless of distance, fairness and equity for all are still a long way off.

As this book was beginning to take shape during 2020, current events dramatically high-lighted the need to focus on the problems that arise from inequity, discrimination, margin-alisation or exclusion. The Covid-19 pandemic was a phenomenon tragically affecting millions of lives across the world. It was to some extent, a common experience we all shared, but also a situation in which disadvantage, marginalisation and poverty were accentuated. In recognition of the important role of the arts and creativity in all our lives, a UNESCO initiative, the inaugural World Art Day, was launched in April 2020. A statement on the UNESCO Twitter feed encapsulated the human need for the arts: 'In times of crisis we need culture to make us resilient, give us hope, remind us that we are not alone' (https://news.un.org/en/story/2020/04/1061802).

Our experiences of crises such as the Covid19 pandemic are completely different, depending on who we are, where we live, and what supports for survival and wellbeing are available to us. Living through the pandemic was a time which highlighted the need for those of us in positions of privilege and power to recognise the importance of working towards a more inclusive world. What was especially fascinating and pertinent to this book were the ways in which so many people responded creatively and artistically to the challenges and difficulties of life in a pandemic. Television, radio, social media and the streets in many communities were full of inspiring examples of the power of the arts to reflect and foster human resilience. We have shared some links to interesting examples in the resources at the end of this chapter.

The inequities and hardships experienced by many children and families during the Covid19 pandemic make the need for more inclusive societies very clear. This has important implications for early years practitioners, Lalvani and Bacon state: 'it is important that educational settings mirror the diversity within which they exist, and actively prepare children for citizenship in a pluralistic democracy through meaningful and sustained opportunities to engage with each other across differences' (2018, p. 1). It has long been recognised that positive childhoods, particularly the early years of life, are key to transforming lives, societies and even nations (UNESCO, 2023). The early years lay foundations for what children might become, and what kind of attitudes and values they develop; thus, early years settings where diversity is welcomed and celebrated can potentially change the world.

INCLUSION AND INCLUSIVE EDUCATION

It is important at this point to introduce the understanding of inclusive education that underpins this book. We understand inclusive education as a philosophy, pedagogy and system in which all children, regardless of gender, ethnicity, ability, cultural, social and economic backgrounds, are welcomed and supported to participate fully as valued members of their educational community (Thomas & Loxley, 2007, 2022). In an inclusive early years setting, all forms of diversity are embraced, and are reflected in the material and social environment, so that the diverse experiences and ways of being of the children and their families become rich resources for everyone's learning and development.

Inclusive education is a contested concept, as well as one where definitions in policy and curricula do not always match the reality. 'Inclusion' is one little word that produces dramatically different responses from varying people, ranging from fear to excitement, and passion to dismissiveness. Along with these diverse emotional responses there are probably even more varied understandings of what inclusion really means, and different experiences influenced by these understandings. Unfortunately, there is a lot that happens that is called 'inclusion', but that is actually *faux*clusion - exclusion masquerading as inclusion. Fauxclusion not only perpetuates confusion about inclusion, but simultaneously prevents inclusion from happening. For example, if we think we are already inclusive, when we are not, then it is much harder to take a step back and see the barriers that are occurring and what we might need to be doing to *actually* become inclusive.

Given the level and implications of the confusion regarding inclusive education, a lot of time and thought has gone into understanding and defining what it actually is. In 2016, the United Nations released *General Comment 4* (GC4) on Article 24 of the *Convention on the Rights of Persons with Disabilities*. GC4 provides a comprehensive and internationally accepted definition of inclusive education. A key aspect of this definition is the clear outlining of the differences between inclusion and integration. As noted in paragraph 11 of GC4 (UN, 2016):

> Exclusion occurs when students are directly or indirectly prevented from or denied access to education in any form. Segregation occurs when the education of students with disabilities is provided in separate environments designed or used to respond to a particular impairment or to various impairments, in isolation from students without disabilities. Integration is the process of placing persons with disabilities in existing mainstream educational institutions with the understanding that they can adjust to the standardised requirements of such institutions.

By contrast, as further explained in GC4:

> Inclusion involves a process of systemic reform embodying changes and modifications in content, teaching methods, approaches, structures and strategies in education to overcome barriers with a vision serving to provide all students of the relevant age range with an equitable and participatory learning experience and the environment that best corresponds to their requirements and preferences. Placing students with disabilities within mainstream classes without accompanying structural changes to, for example, organisation, curriculum and teaching and learning strategies, does not constitute inclusion. Furthermore, integration does not automatically guarantee the transition from segregation to inclusion. (UN, 2016, paragraph 11)

To understand and bring about inclusive education in practice, it is necessary to recognise the difference between integration, or assimilation, and inclusion. Inclusive education is not about children 'fitting in' to a particular setting. It is about the setting 'fitting' the diversities of the children within it. This means that there isn't a 'type' of child or family who is suitable to be included or to 'fit' within existing structures, systems and practices. This would be assimilation, not inclusion. Rather, inclusion and inclusive education involve acknowledging and embracing the diversity of all children and working to make our education settings and experiences fit that beautiful diversity. Consequently, inclusive education involves a process of changing the system, environments, and practices so that all children and families can participate fully and learn, grow, and flourish together. In the words of a five-year-old who participated in some of our research, 'Inclusion is about everyone … and I am a someone in everyone' (Cologon & Cologon, 2023, p. 36).

DEVELOPING INCLUSIVE COMMUNITIES IN EARLY YEARS SETTINGS

Including everyone as learners together aligns with the concept of communities of practice (Lave & Wenger, 1991). This concept recognises learning as a social practice and regards the community of practice as one where relationships and equity form the basis of a positive and fruitful learning environment. An important question for early years practitioners is: How can we form inclusive communities of practice in early years settings and beyond?

Different ways of thinking are crucial to developing inclusive educational settings in which all children's identities are celebrated, where they are welcomed and encouraged to participate as valued members of their learning communities. The creation of equitable and inclusive communities of practice requires critical reflection on aspects of pedagogy, particularly our communication – spoken and unspoken, visible, or hidden. How do we welcome and include diverse languages, cultures, abilities and ways of being? Inclusive communication will mean that no members of the community will be regarded as 'others' – as outside the 'norm' and of low social status – while some remain 'inside' and therefore have higher social status.

The creation of communities of practice includes recognising and understanding how social status is constructed and enacted (Wagner, 2020) and countering any social inequities. Wagner, a US researcher, explored the impact of peer social status on children's developing reading identities in an early years' classroom and found that lower social status was associated with children having less positive perceptions of themselves as readers. Social status in the particular classroom Wagner studied was shown to be linked to the children's linguistic and socio-economic backgrounds. Although not related to experiences of disability, Wagner's findings resonate with research into the experiences of inclusion or exclusion of children who experience disability, who may be similarly regarded as having low social status in their learning communities (Woodgate et al., 2020). Being marginalised can have far reaching consequences, including on children's developing identities as learners. Inclusive approaches, in this case where early years practitioners can focus on ways to equalise children's social status through developing an equitable community of practice, are therefore important in establishing inclusive early years settings, so that inequalities in power and social status are challenged and a more socially equitable community is established. Wagner (2020) mentions Bourdieu's notion of 'symbolic capital' and explored in his case study research how one child used his symbolic capital - knowledge of TV superheroes – to gain social acceptance in imaginative play with his peers. One of the many reasons why creativity and the arts play such a key role in bringing about inclusive education is that they provide ways for children to develop and use symbolic capital to connect with each other and build meaningful relationships.

Thus, arts related activities can be tools for building creative communities of practice that empower children and foster inclusion.

CHILDREN AS ACTIVE AGENTS AND CONTRIBUTORS IN THEIR COMMUNITIES

Inclusion can be understood through the lens of critical theories: as empowering children by respecting and responding to their diverse identities and facilitating opportunities for children to make choices and decisions. Such empowerment involves recognising the right of children to be active agents, developers and creators within their sociocultural environments. In an early years setting, this implies that all aspects of the learning environment are developed in dialog. Such co-construction may mean discussion, but more broadly, it is an underpinning acknowledgement of children's agency. Agency refers to our capacity to make decisions and choices, and to take individual action (Sairanen & Kumpulainen, 2014). Jyrkämä (2008) elaborates the understanding of agency in the light of six modalities, which are:

1 being able to do something,
2 knowing how to do something,
3 wanting to do something,
4 having a possibility to do something,
5 having to do something and
6 feeling, experiencing, appreciating something.

Focusing on the opportunities for children to experience, manifest, and redirect their agency (Jyrkämä, 2008; see also Nummijoki & Engeström, 2010; Sairanen & Kumpulainen, 2014) facilitates the development of an inclusive and caring community.

Therefore, inclusion involves reflection on how the learning environment and everyday life in early childhood settings takes into account each child's preferences, strengths and capabilities. Pedagogical approaches, the learning environment and activities should be responsive to the interests, needs and backgrounds of every child, so that each child accesses an inclusive and safe atmosphere. Differences will be recognised and respected, rather than seen as problems that require fixing so that children are 'normalized'. Secure, respectful and trusting relationships, in which children have rights to express their thoughts and opinions, to be heard and to participate in communities (UN Convention on the Rights of the Child, 1989) are central, as these provide the foundations on which inclusive early years education and care communities can be built. Making choices, perhaps taking risks and trying new things, with supportive adults there to observe, listen and assist when children express their need for support, can be seen as akin to a Zone of Proximal Development (Vygotsky & Cole, 1978). The playful, creative, and collaborative nature of arts play can provide many rich possibilities for children to exercise and build their capabilities and both lead and co-construct their learning with others. As we explore the particular affordances of each art form in this book, and approaches for working equitably with each child's ways of being and doing, we will explore ideas for fostering creation of inclusive communities of practice and supporting children as active agents and contributors in their communities in and through creativity and arts.

WORKING TOWARDS INCLUSIVE PRACTICE

While the right of all children to an inclusive education is recognised in international as well as in national, law, policy and curriculum in many nations, and inclusion as a principle is generally positively regarded, as noted earlier, understandings of what inclusion actually means still vary widely. Thus, the reality in educational practice is at best inconsistent, from early years throughout schooling (Baglieri et al., 2011). Many researchers have sought to understand the reasons for this, in order to pose solutions. While lack of access to the knowledge and resources needed to adequately cater inclusively for all learners is clearly a major issue (Woodcock & Woolfson, 2019), many argue that what is needed most is to change attitudes towards diversity and build understandings of inclusion (Cologon, 2019). John Dewey argued that 'Education is not preparation for life; education is life itself' (1916, p. 239). Dewey also believed that education should aim to help each child to develop to their maximum potential (1934). More recently, others such as Paulo Freire, Nelson Mandela and Martin Luther King Jr. focused their definitions of education not only on individuals but also on social transformation, empowerment and freedom (e.g. Freire, 1996). These thoughts still apply today, highlighting the responsibility of education to be inclusive. We need to create learning environments that widen the possibilities of becoming for all. The question is: How to foster developing inclusive learning environments that approach diversity as a rich resource, offer possibilities of becoming and a sense of belonging for all children? Further reflection on the nature and purpose of education can help in developing answers to this question.

Biesta (2009) suggests viewing education in the light of three functions – qualification, socialisation, and subjectification. In relation to incorporating inclusion into the functions or purposes of education, Biesta's conceptualisation has some relevance, as he notes that learning and teaching convey more than 'academic' skills and knowledge, but also contribute to the development of social and cultural values that are linked to or desired by the broader society. Decisions about pedagogical approaches, curriculum content and resources, positioning, power, and behavioral expectations can all be seen as socially and culturally constructed manifestations of how the three core functions are interpreted. These fundamental themes underpin any reflection on the functions of education and their social and cultural construction – who is included and who is excluded? Whose ways of being are valued and whose are not?

ARTS EXPERIENCES AS INCLUSIVE SPACES

Art [is] a breathing space in our society, a free voice, an alternative world that challenges imagination and shakes our prejudices, a strong subject that invites us in and mobilises our subjective will to create and express, connects with us and challenges our mind and will, and helps communities to grow (Cappelen & Andersson, 2018, p. 635).

There are many different forms of art – each with its own joys. Through art, humans share their stories. As we explore in this book, engaging children in the processes of art making, sharing, and appreciation is a fundamental part of education. Whether for sharing our lives, grappling with our identities, communicating or exploring our experiences or particular events, or expressing thoughts and feelings, '[t]he arts are central to human life' (Nutbrown, 2013, p. 240).

Arts-related experiences offer many benefits for all of us. For example, they create a space for children to celebrate their individuality (Kaufmann, 2006), demonstrate capabilities that defy societal expectations (Band et al., 2011), and experience joy, belonging, acceptance, and connection (Zitomer, 2016). These benefits are not just confined to children or educational settings. The arts are important for all humans, and of course, the diversity of humanity is central to the arts:

> Diversity has the unique ability to refresh, replenish and to stimulate the arts by encouraging new work that challenges, innovates and takes risks. It is not really possible to talk about a modern and relevant arts sector without talking about diversity and equality. (Arts Council England, 2010, cited in Aujla & Redding, 2013, p. 81)

It seems clear that an important and reciprocal relationship exists between human diversity and the arts. One key consideration, though, is that arts experiences must be accessible to, and inclusive of, everyone. Intuitively we may think of the arts as being naturally inclusive, but that assumption is often not matched by reality (Penketh, 2017). Bringing about inclusion within and through the arts, therefore requires careful reflection to ensure that everyone has the opportunity to engage meaningfully with and through the arts. For this, we need to examine our own perceptions of art and art making. We need to recognise the absolute importance of arts processes, and value the many diverse ways of making, doing, and engaging with art that are possible. We also need to think carefully about accessibility. There is much to consider in doing all this, that we will explore throughout this book. To start with, we focus on *why* it is essential to make arts experiences accessible and inclusive.

Arts-related experiences allow us to engage in different ways of being, doing and knowing. They are powerful in giving children multiple ways to express themselves, and to explore their strengths, thoughts and emotions, whilst also offering practitioners access and insight into children's learning, knowing and being (if we are open to it). Engaging in the arts allows us to value diverse ways of communicating. They encourage us to accept diverse bodies, and to celebrate the ways that diverse bodies can enrich the world through the arts. An inclusive approach to the arts enables us to expand our understanding of what the arts can be, who is an artist and how we can all participate in arts experiences. The arts create a potential space for exploring diversity and shifting children's attitudes about themselves and others, facilitating self and peer acceptance (Law et al., 2017). '...[T]he arts bring richness and meaning to all human lives, and ... the diverse modes of expression they afford have the power to provide "voices" for all, regardless of age or ability' (Cologon et al., 2019).

There are so many benefits of the arts for children. For example, engaging children in dance and drama experiences has been found to promote positive self-esteem, social and communicative skills, increased positive social interactions, emotional expression and self-regulation, as well as having benefits for physical health (Emonson et al., 2019; Suppo & Swank, 2020). Early years practitioners can use singing as a way to make a space to create a sense of 'togetherness' or connection, and through this to foster relationships and sense of belonging (Niland, 2015). Collaborative arts processes in dance, drama, storytelling or visual arts can also lead to feelings of belonging.

Clough and Nutbrown (2014, p. 402) write that '[e]ngaging in creative arts experiences is important for the sheer joy it can bring, as well as on account of the self and shared expression that can be enabled through creative processes'. The arts offer remarkable, wonderful and rich opportunities to engage with each other in our shared human journey with genuine and open valuing of our diverse ways of being and doing. They remind us as early years practitioners of the need to 'listen' to the children and families we work with and provide opportunities for every possible avenue of shared expression and joy through art. Through creative, playful arts experiences children can be supported to explore their ideas and identities in their own ways. Artforms can function as 'languages', allowing every child to express themselves through music, painting, sculpting, drawing, dancing, drama, storytelling and more. Open-ended arts experiences allow for connections and collaboration between children as they share ideas and materials in a myriad of imaginative ways. Through the arts, too, we can challenge and problematise the status quo and create space for positive change, including embracing greater diversity of identities and ways of being and doing. Major considerations then become:

a) how we ensure that everyone has the opportunity to engage meaningfully with and through the arts.
b) how the arts might provide opportunities for shared engagement and enrich shared communication and experiences.

CONCLUSION

This chapter has explored why inclusive pedagogy and practice are important in the early years, what inclusion actually means, and the potential of arts experiences for fostering inclusive early years communities. Friedrich Froebel (1782–1852), who inspired the development of early childhood education in Europe and across the world, developed the term 'kindergarten' – children's garden – with the implication that diversity, as in the world of plants and flowers, is precious and wonderful. It is believed that Froebel said, 'Children are like tiny flowers; they are varied and need care, but each is beautiful alone and glorious when seen in the community of peers' (Froebel Web, 1998–2008). However, while inclusive education remains inconsistent, and inaccessible to many, not all children are nurtured in the ways that they need within the 'gardens' of early years settings (Karaolis, 2020). Through inclusive pedagogy and practice in the arts, the beauty of diversity can be nurtured in humanity, as in nature.

─── **To think about...** ───

- Reflect on what you think is the purpose of education. Consider how your ideas could support the need for inclusive education in the early years.
- Think back to your childhood and any creative arts experiences that were especially meaningful to you. What role do you see these having in building your individual and social identity and making you who you are?

RESOURCES

On inclusive education in Australia:
Cologon, K. (2019). *Toward inclusive education*. CDYA

On creativity during the pandemic:
https://www.youtube.com/watch?v=wnW6K-Cbv1M
https://www.youtube.com/watch?v=8cFukLvl7lg

Presentation by Professor Gert Biesta:
https://www.youtube.com/watch?v=h837MDf30A0

REFERENCES

Aujla, I. J., & Redding, E. (2013). Barriers to dance training for young people with disabilities. *British Journal of Special Education*, 40(2), 80–85.

Baglieri, S., Bejoian, L. M., Broderick, A. A., Connor, D. J., & Valle, J. (2011). [Re] claiming 'inclusive education' toward cohesion in educational reform: Disability studies unravels the myth of the normal child. *Teachers College Record*, 113(10), 2122–2154.

Band, S. A., Lindsay, G., Neelands, J., & Freakley, V. (2011). Disabled students in the performing arts–are we setting them up to succeed? *International Journal of Inclusive Education*, 15(9), 891–908.

Biesta, G. (2009). Good education in an age of measurement: On the need to reconnect with the question of purpose in education. *Educational Assessment, Evaluation and Accountability*, 21(1), 33–46.

Cappelen, B., & Andersson, A. P. (2018). Cultural artefacts with virtual capabilities enhance self-expression possibilities for children with special needs. In G. Craddock, C. Doran, L. McNutt, & D. Rice (Eds.), *Transforming our world through design, diversity and education*. IOS Press.

Clough, P., & Nutbrown, C. (2014). *Early childhood cducation: History, philosophy and experience*. SAGE.

Cologon, K. (2019). *Towards inclusive education: A necessary process of transformation*. Report written by Dr Kathy Cologon, Macquarie University, for Children and Young People with Disability Australia (CYDA).

Cologon, K., & Cologon, T. (2023). Children as changemakers. In K. Cologon & Z. Mevawalla (Eds.), *Inclusive education in the early years: Right from the start* (pp. 36–45). Oxford University Press.

Cologon, K., Cologon, T., Mevawalla, Z., & Niland, A. (2019). Generative listening: Using arts-based inquiry to investigate young children's perspectives of inclusion, exclusion and disability. *Journal of Early Childhood Research, 17*(1), 54–69.

Dewey, J. (1916). *Democracy and education*. Project Gutenberg.

Dewey, J. (1934/1989). *John Dewey, The Later Works, 1925–1953, Volume 9: 1933–1934* (pp. 194–204). Jo Ann Boydston (Ed.). Southern Illinois University Press.

Emonson, C., McGillivray, J., Kothe, E. J., Rinehart, N., & Papadopoulos, N. (2019). Class time physical activity programs for primary school aged children at specialist schools: A systematic mapping review. *International Journal of Environmental Research and Public Health, 16*(24), 5140.

Freire, P. (1996). *Pedagogy of the oppressed* (revised). Continuum.

Froebel Web. (1998–2008). https://www.froebelweb.org/web7001.html

Jyrkämä, J. (2008). Toimijuus, ikääntyminen ja arkielämä: Hahmottelua teoreettis-metodologiseksi viitekehykseksi [Agency, ageing and everyday life: A sketch of a theoretical-methodological framework]. *Gerontologia, 22*(4), 190–203.

Karaolis, O. (2020). *Everybody in! Drama as a Pedagogy for inclusion*. Doctoral dissertation. University of Sydney.

Kaufmann, K. A. (2006). *Inclusive creative movement and dance*. Human Kinetics.

Lalvani, & Bacon (2018). Rethinking 'we are all special': Anti-ableism curricula in early childhood classrooms. *Young Exceptional Children, 20*(10), 1–14.

Lave, J., & Wenger, E. (1991). *Situated learning. Legitimate peripheral participation*. Cambridge University Press.

Law, Y. K., Lam, S. F., Law, W., & Tam, Z. W. (2017). Enhancing peer acceptance of children with learning difficulties: Classroom goal orientation and effects of a storytelling programme with drama techniques. *Educational Psychology, 37*(5), 537–549.

Montessori, M. (1948/1973). *From childhood to adolescence* (A. M. Joosten Trans.) (Rev. ed.). Oxford.

Niland, A. (2015). 'Row, row, row your boat': Singing, identity and belonging in a nursery. *International Journal of Early Years Education, 23*(1), 4–16.

Nummijoki, J., & Engeström, Y. (2010). Towards co-configuration in home care of the elderly: Cultivating agency by designing and implementing the mobility agreement. In H. Daniels, A. Edwards, Y. Engeström, T. Gallagher, & S. Ludvigsen (Eds.), *Activity theory in practice: Promoting learning across boundaries and agencies* (pp. 49–71). Routledge.

Nutbrown, C. (2013). Conceptualising arts-based learning in the early years. *Research Papers in Education, 28*(2), 239–263.

Penketh, C. (2017). Children see before they speak: An exploration of ableism in art education. *Disability and Society, 32*(1), 110–127. https://doi.org/10.1080/09687599.2016.1270819

Sairanen, H., & Kumpulainen, K. (2014). A visual narrative inquiry into children's sense of agency in preschool and first grade. *International Journal of Educational Psychology, 3*(2), 141–174.

Suppo, J. L., & Swank, T. (2020). Embracing collaboration through theILens of exceptional needs dance: A mixed methods study. *Journal of Dance Education, 20*(2), 65–77.

Thomas, G., & Loxley, A. (2007). *Ebook: Deconstructings speciale education*. McGraw-Hill Education.

Thomas, G., & Loxley, A. (2022). Groundhog day for inclusive education. *Support for Learning, 37*(2), 225–243.

UNESCO. (2023). *What you need to know about early childhood care and education*. https://www.unesco.org/en/early-childhood-education/need-know

United Nations. (1989). *Convention on the rights of the child*. https://www.ohchr.org/en/instruments-mechanisms/instruments/convention-rights-child

United Nations. (2016). *General Comment No. 4, Article 24: Right to Inclusive Education*. https://www.refworld.org/docid/57c977e34.html

Vygotsky, L. S., & Cole, M. (1978). *Mind in society: Development of higher psychological processes*. Harvard University Press.

Wagner, C. J. (2020). Multilingualism and reading identities in prekindergarten: Young children connecting reading, language, and the self. *Journal of Language, Identity and Education*, 1–16.

Woodcock, S., & Woolfson, L. M. (2019). Are leaders leading the way with inclusion? Teachers' perceptions of systemic support and barriers towards inclusion. *International Journal of Educational Research, 93*, 232–242.

Woodgate, R. L., Gonzalez, M., Demczuk, L., Snow, W. M., Barriage, S., & Kirk, S. (2020). How do peers promote social inclusion of children with disabilities? A mixed-methods systematic review. *Disability & Rehabilitation, 42*(18), 2553–2579.

Zitomer, M. R. (2016). 'Dance makes me happy': Experiences of children with disabilities in elementary school dance education. *Research in Dance Education, 17*(3), 218–234.

2

DIVERSITY AND INCLUSION IN THE EARLY YEARS

Amanda Niland and Kathy Cologon

Chapter objectives

This chapter introduces you to these key ideas:

- Rights and inclusion - an anti-bias approach
- Diversity, identity and inclusion
- Understandings of disability
- Language and inclusion

INTRODUCTION

This chapter continues the discussion of inclusive education in the early years from the previous chapter. Here we explore the link between inclusion and young children's diverse identities, and how early years settings can foster positive self and social identities for all children. We delve further into what inclusion means through focusing on young children's identity formation. This gives the context for exploring the inclusive possibilities of the creative arts in the rest of the book. The importance of inclusion as part of an anti-bias, social justice approach is discussed, as well as the role of language in fostering inclusion.

A CAPABILITY AND RIGHTS-BASED APPROACH TO INCLUSION

Our approach here and throughout the book is capability- and rights-based. This means that we see all children as capable and competent, with potential to develop and learn. We respect every child's right to participate in every aspect of life, especially including education, and the right to experience a sense of belonging and being valued. We regard diversity as intrinsic to humanity, and as a rich resource to be celebrated for the benefit of all. We see children's identities as being socially constructed and understand diversity as differences in aspects of identity. Children's interests, opportunities, abilities, languages, ethnicities, cultures, families, environments and socio-economic backgrounds all play a part in their developing identities in the early years. Identity and diversity sit, alongside justice and activism, at the core of Derman-Sparks and Edwards (2021) anti-bias goals for education in the early years. Derman-Sparks and Edwards (2021, pp. 35–36) propose four core anti-bias goals:

Goal 1, identity:

- Teachers will nurture each child's construction of knowledge-able and confident personal and social identities.
- Children will demonstrate self-awareness, confidence, family pride, and positive social identities.

Goal 2, diversity:

- Teachers will promote each child's comfortable, empathic interaction with people from diverse backgrounds.
- Children will express comfort and joy with human diversity, use accurate language for human differences, and form deep, caring connections across all dimensions of human diversity.

Goal 3, justice:

- Teachers will foster each child's capacity to critically identify bias and will nurture each child's empathy for the hurt bias causes.
- Children will increasingly recognize unfairness (injustice), have language to describe unfairness, and understand that unfairness hurts.

Goal 4, activism:

- Teachers will cultivate each child's ability and confidence to stand up for oneself and for others in the face of bias.
- Children will demonstrate a sense of empowerment and the skills to act, with others or alone, against prejudice and/or discriminatory actions.

Honoring every child's identity, as in anti-bias goal 1, and respecting every child's right to participate fully in early years settings, is intrinsic to inclusion and inclusive pedagogies. Inclusive early years settings are those which welcome all children as valued members of the learning community. The environments of these settings will reflect and celebrate the diversity in children's identities, so that all children feel that their ways of being are reflected in the physical and social environment. In inclusive settings, all children's learning needs are met in ways that foster a sense of belonging, so that each child can flourish. Any inequities and injustices, such as discrimination or marginalisation are actively challenged and disestablished through an anti-bias approach.

Creativity and the arts are integral to all our lives – they give us ways to explore and express our unique and diverse ways of being. An inclusive early years setting can provide rich opportunities for children to engage in playful artistic expression. The arts offer a safe space for children and early years professionals to explore ideas about difference, fairness and unfairness, so that biases and barriers to all children's rights to be included and valued are identified, addressed, and eliminated.

PERSPECTIVES ON DEVELOPMENT IN THE EARLY YEARS

Quality early years education and care aims to facilitate all aspects of young children's learning and development. With the appropriate support, all children can learn and develop in ongoing positive trajectories. Inclusive education will most effectively enable every child to genuinely participate, giving each child a range of opportunities to nurture their development and sense of identity.

The focus of attention in relation to young children's learning and development is often on physical, cognitive, and social/emotional domains. Identity development is not always considered to be integral to understanding and supporting young children's development. In the past, identity has not necessarily been a central concern of developmental researchers, whose research has most often been experimental or quasi-experimental, using mono-cultural sampling and aimed at evaluating children's performance in specific, measurable tasks. However, the field of child development now encompasses a broader range of theoretical perspectives. As the disciplines of social and cultural psychology have grown, new theories consider children more holistically, and recognise the role played by their social and material environmental contexts and their relationships both within and beyond their immediate families. The socio-cultural theory of Vygotsky et al. (1978) and the bio-ecological systems theory of Bromfenbrenner (1979/2009) are especially important and are part of pre-service teacher education in many nations. The work of both these theorists has helped to shift focus away from the individual child and towards understanding the role that social and cultural aspects of life play in shaping children's learning and development, including their identities.

The Influence of Vygotsky's Theories

Vygotsky explored the role of communication with others in the development of children's thinking and understanding of the world. Although he didn't specifically address issues of diverse identities or social groups, working as he did in Soviet Russia during the 1920s and 1930s, Vygotsky's research led him to regard learning as a process that happened through interactions and dialog with others. He also recognised that children learn not only *with* others, but *from* other, more capable peers or adults. This is captured in the theory of the Zone of Proximal Development (ZPD), which describes the process by which children can demonstrate greater capability or understanding when supported by more capable others, and through this gradually demonstrate new knowledge and capabilities independently (Vygotsky et al., 1978). Children enter the ZPD when either adults or peers offer just enough guidance, and only when requested, for the child to extend their capabilities, learning with and from others. The ZPD provides a powerful rationale for inclusive education, as it highlights the potential learning when children of diverse backgrounds, capabilities and levels of development are together in an educational setting.

The Influence of Bronfenbrenner's Ecological Systems Theory

Bronfenbrenner also recognised the need to view children's development as socially and culturally constructed. He regarded children as existing and developing within a complex interwoven set of social and cultural systems that encompass physical, economic, social and cultural aspects of their lives (Bronfenbrenner, 1979/2009). His bio-ecological systems theory provides a framework for analysing and understanding the ways in which children's backgrounds and interactions offer different contexts, resources and possibilities for learning and thus shape their development. This framework is very different from that of developmental psychology, with its focus on quantitative research paradigms which many regard as implying universal common developmental pathways (Shute & Slee, 2015). It also provides a context for considering the relevance of critical theories such as those of Freire or Bourdieu, who highlight the way differences in social and material environments impact people's opportunities to participate fully in the various systems of their communities and nations.

These more holistic theories and the extensive research that they have informed, have transformed understandings of young children's learning and development and have strongly influenced teachers' knowledge, curricula and pedagogies, especially in early years settings. In spite of conflicting pressures from increasingly assessment driven educational systems in many nations, early years practitioners are now encouraged to recognise the importance of understanding and supporting young children's identity development.

YOUNG CHILDREN'S IDENTITY DEVELOPMENT AND INCLUSION

Identity is central to our understanding of inclusion, as being included – feeling a sense of belonging – nurtures a positive sense of identity. Fundamentally the concept of identity centres around the question 'Who am I?'. Identity is not fixed, but can be seen as a process of becoming, influenced by experiences, environments and relationships with others (AGDE, 2022). The importance of supporting the development of positive self and social identities in the early years is advocated in many curricula (e.g. AGDE, 2022; Kuusisto et al., 2021; Te Whāriki, 2017).

Our identities are rooted in our belonging, beginning with the secure relationships between children and their parents/carers in infancy, through which infants gradually begin to distinguish between self and other. As children grow and interact in the world, even in the first two years of life they start to identify themselves and their families with groups, and also show awareness of visible forms of difference between themselves and others, such as differences between genders and between their home language(s) and other forms of spoken expression (Bennett, 2011). And while young children's awareness of these aspects of diversity are developing, so too are their attitudes towards the meaning and relative values attached to diversity by those around them. They can begin to perceive that some types of people or ways of being seem 'normal' or 'better' than others (for example, see Ivy's reflection in Chapter 8). Thus, the seeds for inclusiveness and equity, or marginalisation and oppression, are planted and begin to grow almost from the beginning of life.

To think about...

- Reflect on your earliest memories, to recall how you felt about yourself. What aspects of your identity were most important?
- In your childhood, what aspects of yourself were you proud of? Were there some parts of being you that you wished were different?

Commodified Childhoods

Our connections with others, which contribute to our evolving sense of identity, are based on what we share. This starts within families but moves outward to encompass children's various community contexts, such as early years settings. Young children's social identities are often partly related to material things that they share with others. In urbanised societies, these may for example be stories, music, toys, TV and other digital media characters and related merchandise. For example, consider how common it is in cities across the world to see children dressed in clothing portraying popular children's TV or movie characters. Childhood in many places, particularly in urban environments, has been described as highly 'commodified' (Vanobbergen, 2018), which has implications for equity and for creating conditions for inclusion or exclusion. As Bourdieu states: 'identities should also be seen as associated with differential resources (e.g. material, social, symbolic, etc.) that can play an important role in shaping individuals' opportunities, obligations, actions' (Bourdieu, 1986, as cited in Bennett, 2011, p. 358). This statement is significant because the shaping of children's opportunities is crucial in their experience of inclusion or exclusion.

Another important influence on young children's identities is the stereotyping that can be enacted through material commodities, for example clothes, toys, video games and apps, as well as artistic 'materials' such as songs, books, TV and movies. From cartoon superheroes, through Elsa from *Frozen*, to Peppa Pig and her family, Harry Potter or movie superheroes, a plethora of commodities related particularly to media characters is increasingly available around the world, and heavily marketed to children and families. The ubiquity of white skin, non-disabled bodies and gender appearance stereotypes in these everyday cultural resources, and the absence of other types of visual features, are important signals to young children of what is recognised and valued (Ellis, 2015). It is important to understand the influence of resources such as these and the stereotyping they might lead to, not just because of the influence they may have on children's sense of identity, but because of the impact of stereotyping on shaping expectations of some children depending on their gender, ability or culture.

Physical Diversity

Physical attributes and capabilities also play a part in children's developing identities, but this is dependent on children's perceptions of others' views about them. Values regarding particular physical attributes and capabilities are socially constructed, and are often influenced by stereotypes, with consequent implications for inclusion. If educators or peers in an early years setting have limited expectations for a child because of stereotyped understandings of an aspect of their identity, the child may end up feeling devalued, marginalised or excluded. Inclusive education requires getting to know each child, understanding their backgrounds, interests, strengths and challenges, finding ways to acknowledge and value their unique identity, and engaging in an anti-bias approach in resisting any stereotyped assumptions or inclination to see some ways of being as 'normal' or 'more normal' than others (see the example in Chapter 5 from Zitomer and Reid's research on an inclusive dance program).

Gender

Gender is another important aspect of children's developing individual and social identity in the early years. Reflection on gender, in relation to the arts and beyond, is essential to inclusive education. In considering gender as early years practitioners, it is important to acknowledge our own gender identities and consider how these might impact our perceptions of people in the communities around us, including children. A discussion of the complexities of gender identity construction is beyond the scope of this book; however, growing acknowledgement of the social and cultural constructions of gender identities and attitudes means that reflection on our attitudes and interactions is part of any inclusive journey. While genuine respect for and celebration of gender diversity is growing in many countries, experiences of marginalisation or discrimination still exist. By supporting young children to express their identity, including their gender, in diverse ways and celebrating that diversity, early years settings can lay foundations for more inclusive communities.

Disability

In the 21st century in many parts of the world there is increasing awareness of the inequities caused by some forms of discrimination, particularly racism or sexism. While there is a long way to go, early years curriculum and pedagogy in many countries seek to challenge limiting notions of gender and ensure that ethnic differences are not a barrier for children or families. Cultural diversity may be a learning resource that is utilised in many early years settings, as the importance of multicultural education is increasingly recognised (Barton & Ho, 2020).

Disability, however, still commonly remains outside the 'accepted' and valued forms of human diversity. Therefore, children may encounter the oppression that constitutes disability through the experience of having their identities defined in the eyes of others primarily, and negatively, by their impairments. Such definitions are often underpinned by stereotyped assumptions about diagnostic labels and by others' implicit beliefs about impairment and the experience of disability. We, who do and do not experience disability, see disability as a positive form of diversity, not as a problem or a tragedy. We understand though, that this way of viewing disability can be more challenging for some to grasp in comparison to other forms of diversity. This is perhaps why many children and families experience disability as discrimination or stigma, even in generally friendly and welcoming settings such as early years education and care. For this reason, we now focus specifically on understandings of disability.

Defining Disability

Definitions and understandings of disability, as with any form of diversity, have been socially and culturally constructed over time. These understandings are reflected in many explicit and implicit ways throughout our lives, so that it is only with deep critical reflection that we may be able to identify our underlying feelings and beliefs and begin to see how they have been formed. In the past, children who experience disability were mainly educated in special schools, segregated from their peers and communities (a practice still advocated by some), and up until late in the 20th century it was not uncommon for children who experience disability to be in institutional care rather than at home with families. These practices were all related to understanding disability *as* impairment akin to illness that needed to be cured or eliminated, and the lives of people who experience disability as not worth living and necessitating being hidden from society.

Recognising such social attitudes as problematic, with deep and broad implications for people's lived experiences, disability activists began to refer to this generally accepted and deeply embedded negative view of disability as a medical model. In working to help others understand the challenges that are part of the everyday, and the problems with attitudes and systemic barriers, a social model of disability was developed as an alternative way of under-standing disability. It is only through the development of the social model that the medical model was identified. However, in identifying this (still pervasive) model, disability activists identified its key features – that a medical model views disability as existing within a person and as a tragedy or aberration, and a medical problem to be remediated or 'fixed'.

Medical Model Thinking

The term 'medical model' was not ever intended as a suggestion that medicine and *medical care* is a problem. In fact, a medical model of disability often underpins decisions to withhold medical treatment, and the fight for equitable medical care is a key aspect of the application of the social model. Instead, the term medical model is intended to illustrate that, rather than viewing impairment as a natural part of human diversity, a medical model of disability views people as 'broken' and needing to be fixed or eliminated, and fails to recognise the oppression that people face on every day.

Viewing some people as 'broken' leads to ableism - forms of thinking that result in stigma and discrimination of people on the basis of disability. Ableism can be directly paralleled with racism, ageism, sexism, homophobia, transphobia, and so forth. In essence, it is a process by which we create a 'them' and 'us', with 'us' being seen as superior to 'them'. 'Ableism plays out insidiously in everyday situations. The sense that an interaction or relationship between a person who does and a person who doesn't experience disability is somehow benevolent on the part of the non-disabled person; the frequently unquestioned inaccessibility of places, events and materials; patronising interactions such as the often cited congratulatory remarks that a person who experiences disability may receive from strangers for simply being out and about – these are all examples of ableism' (Cologon, 2019, pp. 35–36).

Disability studies scholar Rosemary Garland-Thomson wrote that disability is 'a culturally fabri-cated narrative of the body, similar to what we understand as the fictions of race and gender' (Garland-Thomson, 2002, p. 5). From an ableist perspective it is a narrative 'benevolent prejudice' – one of tragedy and suffering necessitating sympathy, pity, cures, treatments, and preventions. The ableist perpetuation of exclusion and segregation is based on the myth of the 'normal person', which results in a division of people into 'normal' and the inferred 'Other', which is constructed as 'abnormal'. From an ableist viewpoint, therefore, a child who experiences disability is negatively constructed as 'abnormal'. This difficult to shake belief is deeply entrenched as the basis of many approaches to and beliefs about education (Campbell, 2012). It is thus important to acknowledge that ableism and anti-ableism can occur alongside each other. As we engage with proactive efforts towards anti-ableism, we 'dip in and out'; of ableism and anti-ableism as our awareness grows.

Social and Social-Relational Model Thinking

To challenge the pervasive ableism in society, disability studies scholars have posed a social model of disability. This holds that disability is created by society and caused by attitudes, policies and social provisions (or lack of provisions) that cause discrimination and exclusion of those of us labeled as disabled (Oliver, 1983). In the field of disability studies, there is ongoing discussion and debate about how best to understand and conceptualise the experience of disability. While all advocate strongly against medical model understandings, and for the need for fuller honoring of the rights of those experiencing disability, not all see the social model definition as fully encompassing the lived experience of those seen as disabled (Corker & Shakespeare, 2002; Thomas, 2009).

A perspective on disability that is valuable for early years practitioners is the social relational model (Thomas, 2009). This takes aspects of social model thinking as its starting point – in particular the idea that those of us without impairments are more powerful than those of us with impairments, leading to the experiences of oppression and exclusion. According to the social model, this oppression and exclusion is the sole cause of the experience of disability. However, Thomas argues that this power inequity, while certainly a crucial part of the experience of disability, is not the whole story. She stressed that the effects of impairments should not be ignored – life is experienced differently by those of us with visual impairments, or who use wheelchairs for example. Thomas and others point out the dangers of ignoring bodily experience and over-simplifying or generalising the experience of disability: 'The global experience of disabled people is too complex to be rendered within one unitary model or set of ideas' (Corker & Shakespeare, 2002, p. 15). Thomas also provides an important extra perspective on the oppression identified by social model thinkers. She states that 'The oppression that disabled people experience operates on the "inside" as well as on the "outside": it is about being made to feel of lesser value, worthless, unattractive, or disgusting as well as it is about "outside" matters such as being turned down for a job because one is "disabled", or not being offered the chance of a mainstream education because of "special needs"' (Thomas, 2004, p. 31). Thomas, taking a social-relational perspective, terms the 'outside' experience of disability 'barriers to doing', the 'inside' effects 'barriers to being' and regards these two, along with the bio-social effects of bodily or cognitive impairments, as jointly constituting the experience of disability. If you would like to read more about this debate over understandings of disability and its history, a link to Thomas's 2019 article is available at the end of this chapter.

The social-relational model has important implications for early years practitioners aiming to facilitate inclusive education. While it was developed in relation to the experience of disability, some aspects are relevant to any experience of difference that involves exclusion or social oppression. It provides principles that can guide us in reflecting on our environments, curricula, resources and pedagogy. We can use these principles to work towards the removal of any barriers to doing or being, and any impairment effects that may relate to physical, cognitive, linguistic or cultural differences. Social relational thinking highlights the importance of inclusive educational provisions, so that no child is disempowered because they are in some way different from some of their peers. Social relational thinking can guide us for example in implementing creative arts play using open-ended resources that reflect all the interests, languages, cultures, ethnicities and abilities of the children in our early years education and care communities. Thus, when engaging in the arts children will not experience any barriers to being or doing – all children will be able to participate fully in their own ways and experience a sense of belonging.

The exploration of identity development and discussion of understandings of disability in this chapter provide a basis for recognising the importance of inclusive education, so that differences do not lead to barriers to participation or hinder the development of a positive sense of identity by all children. Social-relational model thinking can guide early years practitioners in providing inclusive early years education and care that will nurture positive identities and a sense of belonging for all. Given young children's interest in creative and artistic play, and the diversity inherent in artistic expression, the arts can be appropriate and useful for removing those barriers to doing and being that can impede the development of positive identities. When children feel recognised and valued for whom they are, and relationships are based on mutual respect and trust, participation is possible in a wide range of ways. When curriculum and resources are representative of the range of ways of being of everyone in an educational community, every child can develop a positive sense of identity as a person and as a learner.

WE ARE NOT THE SAME, BUT WE ALL BELONG: LANGUAGE AND INCLUSION

The ways that we talk about and with each other, for children and adults, will both reflect and create ways of thinking about identities and diversity. Language can bring us together or keep us apart; it can challenge bias or create it. Discriminatory language – sexist, racist or ableist for example – can create the 'barriers to being' that Thomas speaks about (2009). There are many examples in history, politics and news media of where language, particularly labeling of people or ways of being, can lead to dehumanisation that then makes discrimination acceptable. The focus on human rights during the 20th century has led to increased public awareness in many parts of the world of the importance of language and terminology that convey respect or equity in relation to race, gender, religion and ability. For example, the rise of feminism in the 1970s led to a push for less discriminatory forms of address, and any exploration of media reporting on same sex relationships will reveal significantly different terminology now as compared to 50 or more years ago, when this way of being was regarded as aberrant and was often illegal. In relation to disability too, language has changed as social attitudes, laws and policies have recognised the unfairness, marginalisation, discrimination and even cruelty imposed on people labeled as disabled. One example of this is the debate amongst disability rights activists and disability scholars about 'person-first' (a child who experiences disability) versus 'identity-first' language (a disabled child) (Botha et al., 2021). There is still a distance to travel in terms of widespread use of inclusive, respectful, rights-based language. Early years practitioners, informed by the anti-bias goals, can reflect on their language use around diversity, with the aim of supporting every child's sense of belonging.

Early years practitioners are role models for children during a critical time for language and identity development; the words we use to talk with and about children will influence their individual and social identities and their attitudes towards peers. Using language that is respectful and inclusive will help us to develop welcoming, positive and trusting relationships in early years communities.

The Languages of the Arts

The need to communicate and connect with others is part of being human. The open-endedness inherent in creativity and the arts means that children can explore and communicate their different interests, ideas and feelings through the 'languages' of the arts. Children can also develop and express aspects of their identities through art forms such as music, dance, drawing, painting, storytelling and drama. In the case study below, two children of different ages, backgrounds, genders and abilities express their identities and connect with each other through music.

Mika (aged five) and Tommy (aged four), play together regularly while at preschool. Their personalities, developmental capabilities and communication styles are quite different - while Mika is talkative and sociable, Tommy is a mostly non-verbal communicator who often plays alone. Their bond began with musical play, which both children choose to do often, and now they often make music together. During free play time soon after the children's arrival at preschool one morning, Mika was playing on the colourful xylophone. Tommy noticed and started to imitate what she was doing, taking over the xylophone from her. Since Mika likes playing with Tommy, she let him play the xylophone and she started playing the clap sticks. Every time Tommy played two or three different notes and stopped, Mika would tap two or three times. Both realised they were making a pattern and repeated it a couple of times. This way they created their own music, communicating just through eye contact and listening to each other's sounds. (Niland, 2020, Early years educator's observation notes)

CONCLUSION

In this chapter we have outlined the inclusive perspective on diversity and difference that underpins this book. Our aim in writing a book about the many inclusive possibilities offered by the creative arts, is to take a positive approach; however in this chapter we have also acknowledged the importance of recognising that some attitudes and practices in early years settings and communities can present significant challenges for the development of inclusive education and care. We hope that the issues and questions raised will inspire you to look deeply as you work towards building inclusive settings in which every child experiences a sense of belonging and being valued for whom they are.

To think about...

- Thinking back to your early childhood, how was your identity and those of your peers reflected in your preschool or early school classrooms? Were all children's identities recognised or valued?
- What are your thoughts about how the words you use as an early years professional can communicate to children that everyone's identities are welcome?

FURTHER READING AND RESOURCES

United Nations Convention on the Rights of the Child:
https://www.ohchr.org/Documents/ProfessionalInterest/crc.pdf

- In relation to the arts see Article 13
- In relation to children with disabilities see Article 23
- In relation to education see Article 28
- In relation to children's diverse identities see Article 29

The anti-bias principles:
https://www.naeyc.org/resources/pubs/yc/nov2019/understanding-anti-bias

A deeply reflective article by Carol Thomas on the social relational model of disability:
Thomas, C. (2019). Times change, but things remain the same. *Disability & Society, 34*(7–8), 1040–1041. https://www.tandfonline.com/doi/full/10.1080/09687599.2019.1664074

A useful resource that aims to eliminate barriers that language can impose:
United Nations. (2021). *Disability-inclusive language guidelines.* https://www.ungeneva.org/sites/default/files/2021-01/Disability-Inclusive-Language-Guidelines.pdf

REFERENCES

Australian Government Department of Education [AGDE]. (2022). *Belonging, being and becoming: The early years learning framework for Australia (v 2.0).* Commonwealth of Australia.

Barton, K. C., & Ho, L. C. (2020). Cultivating sprouts of benevolence: A foundational principle for curriculum in civic and multicultural education. *Multicultural Education Review, 12*(3), 157–176.

Bennett, M. (2011). Children's social identities. *Infant and Child Development, 20*(4), 353–363.

Botha, M., Hanlon, J., & Williams, G. L. (2021). Does language matter? Identity-first versus person-first language use in autism research: A response to Vivanti. *Journal of Autism and Developmental Disorders,* 1–9.

Bronfenbrenner, U. (1979/2009). *The ecology of human development: Experiments by nature and design.* Harvard University Press.

Campbell, F. K. (2012). Stalking ableism: Using disability to expose 'abled' narcissism. In *Disability and social theory: New developments and directions* (pp. 212–230). Palgrave Macmillan UK.

Cologon, K. (2019). *Toward inclusive education*. CDYA.

Corker, M., & Shakespeare, T. (2002). *Disability/postmodernity*. Continuum.

Derman-Sparks, L., & Edwards, J. O. (2021). Teaching about identity, racism, and fairness: Engaging young children in anti-bias education. *American Educator*, 44(4), 35–40.

Ellis, K. (2015). Our moment in time: The transitory and concrete value of disability toys. In K. Ellis (Ed.), *Disability and popular culture: Focusing passion, creating community and expressing defiance*. Routledge. http://ebookcentral.proquest.com/lib/usyd/detail.action?docID=1843655

Garland-Thomson, R. (2002). Integrating disability, transforming feminist theory. *National Women's Studies Association Journal*, 14(3), 1–32.

Kuusisto, A., Poulter, S., & Harju-Luukkainen, H. (2021). Worldviews and national values in Swedish, Norwegian and Finnish early childhood education and care curricula. *International Research in Early Childhood Education*, 11(2).

Ministry of Education. (2017). *Te Whariki: He whariki ma⁻tauranga mo⁻nga⁻mokopuna o Aotearoa. Early childhood curriculum*. Learning Media.

Niland, A. (2020). *Making music together: Using music to support belonging and peer relationships in an inclusive Early Childhood setting*. Unpublished research data. Ethics approval number 2020/123. The University of Sydney.

Oliver, M. (1983). *Social work with disabled people*. Macmillan.

Shute, R. H., & Slee, P. T. (2015). *Child development: Theories and critical perspectives*. Routledge.

Thomas, C. (2004). Developing the social relational in the social model of disability: A theoretical agenda. In C. Barnes & G. Mercer (Eds.), *The social model of disability theory and research*. The Disability Press.

Thomas, C. (2009). Rescuing a social relational understanding of disability. *Scandinavian Journal of Disability Research*, 6(1), 22–36.

Thomas, C. (2019). Times change, but things remain the same. *Disability & Society*, 34(7–8), 1040–1041.

Vanobbergen, B. (2018). Children as consumers. In *The international handbook of philosophy of education* (pp. 1337–1348). Springer.

Vygotsky, L. S., Cole, M., John-Steiner, V., Scribner, S., & Souberman, E. (1978). *Mind in society: Development of higher psychological processes*. Harvard University Press.

3
CREATIVITY AND ARTS IN YOUNG CHILDREN'S LIVES

Laura Huhtinen-Hildén

Chapter objectives

This chapter introduces you to these key ideas:

- Meanings of creativity and arts in young children's lives
- The child as an artist
- Creative group processes enhancing inclusion

INTRODUCTION

This chapter focuses on perspectives on creativity and arts in young children's lives and discusses the ways in which children use them in their play as tools for communication, expression and meaning-making. The chapter explores meanings of creativity, the role of arts in children's lives, and the implications for their sense of identity, learning and development, and for early years education and care environments. Creativity is viewed as intrinsic to all of us, and children as inherently artistic beings who use their senses to explore the world through a form of 'aesthetic attending' (Clough, 2002, p. 85). From very early in life, children show interest in some experiences and sensations over others, seeming to develop sensory and aesthetic preferences. These are very different for each child, although of course they are shaped by the physical and sensory environment that surrounds them. Given that children also express their creativity in diverse ways unique to them, with their processes being the focus during the early years, creativity is presented here as potentially inherently inclusive.

CREATIVITY AND THE ARTS AS PART OF LIFE

We live in a sea of creativity from the very beginning of our lives. A curious, creative approach to life is the child's companion as they begin to navigate and play in this wonderful sea, to make sense of its various elements. This, as Winnicott (1971, p. 53) points out, is why we need play in our lives. Our wellbeing depends on the flexibility that is inherent in imagination and playfulness. These are the underpinnings of creativity, which make it an essential part of a good life.

The holistic nature of children's ways of experiencing the world explains why they so easily use different modes of communication and expression during arts play and playfulness in their daily lives. This is why play is so valuable for learning and development. Play can encompass as many different modes as children need it to at any given moment. These often include art forms. The meaning, power and pleasure all humans find in the arts, as creators or audiences, makes it clear that there are things we may want or need to 'say' that cannot be conveyed through words alone. The arts open these wider communication possibilities for young children, celebrating all their unique ways of using them, and valuing their capabilities (Niland, 2016). Figure 3.1 illustrates the different ways that creativity and the arts are part of children's lives.

Figure 3.1 Meanings of creativity and arts in young children's lives

Artistic and Creative Communication Begins at Birth

We are born with huge creative capacities as well as needs. Newborns are already skilful communicators, using the range of their voices, bodies and expressions as vehicles for communication and survival. Bonding with their caregiver is a crucial endeavor, so babies do everything possible to get the attention that ensures they are taken care of. In response to babies' communications, caregivers use a special, musical and creative expression in this duet. This has been named 'motherese' (Fernald, 1985) – a special kind of singing and playful speech reserved only for babies and very young children (although often also for cute animals that raise the carer instinct in us!). The role of this creative expression is to show responsiveness to the baby's style of communicating, and it serves to ensure that the baby focuses on the caregiver. It is a very special and crucial part of creating the bonding between babies and their closest caregivers.

The way our musical expression capacity is utilised creatively in these early interactions is a powerful example of humans' innate musicality. Babies need caregivers to keep them alive both physically and mentally. Life and its affordances are overwhelming and incomprehensible without a caregiver to assist in making sense of them. When we look at a frustrated, crying baby and a sensitive parent this can be understood: The crying baby is soothed with the musically descending melody and slow pulse of the caregiver's speech, often accompanied with slow, gentle movements, gestures and touch. Stern (1985) called these first emotional energy bursts 'vitality affects' (p. 53) which he regarded as playing an important role in tuning the caregiver and baby to a shared feeling-state. In a way this early communication 'drama' reveals the roots of our creativity. It helps us understand our fundamental human need for shared experiences in the sea of creativity and arts through our life span. We have an innate need to bond and belong to a community. This is conveyed through non-verbal, often creative or artistic elements or behaviors in our interactions. According to Trevarthen and Malloch (2000) we are born with *communicative musicality* – a special interest and capacity for interaction in and through music. Our need to connect and respond to each other is also at the heart of our various forms of mark-making (visual art forms and writing) and dance. Likewise, it drives our need to create shared narratives through various forms of storytelling and drama.

Making Sense of the World

Curiosity, exploration and imagination lead children to adventures, experiences and of course learning. They approach their environments with all their senses and aesthetic, artistic ways of engaging: touching, tasting, moving in the space, trying out their voices in it or playing with possibilities for making all the sounds it possesses and creating stories. These creative performances occur naturally, they seem innate to our ways of being. Children use creative, artistic expressions to gain and organise information about the world around them. This creative approach to making sense of their world and discovering its secrets is realised through curious exploration and play.

Our creative capacity is in use in our daily lives ('little c' creativity) for example when we solve problems or express ourselves with creative acts (Craft, 2001; Richards, 2010). Everyday creativity enables utilising our mental capacities and mind-body connections (Richards, 2010, p. 208). Therefore, it is very important to nurture everyday creativity in childhood, as this is when children are shaping their ideas of the world and its possibilities (Craft, 2001; Niland, 2016). Craft (2001) also highlights the value of questioning - 'What if …?' – as an approach for encouraging children to use their creativity. She depicts the features of this 'possibility thinking' as imagination, self-determination and direction, innovation, action, development, depth, taking risks, being imaginative, posing questions and playing -toying with possibilities (Craft, 2001, pp. 56–59).

The environment sets the dimensions in which playing with possibilities or artistic explorations can occur. The possibilities that open up, or the restrictions a child encounters can be concrete or abstract in nature. For example, the child can be offered lots of materials for play, but if educators' or society's values and attitudes are concerned mostly with talent, technical aspects of arts learning or the achievement of visible/audible outcomes, these may end up causing barriers for artistic expression and creativity. Therefore adults – early years practitioners, parents and caregivers – play a vital role in opening up the possibilities for learning in and through creativity and the arts (Huhtinen-Hildén, 2017; Huhtinen-Hildén & Pitt, 2018).

Kurkela calls the dimension that music creates *music reality*. This world beyond our everyday life, can be entered only by concentrating on the experience and letting the magic touch and affect you (Kurkela, 1993, pp. 48–49). Artistic, playful and imaginative dimensions can open for us through a range of art forms and creative actions and provide safe spaces in which curiosity, exploring possibilities and creativity form a solid ground for learning.

The environment created by arts and creative explorations is closely linked to the role of play in a child's life. Play leads children to territories where they negotiate and make sense of new or uncomfortable experiences.

> Alex, aged 2 years old, used dramatic role play to deal with needing to take a very bad-tasting medicine when he was ill. He found a small measuring cup and sat down with Maurice, his favourite teddy bear. Repeating the strategy his parents had adopted with him, he held the cup to the teddy's mouth, voiced the teddy's 'Noooo..' and then said 'Your medicine will make you better'.

Freud and Jung proposed that children's play serves important emotional purposes in their lives, as they meet the challenges of a world they are gradually learning to understand. Children use their artistic creativity in play to work through strange, uncomfortable or distressing or interesting situations, as Alex did in the story above.

Emotions, Self-Regulation and the Arts

The arts can play a powerful emotional role in our lives. For example, stories, paintings or music may meet our emotions as a mirror, as if someone has understood just how we feel and shared their emotions with us in the form of a creative artifact!

Music by its acoustic, time-based and atmospheric nature differs from other art forms and is especially powerful at arousing our emotions, even if we are not consciously listening. For example, there can be times in our lives when hearing something played in a minor key is too much, and tears find their way out. There emotional experiences evoked by music and music assisting to regulate these emotions has been studied intensively (e.g. Peltola & Eerola, 2016; Saarikallio & Erkkilä, 2007; Saarikallio et al., 2018, 2020). When we listen to music it affects us in many ways. We may encounter shared emotional material in music that matches our mood and helps us discover this as well as find a way to negotiate with this feeling. Music can also connect us with past experiences or emotions and give us the opportunity to relive the experience through the music even if the emotion has no relationship to our lives at that moment.

Children can actively use drawing, painting, dancing, singing or sound explorations as vehicles for self-regulation. Artistic activities may offer the child a needed pathway for adjusting emotions and behavior to suit the needs or demands of a current situation. For example, drawing can be calming for taking a distressed child. Children also use humming, singing or playing with their voice for this purpose. This ability to use creative and artistic actions in self-regulation can also be supported by parents, educators and caregivers. Calmly humming or making swaying movements are used naturally to soothe an upset child or comfort him/her after frustration.

> Susie was used to hearing a special song sung to her by her mother when she cried. This happened daily and the reasons for crying were – as often in children's lives – various: from a broken toy or having to stop her play for mealtime to hurting herself while hopping outside. For Susie the song had the power of easing the pain, mental or physical. One day her mother used the song in a situation that was not so dramatic in Susie's view. When she heard mother singing the song that was usually sung to comfort her when she cried, she told her mother very firmly to stop singing:' If you keep singing, I'll start crying because that's the crying song'.

In this example, for Susie this song was connected with her processes of self-regulation. The song meant time to cry, breathe and be soothed by the calming voice and music as well as the touch of her mother. When she had learned how the power of the crying song worked, she may hum the song herself to find comfort.

Creativity, Social Bonding and Communities of Practice

Creative actions and arts activities are some of the means through which we become part of our communities and develop feelings of belonging. In all cultures around the world, arts play a vital role in forming a sense of community. Cultural or artistic rituals and traditions carry meanings beyond words and can be understood at a very deep level. Our creative capacity allows us to position ourselves and negotiate verbally and non-verbally as part of communities of practice (see Lave & Wenger, 1991; Wenger, 1998): the various groups or communities we belong to in different areas of our lives. These communities operate to create norms, shared repertoire and traditions, often utilising creative interactions. These norms can consist of behaviors, attitudes and values, which can make communities of practice inclusive. There is also a possibility that the norms may sometimes make groups exclusive, so not truly a community of practice.

The role of the arts in creating communities of practice that are welcoming and inclusive is explored extensively in this book. As you will see in other chapters, creative and artistic experiences in the lives of children open up spaces where they can on one hand be invited into the community and on the other hand take part in shaping its values and boundaries, in essence its inclusivity.

> Matti, the early years practitioner, was to start with a new group of three- to four-year-old children. He had been informed beforehand of the multi-faceted backgrounds, challenges and needs of the children in the group. He wanted to construct a working culture that would recognise all the capabilities in the group and facilitate developing

empathy among the children. For the first day he collected as many different teddies as he could find. There we big and small, with stripes, squares and of various colours. Not all the teddy bears were in the same condition: some lacked a limb or an ear or were otherwise incomplete. The theme of the first week was to identify the secret powers and uniqueness of each teddy. These were then woven into singing activities, games, drawings, and a dance that celebrated the best suitable movement for each of the bears.

This case study shows one practitioner's approach to forming a creative, welcoming community of practice in an early years setting. The creative activities used the diverse teddy bears as a metaphor, to sing a playful song that celebrated something special from each child and to engage in a drama activity using 'the secret powers' of each participant.

The importance of creative inclusion should not be underestimated. We receive much of our information about the world around us in forms other than spoken language. A dance that is collaboratively created with movements from each participant, or a story consisting of every-one's input, carry a strong message: 'I belong to this group, everyone is needed, and we are all unique'. Creative activities that open up possibilities for bonding, belonging and self-expression form a safe and inclusive environment where possibilities and strengths are emphasised. These ideas can guide us in developing creative, child-centred and inclusive pedagogy. Throughout this book you will find principles, suggested strategies and short case studies to facilitate your inclusion journey through the arts.

THE CHILD AS AN ARTIST

Who can be called an artist? This is a fundamental question not only in the adult world of labor markets or arts institutions, but also in education and care. If we approach a child as an artist with artistic needs and capacities and their own 'voice', we end up in taking different pedagogical pathways than if we see a child as someone lacking an artistic education and therefore not as an equal in artistic expression. Anyone with formal music or visual arts training can impress with their instrumental performance, singing, drawing or painting; but on the other hand, the need to tell a story or convey a message through music or art does not primarily come from education: it comes from the creativity and desire to connect and express ourselves that is within each of us. Therefore, developing creative, inclusive arts pedagogy is combining the respect and cherishing of children's innate artistry and at the same time facilitating learning that gives children tools for the artistic expression they search for.

Being seen and appreciated as a unique human being is a fundamental need. Creative activities always embody this need: they can be captured as outbursts of our uniqueness, a 'vehicle for human flourishing' (see Elliott & Silverman, 2015, pp. 17–18). This makes creative and artistic exploration also a very vulnerable environment, in which emotional safety is essential.

Tuiku was absorbed in drawing in the corner of the room. Drawing was carried out with deep concentration, and 'flow' in this creative moment could be seen in the child's intense focus on the paper, careful choices of colours and purposeful crayon strokes. Early years teacher Mona approached the child, looked at the drawing and asked, 'What is it?' The child looked puzzled – for Tuiku the purpose of drawing today was not to make a picture of something, but to express Tuiku's way of being in the world at that moment.

Children need adults who are sensitive and respectful of their artistic worlds. We can never fully know what being in the world feels like for another human being, although their artistic expression can give us some insights. Therefore, how we approach these private, creative outbursts conveys strong messages about what we value.

The World of Possibilities Beyond

Three-year-old Tom is frustrated with his dad regulating his life in so many ways. Tom comes up with all kinds of ideas, actions and creative outbursts that very often crash into dad's rules and reality. The situation for Tom is difficult, but there is something that eases his being: he draws a picture of himself and his dad: One person in the picture is very tall and the other very small. He proudly presents this to his mother: 'Look, here is dad as a child and Tom as a grown up!'

This case study shows beautifully how creativity and artistic expression can assist in exploring emotions and working through difficult situations. Drawing gave Tom space to explore his feelings and find a way of coming to terms with the uncomfortable fact that he is just a small child, and his dad is the tall and capable adult making all the important decisions in his life (like when to go to sleep and what to eat for breakfast). Creativity eases this painful reality. He draws his creative solution to this impossible situation. At least in the imaginative world of his drawing he can change things and make them the way he'd like them to be.

Tom's use of drawing shows creativity as well as play. Creative and artistic actions offer a playful space where children can try different options and perhaps come to terms with reality or experiences. However, this space exists not just as a learning environment but also for its own sake: this imaginative world of possibilities enables a child to escape facts, realities and boundaries. This play world is constructed from inside the child and whether or not it is visible to others, it needs to be respected, valued and nurtured. In this way a child's artistic creativity may strengthen dispositions such as resilience that can act as a buffer against some of life's challenges (see e.g. Huhtinen-Hildén & Isola, 2019a).

Being able to move freely in the imagination can also be a matter of equity or power. Do we have equal possibilities to explore our power, or do others put us in our places? This relates both to equity and to inclusion: for example, children with disabilities can be seen only through the lens of their disability, or also as artists or creative beings.

To think about...

- What role has creativity played in your life, from childhood onwards?
- Have you experienced creative activities fostering a sense of belonging?

CONSTRUCTING THE CREATIVE ENVIRONMENT FOR INCLUSION

A group is an important environment for joining in and facilitating creativity and arts in early years settings. Creative processes as part of a group also have great potential for enhancing inclusion and experiencing, evolving and redirecting one's agency. Below, *the model for creative group processes* (Huhtinen-Hildén & Isola, 2019b) is used as a lens and explore its implications and theoretical underpinnings in early childhood education and care settings and practice.

Creative Group Processes Enhancing Inclusion

Playful, creative and artistic expression in collaborative group processes, can be conceived as a dialog where initiatives, power and contributions are shared and negotiated within the community of practice (Lave & Wenger, 1991; Wenger, 1998). These artistic journeys are common in early childhood education and care. The model shown in Figure 3.2 unravels the elements of a creative group process (Huhtinen-Hildén & Isola, 2019b). Studying this model and its theoretical underpinnings helps us to articulate and appreciate the importance of early years practice. In creative activities, life experiences and their significance can be reflected verbally and through creative experiences and actions such as singing, playing, improvising, moving, dancing, storytelling, painting, drawing rhymes, etc.

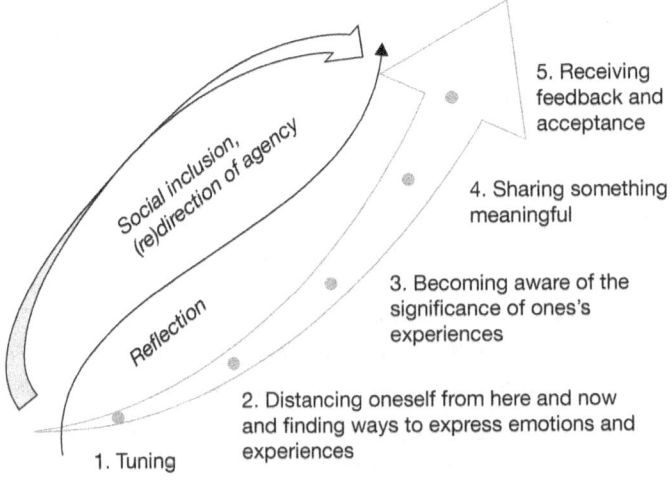

Figure 3.2 Model of creative group processes (Huhtinen-Hildén & Isola, 2019b)

This model explains how creative group activities enhance social inclusion and enable (re)direction of the agency of those participating. The process can be illustrated through phases of:

1 tuning in,
2 distancing oneself from here and now (transcendence) and finding ways to express emotions and experiences,
3 becoming aware of their significance,
4 sharing something meaningful and
5 receiving feedback and acceptance.

We will now look at each element or phase through the lens of early childhood education and care practice.

Tuning in

An early childhood group experience often begins with coming together to share something that is familiar to participants – a song, rhyme or other kind of ritual for coming together. Building an emotionally safe atmosphere and learning environment is a very important phase of creating a space where everyone feels accepted as they are (see Huhtinen-Hildén & Pitt, 2018, p. 75). Songs or name games in a circle are often used here for greeting and welcoming participants. We tune ourselves towards the group, the activities, the present moment and the shared journey to come. Creating a sense of togetherness in a group can also be facilitated without words – perhaps by passing a toy from hand to hand, welcoming or introducing everyone as part of the group with a gesture or signing. The most important element of tuning in is equity: all participants should be able to introduce themselves in the way they feel comfortable and able - everyone is respected as a unique and vital part of the specific group gathered. This conveys a message of being safe and protected. A form of tuning in that has become integral to coming together in many early years settings in Australia is the first nations traditional practice of 'acknowledgement of country', which is a way of honoring the history and traditional custodians of the place on which people are gathering together (see weblink at the end of this chapter).

Creative Activities and Distancing From Here and Now

After the welcoming ritual, the shared journey of creativity begins, and the group is drawn to the creative process. The expressive and creative pathways enable us to become part of the co-created moment. The *Tune of my life* research project deepens understanding of how in creative processes we reflect upon ourselves, whether unconsciously or consciously (Huhtinen-Hildén & Isola, 2019b). Creative activities, especially those inviting us to create something can open up this kind of space for self-inquiry, self-expression and emotions.

For children, living in a story, playing in their imaginative world, is their natural way of being, which may also feel very real and serious. For example, experiencing being scared of a monster or a dark cave while on a shared 'journey' offers an important chance to become familiar with this emotional experience in a safe context.

Kuura, aged 4, had difficulties falling asleep in the evening. The child's mother reported this after hearing that Kuura also had been afraid of sounds and shadows during sleep time at her early years centre. Apparently, many children had been feeling uneasy when trying to fall asleep there and this gave educators the idea of developing a creative group experience around this theme.

The starting point was a Teddy bear, who was worried about sounds, lights, shadows and thoughts going to sleep. The children each chose each a picture from a selection to represent something that frightens Teddy. After that they all selected an instrument to create sounds for their picture., and these sounds of scary things were shared in a circle. This opened up an animated discussion about the sounds, being scared and Teddy. The next thing was to create something that could help and comfort Teddy. The group co-created a safe and calming sound, gesture, spot in the room, rhyme or other element for each scary sound. The highlight of the process was the story made together connecting and using all the elements, which was performed to another group of children in the setting.

Creative experiences 'offer opportunities to encounter genuine emotions at the heart of our being' (Huhtinen-Hildén & Pitt, 2018, p. 89). Using our imagination and being in the world of stories and creativity enable us also to express our emotions through artistic activities and interpretation. In the case study above, the children worked together creatively to solve a shared problem, to help Teddy work through imaginary fears. This then gave Kuura the opportunity to reflect on her own real feelings of fear.

Becoming Aware of the Significance of Experiences

Living through a creative adventure raises fresh thoughts, perspectives and impulses. Meeting them through arts or creative experiences can allow us to become more aware of their significance in our lives. This emergent awareness is not necessarily verbal or spoken in nature. Meanings can also be conveyed through created artifacts or artistic interactions. This is tangible when we observe children in playful, creative group activities or in their shared play. Being aware of the importance of collaborative activities from this point of view challenges those of us working with children to use our pedagogical sensitivity. This inspires us, as practitioners in Kuura's early years setting did, to look for opportunities to take impulses and initiatives that children show us and use them to create a shared process that lives and breathes in the rhythm of all participants.

Sharing and Being Accepted

In creative experiences, emotions are always present. Communal experiences offer natural opportunities for expressing and sharing something that is meaningful for the participants - thoughts, ideas, musical impulses, dance movements, playing an instrument, singing, creating stories together or just smiling. Thus, any group situation needs to be facilitated with sensitivity and care, through inclusive and sensitive pedagogical approaches.

When cherished with this sensitivity and care, creative group experiences may offer children a safe environment for sharing as well as receiving acceptance. Being accepted in a group and receiving positive and supportive feedback on our ideas or creative expressions are innate needs for every one of us. These are crucial elements for learning and development at all ages. Nurturing a positive identity for every child as a unique person, artistic being and learner is a central aim of inclusive creative arts pedagogy.

Creative expressions open various possibilities for getting feedback and receiving or conveying acceptance. Feelings of empathy, compassion, togetherness as well as encountering and understanding one another are expressed and received through gestures, actions, artistic expression and words. This strengthens self-esteem and invites us to become part of the positive interaction in the group.

Social Inclusion and Redirecting One's Agency

The five vital elements/phases outlined above illustrate how creative group experiences can enhance social inclusion and redirect the agency of those participating in the process. These phases can be reflected upon and utilised flexibly when developing arts curriculum and in daily practice in early years settings. The guiding thought for early years practitioners could be, to honor children's multimodal ways of responding to the world through facilitating a creative environment and approaching everyday life through the lens of arts activities. Central to this is providing space for children to experience and evolve their agency.

Creativity and its role in our lives is very much linked with the concept of agency (see Jyrkämä, 2008; see also Nummijoki & Engeström, 2010; Sairanen & Kumpulainen, 2014). Being able to create, express yourself, explore possibilities and be playful strengthens children's experience of their agency and helps them to make sense of the world around them and express their feelings.

Valuing children's agency supports inclusion as it leads educators to look for ways to create opportunities for experience, implement and evolve their agency. Some of the conditions that support this may be easily provided and appropriate for all children, such as providing access to a selection of creative resources during free play. However, the most important aspect required is being responsive to uniqueness, and understanding the particular capabilities and needs of all children. This involves considering each child's interests, preferences and abilities, in order to provide a range of creative opportunities, and develop inclusive pedagogical approaches.

To think about...

- Take a moment to recall an arts-related group situation from your childhood, where you felt especially safe and accepted.
  - What were the elements and approaches that enabled your positive feelings?
  - Use these notions as a lens through which to reflect on your own early years practice: Identify a situation in your everyday practice that are linked to the same elements or approaches.

CONCLUSION

This chapter has shared our perspective on creativity and the arts as central to life and learning. Young children are on a voyage of discovery as they make meaning of their world. Their journey begins with curiosity, which drives their playful exploration, and creativity is ever-present on this voyage. The arts give children possibilities to explore and express their discoveries, thoughts and feelings. In early years settings, creativity as a group process helps build a sense of togetherness and community. When early years practitioners develop a safe, welcoming environment in and through creativity and the arts, this lays the foundations for inclusive environments in which each child's uniqueness is valued, and every child can flourish. The ideas in this chapter form the basis for the exploration in the following chapters of the creative and inclusive possibilities afforded by the various art forms offered to children in early years settings.

FURTHER READING AND RESOURCES

Acknowledgement of country in Australia
https://www.indigenous.gov.au/contact-us/welcome_acknowledgement-country

REFERENCES

Clough, P. (2002). *Narratives and fictions in educational research*. Open University Press.
Craft, A. (2001). Little c creativity. In A. Craft, B. Jeffrey, & M. Leibling (Eds.), *Creativity in education* (pp. 45–61). Continuum.

Elliott, D. J., & Silverman, M. (2015). *Music matters: A philosophy of music education* (2nd ed.). Oxford University Press.

Fernald, A. (1985). Four-month-old infants prefer to listen to motherese. *Infant Behaviour and Development, 8*(2), 181–195.

Huhtinen-Hildén, L. (2017). Elävänä hetkessä. Suunnitelmallisuus ja pedagoginen improvisointi. T. A. Lindeberg-Piiroinen & I. Ruokonen (toim.). *Musiikki varhaiskasvatuksessa -käsikirja,* 389–411. Classicus.

Huhtinen-Hildén, L., & Isola, A.-M. (2019a). Reconstructing life narratives through creativity in social work. *Cogent Social Sciences, 5*(1). https://doi.org/10.1080/23311886.2019.1606974

Huhtinen-Hildén, L., & Isola, A.-M. (2019b). *Luova ryhmätoiminta lisää hyvinvointia. Tutkimuksesta tiiviisti.* Terveyden ja hyvinvoinnin laitos. http://urn.fi/URN:ISBN:978-952-343-329-8

Huhtinen-Hildén, L., & Pitt, J. (2018). *Taking a learner-centred approach to music education: Pedagogical pathways.* Routledge.

Jyrkämä, J. (2008). Toimijuus, ikääntyminen ja arkielämä: Hahmottelua teoreettis-metodologiseksi viitekehykseksi. *Gerontologia, 22*(4), 190–203.

Kurkela, K. (1993). *Mielen maisemat ja musiikki. Musiikin tutkimuslaitoksen julkaisusarja 11.* Sibelius-Akatemia.

Lave, J., & Wenger, E. (1991). *Situated learning: Legitimate peripheral participation.* Cambridge University Press.

Niland, A. (2016). *Creativity and young children: Wondering, exploring, discovering, learning.* Early Childhood Australia.

Nummijoki, J., & Engeström, Y. (2010). Towards co-configuration in home care of the elderly: Cultivating agency by designing and implementing the mobility agreement. In H. Daniels, A. Edwards, Y. Engeström, T. Gallagher, & S. Ludvigsen (Eds.), *Activity theory in practice: Promoting learning across boundaries and agencies* (pp. 49–71). Routledge.

Peltola, H.-R., & Eerola, T. (2016). Fifty shades of blue: Classification of music-evoked sadness. *Musicae Scientiae, 20*(1), 84–102.

Richards, R. (2010). Everyday creativity: Process and way of life – four key issues. In J. C. Kaufman & R. J. Sternberg (Eds.), *The Cambridge handbook of creativity* (pp. 185–215). Cambridge University Press.

Saarikallio, S., & Erkkilä, J. (2007). The role of music in adolescents' mood regulation. *Psychology of Music, 35*(1), 88–109.

Saarikallio, S., Maksimainen, J., & Randall, W. M. (2018). Relaxed and connected: Insights into the emotional-motivational constituents of musical pleasure. *Psychology of Music, 47*, 644–662. https://doi.org/10.1177/0305735618778768

Saarikallio, S. H., Randall, W. M., & Baltazar, M. (2020). Music listening for supporting adolescents' sense of agency in daily life. *Frontiers in Psychology, 10.* Article 2911. https://doi.org/10.3389/fpsyg.2019.02911

Sairanen, H., & Kumpulainen, K. (2014). A visual narrative inquiry into children's sense of agency in preschool and first grade. *International Journal of Educational Psychology, 3*(2), 141–174.

Stern, D. N. (1985). *The interpersonal world of the infant: A view from psychoanalysis and developmental psychology*. Basic Books.

Trevarthen, C., & Malloch, S. (2000). The dance of well-being: Defining the musical therapeutic effect. *Nordic Journal of Music Therapy, 9*(2), 3–17.

Wenger, E. (1998). *Communities of practice: Learning, meaning, and identity*. Cambridge University Press.

Winnicott, D. W. (1971). *Playing and reality*. Tavistock Publications.

INTRODUCTION TO PART II

In Part Two, each chapter focuses on one art form, and combines research-informed discussion, case studies from practice and research, and suggestions to facilitate professional reflection and the implementation of inclusive arts practice. The art forms explored are those that children most commonly engage with in their daily lives and in early years settings.

When young children play, they actually often move seamlessly between several art forms. For example, while creating an imagined world and stepping into character roles during dramatic play, a child may sing, dance, tap out rhythms, create sound effects and engage in mark-making and creative construction. In spite of this creative flexibility, it is valuable for us as early years practitioners to consider the particular qualities of each art form individually. This specific focus allows for more effective facilitation of children's participation in ways that can support them in building their knowledge of the elements, materials and techniques of each art form. Our understanding of each art form can enable us to offer children rich and varied opportunities for creative exploration and expression. Most importantly, our understanding of, and confidence in, engaging with each art form can support our awareness of the possibilities that each offers for inclusive pedagogy and practice.

4

MUSIC AS AN INVITING ENVIRONMENT FOR CONNECTING AND BELONGING

Laura Huhtinen-Hildén
and Amanda Niland

Chapter objectives

This chapter introduces you to these key ideas:

- Experience and expression in and through music
- Music and learning
- Music experiences as an environment for exploring who we are and how we connect with others

INTRODUCTION

In this chapter, we share examples of experiences that help us explore music as an innate part of life, with great potential for interaction, connection and relationships, especially in early years settings. We present early childhood music practice as a means to open up possibilities for inclusion, creative experiences and learning.

MUSIC AS A COMPANION IN LIFE

Regulation of Emotions and Actions

The baby, unsettled, makes some frustrated sounds. The mother is occupied and does not respond. The whining gets louder and the baby throws the dummy to the floor. The mother picks it up and gives it back, but does not pay full attention until the baby's little round face turns red with screaming. At that point the mother takes the baby from the pushchair, and uses a soothing voice, humming-like speech and movements, easing the baby and herself with the shared, slowing down tempo.

This scene, familiar to many, illustrates the musical elements present in early infant/carer interactions. In this soundscape, rhythm, melody, playing with intensities of sounds and possibilities for vocal expressions and movement create musical self-regulation. Although for most caregivers this mother's behaviour happens instinctively, the interaction can also be viewed through a developmental lens. Using vocal expressions to facilitate regulating babies' emotions can later become a tool for the child to use on her own – humming or singing can be means of self-regulation. This is one important role that music can have in children's lives.

The power of music relates very much to its potential to evoke or match our emotions. For example, music that evokes sorrowful feelings may feel comforting (Peltola & Eerola, 2016) and help us work through our experiences and emotions or share them with others. This can be used with young children – finding names for the emotions that music evokes and getting to know them builds an important basis for coping with feelings throughout life. Musical play can facilitate exploring the essence of emotions, making them more tangible for the child.

Music can assist in organising the world in an understandable way, which also supports children's self-regulation. Early childhood takes children on a journey of discovery through a fascinating world full of distractions and temptations. To resist or decide between the immediate call of various impulses children need the ability to regulate their behaviour to suit the situation at hand. Music such as action or transition songs gives a sense of managing time and actions, supporting the development of self-regulation skills (Eklund & Heinonen, 2011). The way music progresses in time gives a feeling of knowing what to expect. Similarly, the lyrics of a song can guide children's actions, supporting their focus on the task at hand.

Making Sense of the World and Learning Through Music

What do we mean by musical learning during early childhood: learning *about* music, or *in and through* music? The first implies developing skills such as 'keeping the beat', singing in tune, reading musical notation or playing a musical instrument. The second means being and becoming, sharing, connecting, interacting and experiencing the musical worlds of children, their families and communities. Therefore, answering the question of what actually constitutes learning means reflecting on the purpose and value of music in the early years generally, and within education and care.

Research on infants' responses to music has shown that an urge to connect musically with others seems to be an essential human instinct (e.g. Malloch & Trevarthen, 2009; Trainor & Schmidt, 2003). Malloch and Trevarthen explored the musicality inherent in vocal interactions and identified reciprocal synchronisation of the beat (pulse) between adults and infants. They found that infants and adults match sound quality (pitch and dynamics) with each other, in a sort of musical 'call and response' that creates a shared narrative. Research with deaf mothers and their infants showed corresponding findings, with embodied 'narratives' related to the rhythmic qualities of the mothers' signing (Trehub & Nakata, 2001/2002). These findings have been acknowledged widely as evidence of our innate musicality (Dissanayake, 2011). It is significant also that many characteristics of early adult/infant musical interactions are shared across cultures and throughout history. For example, the use of lullabies – slow, quiet music, mostly singing, with a narrow pitch range – to soothe an infant is widespread.

The idea that music is an innate part of our humanity suggests the need for a child-focused approach to music education in early childhood that combines learning *in* and *through* music. In such an approach, each child's uniqueness and connectedness to their cultures (family, community and beyond) provide starting points for music pedagogy. Getting to know children and their families, encouraging the sharing of songs and other music from home, and observing children's musical interests and preferences during free play and group times can guide educators with their musical/pedagogical planning and provisioning.

Exploring Who We Are

Musical activities open rich territory for exploring our being in the world. We can play with possibilities of sounds, emotions and expression – being active in singing, playing, moving and listening. Children's imaginations and stories are nurtured by music, offering rich possibilities for curiosity and exploration. Music allows us to make sense of the world and play with different ways of being part of it.

Musical experiences serve as a playground for finding out who we are, where we belong and how we can be with others. Musical actions convey cultural features, traditions and values which also help us appreciate differences, thus music can bring about inclusion. Songs that belong to a specific cultural context or an instrument that is used in it open up new perspectives and widen the experiences of something previously unknown to us. All elements in music that introduce us to something new, such as genres, styles and sounds of music across cultures serve as preparation for other areas in life where we encounter something or someone unfamiliar to us. In early years settings, forming an inclusive atmosphere in a group needs a strong sense of acceptance. Social and cultural inclusion also involves learning about the musical traditions of all community members in the early years setting. In many nations with multi-ethnic and multicultural populations, music has an important role to play in building understanding and social inclusion. The case study below illustrates a child who feels safe sharing music of his culture with his peers.

> On arriving at preschool, Paulo (aged 4) went straight to the musical instrument area and joined Matias (4) and Mara (5). Mara was playing the bongos and Matias the castanets. Thomas chose the tambourine.
>
> They played their instruments for a while, exploring different sounds, sometimes loudly and sometimes softly. Suddenly, Paulo asked his friends to be quiet because he wanted to show them and me (educator) a song from Colombia.
>
> With the tambourine on his right hand, Paulo started singing and playing "Estrellas de Belen" in Spanish, following its beat.
>
> Then he asked me to make a video to show his mum and began again. He gave the camera a big smile and occasionally looked at himself in the large mirror nearby, watching how he looked while playing and singing. His friend Matias started to accompany him with castanets.
>
> EDUCATOR'S REFLECTIONS: "Estrellas de Belen" is a religious song which makes me think this song goes deeply into the cultural beliefs of Paulo's family and is probably a song that he has sung and listened to repeatedly. I noticed that at all times Paulo had a smile on his face, seeming happy and proud of himself and his culture. (Niland, 2020, Early years educator's observation notes)

This case study is from data gathered by Amanda in a study of the potential of music for connection, communication and relationship building in an early years setting (Niland, 2020). In this setting in an ethnically diverse inner suburb in Sydney, Australia, music is an important part of the children's days. A musical play area is always available, with provisions carefully selected and positioned to be responsive to children's musical interests and preferences. Educators plan and interact intentionally to be responsive to and inclusive of each child.

The children featured in the case study often start their day by gathering in the music play area. As first-language Spanish speakers, they often share Spanish songs with each other and the class. The educators have taken time to learn about the songs, asking the children's families and searching the internet. They have also sourced some instruments used in South American music, such as castanets and a small cajon (box drum), that the children use regularly. The importance of music to Paolo and the sense of belonging generated by the use of the familiar, meaningful song, seems obvious. It is interesting to note his wish to create a link between his musical play and his home, by singing a favourite song with his friends and sharing the moment with his mother via a video.

Music Widening the Possibilities of 'I Can'

The agency has been defined as children's capacity to make decisions and choices and take independent action (Sairanen & Kumpulainen, 2014). Experiencing music and being nurtured to express oneself within a creative musical world foster children's experiences of their capabilities and possibilities to function, helping them to make sense of their world and express their feelings. This strengthens their agency beliefs that, according to Leemann et al. (2021, p. 4), determine largely the experiences of social inclusion. Children's opportunities to be creative and to use music for interaction, expressing themselves, communicating and connecting with others, as Paolo did in the example above, opens up possibilities for experiencing, evolving and redirecting one's agency (see Jyrkämä, 2008; see also Nummijoki & Engeström, 2010; Sairanen & Kumpulainen, 2014). This builds children's confidence, empowering them to play, take risks or experiment. Providing a safe space for music activities means combining respect for and cherishing of children's innate musical 'voices' with facilitating learning that gives children tools for musical expression and interaction they search for.

Music Supporting Communication and Language Skills

A growing body of research suggests that music has an impact on the brain and may contribute to many aspects of development (Peretz & Zatore, 2003; Schellenberg, 2020). The value of music, especially singing, for supporting early language and literacy development is widely anecdotally acknowledged. Many educators, music therapists and speech and language therapists regularly use songs, rhymes and rhythms in their work with young children, aiming to facilitate speech or literacy learning. Linnavalli et al. (2018, p. 1) confirm that 'a growing body of evidence from behavioural research suggests that there are also causal links between music and language'. This relationship has been demonstrated for example by research using sonic analysis technology that identified musical elements in speech such as rhythm, meter and pitch (Brandt et al., 2012). Analysis of recordings of mother/infant vocal interactions also show these elements, and importantly, the reciprocal musical synchronisation of adults and infants (Malloch & Trevarthen, 2009).

Given the intrinsically musical nature of speech, it becomes clearer why songs, rhymes and musical games have been linked to language development. A rich musical environment in everyday activities has beneficial effects on the development of sensitivity to auditory changes (Putkinen et al., 2013). Both the informal musical activities such as musical play and parental singing (see Putkinen et al., 2013) and regular, organised music sessions in early years settings (Linnavalli et al., 2018, 2021) are valuable for many aspects of children's learning and development of communication and linguistic skills.

To think about...

In the daily practice of early years education and care:

- Are the musical items available physically accessible to every child, with adaptations and choices provided?
- Do these items offer a range of sound possibilities to suit diverse sensory interests and preferences?
- Are the music activities facilitated with various means of communicating choices or ideas (e.g. visuals or tactiles) to meet the interests, needs and preferences of every child?

MUSIC EXPERIENCES - INVITATIONS TO CONNECT

Bonding - We Are Drawn to Musical Interaction

Music is present in our lives from very early on. Even in the womb, rhythms and sounds surround the child. In early interactions, musical elements play an important role in infant/carer communication. According to Malloch and Trevarthen (2009), we are born with communicative musicality – a special interest and capacity for interaction in and through music. Therefore, music is an essential companion in early years education and care.

Music offers a non-visible space where we can experience togetherness in a very strong and unique way.

Music can be both inside and outside us – at the same time tangible and incomprehensible. Music experiences provide a way to communicate ideas, join with others and create an environment for learning in and through interaction.

Joining in

In an early years setting, the group is gathering in a circle. The invitation to join is conveyed through a song and the open arms of a teacher. Children copy the welcoming gesture and form a singing circle holding hands.

This common scene shows our mirror neurons at work. These are activated by even watching each other perform a task or express an emotion – they help us to tune to each other (Livingstone & Thompson, 2009). Music, as something we experience through our bodies, senses and emotions, assists this beautifully; we share the same tempo of a song and synchronise movements with others, in a reciprocal process akin to the 'communicative musicality' of infants and carers mentioned earlier. All this facilitates feelings of acceptance, sharing and belonging, being part of this group.

In the introduction, Laura shared her vision of music as a 'lap' that draws everyone in, which describes the feeling of how music creates a sonic environment around everyone in the space. This special feature could explain why music, especially singing, is part of social gatherings across the world, including in classrooms, as a way of welcoming people and experiencing togetherness. Singing or moving to music with others brings a strong emotional response that seems to speak to our innate human urge to connect. In early years settings, this musical coming together often takes the form of greeting songs at the start of group times. These welcoming experiences invite children to feel safe to join a group with their peers, to interact creatively and build a musical community of practice (Lave & Wenger, 1991). Placing a child's name in a greeting song is particularly important – a public acknowledgement of that child as an individual, who is valued in the group.

Traditional welcoming rituals, such as the Australian acknowledgement of country mentioned in Chapter 3, are also part of the daily routine in many early years settings in Aotearoa New Zealand, and involve music. The early childhood curriculum of Aotearoa New Zealand is called *Te Whāriki* (Ministry of Education, 2017), which means a woven mat. This symbolises the interweaving of the diverse cultural threads of Maori, Pakeha (white) and Pacific island people and traditions. Early years musical welcoming rituals often follow Maori practices. Bodkin-Allen (2012) describes a welcoming ritual she observed:

> they sit in a circle with their teachers for the morning karakia (prayer) and mihimihi (ritualized self-introduction). A waiata (song) is sung after each child's mihimihi, emulating the protocol of the marae, and is accompanied by a teacher playing the guitar. Each child selects the waiata that follows his or her speech, and everyone joins in the singing. In this way the group shows their support to the child, and they all become one group or whanau (family). (p. 4)

This particular welcoming ritual, while following a predictable sequence, allows each child to choose their own waiata (song), which invites everyone to join in and contribute. The following case study from Australia shows a welcoming ritual, with visual modes of communication used as part of an inclusive approach.

Mara (5.5) and Juni (4) took the bongo and started to sing "let's sing hello to everyone". Mara decided that they were going to be in charge of group time that day, so the educator brought them the big felt board. Juni chose song choice pictures to put on the board. "No, no, no" said Mara "we need to start with the Acknowledgement". Both girls looked for the Aboriginal flag picture in the song basket but couldn't find it, so asked the educator. The educator brought it and the welcome song symbol. They put the Aboriginal flag, the welcome song symbol, the symbol for bongo and then their chosen songs. A small group gathered as the two girls started the Acknowledgement. They included key-word signs as we always do in group time and Chen and the educator followed, then continued with the welcome song "Let's sing hello to…" using the bongos. Tommy also participated and played the bongos while the group sang "let's sing hello to Tommy". After that, the girls asked other children to choose songs from the board and we sang them together. Suddenly, the board fell off its stand, causing a big giggle around the group. Chen decided to assist Mara and Juni and stood behind them holding the board while they continued their group time which resulted in more giggles. Mara decided it was Tommy's turn to choose a song. As Tommy didn't stand up when his name was called, Mara took his hand and walked him towards the felt board to help him choose. When Tommy didn't point at any songs, Mara chose Row, Row your Boat, saying it was Tommy's favourite. (Niland, 2020, Early years educator's observation notes)

As part of regular rituals in an early years setting, musical greetings can sometimes be used beyond routine group times to welcome individual children as they arrive for the day. For infants and toddlers forming their first relationships with adults outside their home and family, being greeted by a song containing their name can be an intimate and caring way to begin their day. Through this, educators can create the secure relationships that very young children need to build their sense of belonging in this new community. Familiar greeting rituals make us all feel safe and relaxed, but this predictability is especially important to infants and toddlers – this special musical moment can make a warm and friendly arrival ritual.

A song used for greeting in an early years setting might be adapted from one that practitioners know is a favourite of the group or of individual children, or perhaps a song that family members have shared. Sharing songs and music from children's home and community cultures is one of the ways that music can create a bridge between home and early years settings as one element of inclusive pedagogy. Children are more likely to feel a sense of belonging in an early years setting when aspects of their home cultures are acknowledged and enjoyed by their educators and peers.

To think about...

- Take a moment to reflect on welcoming rituals in your practice:
  - What kind of musical elements are utilised in these greetings?
  - What meaning or significance might these rituals have for children and families?
- Make a list of all the modes of communication used by children and families in your setting's community. Consider the first languages of all, both spoken and non-spoken, reflecting on children's play, creative expressions and general communication of children's feelings, ideas and needs throughout the day.
  - How do these modes of communication relate to the group gatherings in your setting? What kind of invitations for interaction do these situations provide?
  - What modes of communication – other than words – are used (e.g. visuals, key word signing, gesture, facial actions, movement and sound makers), and how do these meet the needs of the group?
  - How can multiple languages and modes of communication be incorporated into musical practice?

Connecting Cultures

Including a range of cultures in early years settings enables relationships founded in mutual valuing and respect for multiple ways of being. Everyone's sense of belonging is strengthened when children feel that their lives outside the setting are reflected in its environment, play provisions and daily practices, when they can connect with and share each other's cultures. Music is one of the ways to make these connections. There are two main reasons for exploring and sharing music from many cultures with children. Firstly, it is fascinating to hear and engage with the amazing diversity of music from around the world and past times. Secondly, it symbolises our common humanity and the many unique musical differences between us. Diversity in relation to music also encompasses the many ways that we may experience music. Music involves vibrations, which can be felt through our hearing and in other embodied ways. Musical provisions, such as speakers and floor surfaces that carry vibrations, encouraging movement with music, using instruments with rich vibrations such as drums, the use of signing as a form of singing and exploring digital visual representations of music, represent some of the richness of deaf musical cultures (see resources at the end of this chapter). Encountering, enjoying and valuing diverse music in a variety of ways provide a model of openness and inclusiveness.

Music can also be part of processes of reconciliation on a path to social justice. Each nation has a diverse musical history. For those with a colonial history, such as Australia, the musical cultures of the indigenous peoples are often enmeshed in that history. For nations such as the USA, Australia, New Zealand and Canada, where first nations peoples are not the majority, in small but meaningful ways, reconciliation and inclusion are being fostered by educators who share with children the stories behind the music of their nations' past. Also for example in the USA, many beautiful songs from the times of slavery have long been sung and enjoyed in schools and summer camps but not necessarily contextualised for children in relation to their history and full meaning. However, when teachers tell children the stories behind such songs, a process of social healing may be possible. Occasionally, teachers may also decide not to use a song if its history and meaning directly conflict with the inclusive culture of the setting and the anti-bias goals of their pedagogy. There is an important difference between a multicultural music curriculum, where music of many cultures is shared for its musical interest, and an inclusive, culturally affirming music curriculum, where the lives of the people who created this music and social justice aspects of the music's history are explored.

In Australia, early years policies and curricula aim to contribute to a more socially just and inclusive nation and building Aboriginal cultural knowledge is stressed in the national early childhood curriculum (AGDE, 2022). Gradual progress towards cultural respect and inclusion in Australia is illustrated in the story of the recent history of the song, Taba Naba. This song, from Thursday Island, in the Torres Strait Islands in the far north of Australia, was recorded by children's group The Wiggles and is popular in early years settings. However, until quite recently, the full story of its origins was not known, and it was falsely labelled as 'traditional'. The Torres Strait Islands were settled by Christian missionaries after white settlement and many islanders became slaves on Queensland sugar cane plantations. Taba Naba's story is enmeshed in the recent history of these islands (see Taba Naba YouTube video).

Creating a Caring Community

Musical experiences can provide child-centred and inclusive ways to develop vital skills and understandings through planned or spontaneous interactions that lay a foundation for the rest of life. The following case study shows children developing new social connections and their capacity for empathy through their physical and perceptual experience of music and movement.

> JJ was feeling a bit upset so I invited him to sit on the jumping board to sing and play "Five Cheeky Monkeys", which is a music experience that has a soothing effect on him. JJ and I sat and I sang while we bounced. Very soon we were joined by five other children. We continued singing "Five Cheeky Monkeys" together, bouncing the board so energetically that some of the children were jumping while sitting. Giggles accompanied the chant as all the children enjoyed the game together. Everyone was very caring too, adjusting their strength so that JJ didn't feel scared. Maya hugged and tickled JJ while singing, which made him laugh. At one point, Juni and Carl pretended to be cheeky monkeys and jumped from the board to the ground. Then Carl, Freya and Juni did some monkey dancing, while the rest of us continued bouncing on the board and singing the song.

> Educator's reflection: This was a wonderful, unplanned music experience that connected children to each other. Children who don't usually play together joined in - bouncing, dancing and pretending to be monkeys, and interacting through facial expressions, body language and giggles. The connection between them was full of energy and excitement. The song was a way to play together which included being very careful for their friends who are learning how to balance. (Niland, 2020, Early years educator's observation notes)

Structure and Pedagogical Improvisation

Playful musical activities create a wonderful, exploratory world where a whole class or group can join in and share a special kind of being together. This can bring challenges for early years educators who need to balance a guiding structure for the session with respect for, and responsiveness to the initiatives of participants. Weaving in ideas, thoughts and needs of the group calls for pedagogical improvisation (Donmoyer, 1983; Sawyer, 2011). To facilitate creative activities in a group setting means navigating for a balance of structure and improvisation (Huhtinen-Hildén, 2017; Huhtinen-Hildén & Pitt, 2018), as the case study below illustrates.

> Vili is becoming more comfortable to participate in our music group times. When he first started at preschool, he often cried and wanted to be outside. Respecting this, for a while an educator would sit near the door with him as he observed the group from outside.
>
> Recently, Vili came and sat with Cara (Educator) as she took the group. He tapped with the stick when we sang "Let's sing hello to everyone", a smile on his face. Vili also chose a song from the visuals when invited - 'Eency weency spider'.
>
> Now he often chooses to sit closer to the group. Today, when we sang 'Let's sing hello to everyone', he played the drum independently with some soft sounds and some loud sounds.
>
> Educator's reflection: Vili finds some changes hard in the routine. With music, which he enjoys, he has made some steps toward participating in a new routine. I reflected on how the use of visuals can help. We also have some predictability in our group times, which seems to assist many children, including Vili, to join in. (Niland, 2020, Early years educator's observation notes)

Musical elements themselves as well as music related activities can offer structure and predictability. This can be very helpful for children whose ways of being are challenged by the transitions and changes that are part of everyday life. Using music purposefully to create a sense of here and now and structure time supports all children in various other aspects of life as well. Music also offers non-spoken means to connect, as case studies in this chapter have shown. The case study of Vili's steps towards feeling confident to join in shows how a sense of belonging can be fostered through the familiar structures of music.

Conclusion

In this chapter, we have introduced some of the particular features of music and music-related activities that make it such an important part of early years education and care. We have drawn on the growing body of research into the innate musicality of humans and the role of music in young children's lives, learning and development. We have shared examples of inclusive musical experiences from early years settings, with the aim of providing opportunities to reflect on the meaning of music-making for young children, and on the ways that music can be inclusive of all children, celebrating their ways of experiencing and expressing themselves in and through music and supporting their sense of belonging, while also contributing to their learning and development. We have also shared some musical ideas for you to explore with young children, which we hope you will find useful in your inclusive education toolkit.

To think about...

- What kinds of memories do you recall related to music or music activities from your childhood?
- How do those memories resonate with the themes explored in this chapter?
- Thinking of your daily practice, what kind of experiences and possibilities could music activities open up for children?

RESOURCES

Digital visualisations of music:

Trepak from Tchaikowsky's *The Nutcracker Suite*.

https://www.youtube.com/watch?v=HfUz0NBOBEs

Winter from Vivaldi's *The Four Seasons*.

https://www.youtube.com/watch?v=Qqe0GdUpJHs&list=PLCY0YtwvPCkWll-0RXwTqbEQwT-l8yoz-b&index=4

Taba Naba YouTube video: *The story of Taba Naba*.

https://www.youtube.com/watch?v=JBMyHVPOQqE

REFERENCES

Australian Government Department of Education [AGDE]. (2022). *Belonging, being and becoming: The early years learning framework for Australia (v 2.0)*. Commonwealth of Australia.

Bodkin-Allen, S. (2012). The interweaving threads of music in the Whariki of early childhood cultures in Aotearoa/New Zealand. In *The Oxford handbook of children's musical cultures*. https://www.oxfordhandbooks.com/view/10.1093/oxfordhb/9780199737635.001.0001/oxfordhb-9780199737635-e-23?mediaType=Article&q=a%E2%80%99oga+amata

Brandt, A., Gebrian, M., & Slevc, L. R. (2012). Music and early language acquisition. *Frontiers in Psychology, 3*, 327.

Dissanayake, E. (2011). Homo Musicus: Are humans predisposed to be musical. *Encuentro de Ciencias Cognitivas de la Música, 10*, 17–21.

Donmoyer, R. (1983). Pedagogical improvisation. *Educational Leadership, 40*, 39–43.

Eklund, K., & Heinonen, J. (2011). Lapsen itsesäätelyn tukeminen arjessa. In T. Aro & M.-L. Laakso (Eds.), *Taaperosta Taitavaksi Toimijaksi. Itsesäätelytaitojen Kehitys ja Tukeminen* (pp. 216–235). Niilo Mäki Instituutti.

Huhtinen-Hildén, L. (2017). Elävänä hetkessä. Suunnitelmallisuus ja pedagoginen improvisointi. In A. Lindeberg-Piiroinen & I. Ruokonen (Eds.), *Musiikki varhaiskasvatuksessa – käsikirja* (pp. 389–411). Classicus.

Huhtinen-Hildén, L., & Pitt, J. (2018). Taking a learner-centred approach to music education. In *Pedagogical pathways*. Routledge.

Jyrkämä, J. (2008). Toimijuus, ikääntyminen ja arkielämä: Hahmottelua teoreettis-metodologiseksi viitekehykseksi. *Gerontologia, 22*(4), 190–203. (Title in English: Agency, ageing and everyday life: A sketch of a theoretical-methodological framework)

Lave, J., & Wenger, E. (1991). *Situated learning: Legitimate peripheral participation*. Cambridge University Press.

Leemann, L., Martelin, T., Koskinen, S., Härkänen, T., & Isola, A.-M. (2021). Development and psychometric evaluation of the experiences of social inclusion scale. *Journal of Human Development and Capabilities*. https://doi.org/10.1080/19452829.2021.1985440

Linnavalli, T., Putkinen, V., Lipsanen, J., Huotilainen, M., & Tervaniemi, M. (2018). Music playschool enhances children's linguistic skills. *Scientific Reports, 8*(1), 8767. https://doi.org/10.1038/s41598-018-27126-5

Linnavalli, T., Soni Garcia, A., & Tervaniemi, M. (2021). Perspectives on the potential benefits of children's group-based music education. *Music and Science, 4*, 1–14. https://doi.org/10.1177/20592043211033578

Livingstone, S. R., & Thompson, W. F. (2009). The emergence of music from the Theory of Mind. *Musicae Scientiae, 13*(2_Suppl. l), 83–115.

Malloch, S., & Trevarthen, C. (2009). Musicality: Communicating the vitality and interests of life. In S. Malloch & C. Trevarthen (Eds.), *Communicative musicality: Exploring the basis of human companionship* (pp. 3–11). Oxford University Press.

Ministry of Education. (2017). *Te Whāriki. He whāriki mātauranga mō ngā mokopuna o Aotearoa. Early childhood curriculum*. https://www.education.govt.nz/assets/Documents/Early-Childhood/Te-Whariki-Early-Childhood-Curriculum-ENG-Web.pdf

Niland, A. (2020). *Making music together: Using music to support belonging and peer relationships in an inclusive Early Childhood setting*. Unpublished research data. Ethics approval number 2020/123. The University of Sydney.

Nummijoki, J., & Engeström, Y. (2010). Towards co-configuration in home care of the elderly: Cultivating agency by designing and implementing the mobility agreement. In H. Daniels, A. Edwards, Y. Engeström, T. Gallagher, & S. Ludvigsen (Eds.), *Activity theory in practice: Promoting learning across boundaries and agencies* (pp. 49–71). Routledge.

Peltola, H.-R., & Eerola, T. (2016). Fifty shades of blue: Classification of music-evoked sadness. *Musicae Scientiae, 20*(1), 84–102.

Peretz, I., & Zatorre, R. (Eds.). (2003). *The cognitive neuroscience of music*. Oxford University Press.

Putkinen, V., Tervaniemi, M., & Huotilainen, M. (2013). Informal musical activities are linked to auditory discrimination and attention in 2–3-year-old children: An event-related potential study. *European Journal of Neuroscience, 37*(4), 654–661.

Sairanen, H., & Kumpulainen, K. (2014). A visual narrative inquiry into children's sense of agency in preschool and first grade. *International Journal of Educational Psychology, 3*(2), 141–174.

Sawyer, R. K. (2011). What makes good teachers great? The artful balance of structure and improvisation. In R. K. Sawyer (Ed.), *Structure and improvisation in creative teaching* (pp. 1–24). Cambridge University Press.

Schellenberg, E. G. (2020). Correlation = causation? Music training, psychology, and neuroscience. *Psychology of Aesthetics, Creativity, and the Arts, 14*(4), 475.

Trainor, L. J., & Schmidt, L. A. (2003). Processing emotions induced by music. In I. Peretz & R. Zatorre (Eds.), *The Cognitive neuroscience of music*. Oxford University Press.

Trehub, S. E., & Nakata, T. (2001/2002). Emotion and music in infancy. *Musicae Scientiae, 5*(1_Suppl. l), 37–61. https://doi.org/10.1177/10298649020050S103

5
ENHANCING INCLUSION THROUGH MOVEMENT AND DANCE

Amanda Niland and
Laura Huhtinen-Hildén

Chapter objectives

This chapter introduces you to these key ideas:

- Exploring the world through our bodies
- Movement, dance and emotions
- Movement and dance in early years settings
- Movement and dance as social and cultural narratives
- Planning and implementing inclusive dance play activities

INTRODUCTION

In this chapter, we delve into the world of expression through bodily movement and explore the role of creative movement and dance in young children's lives and early years of education and care. We present creative movement, bodily expression and dance as 'languages' used by children, as suggested by the educators of Reggio Emilia. We explore the many ways that children use the possibilities of movement and dance to make and express meaning, individually and collaboratively. We discuss the potential of creative bodily expression for connection and communication between children with diverse ways of being in the world. Our aim is to facilitate understanding of the potential of movement and dance as forms of inclusion in action, thus valuable within inclusive arts pedagogy.

EXPLORING THE WORLD AND LIFE THROUGH OUR BODIES

Our unique and diverse bodies are fundamental to how we perceive the world and express ourselves. As Merleau-Ponty states: 'The body is our general medium for having a world' (1962, p. 169). From infancy, our bodily expressions reveal our moods and emotions, and we communicate with gestures and movements throughout our lives, even if we don't realise it. We can listen, feel, play, learn, interact and create with our bodies and their movements. In recognition of children's aesthetic awareness and the aesthetic aspects of movement when used expressively, we also use the word *dance* to refer to creative body movement that encompasses all bodies and ways of moving.

Children may be drawn to dance as a form of expression, given their innate desire to move. Movement is sometimes defined as a 'sixth sense' termed proprioception (Schiller & Meiners, 2012) – the physical experience of moving through space and the body's 'sensing of the skin surface, muscle, tendon and joint motion, weight balance, resistance to gravity and acceleration/deceleration' (Schiller & Meiners, p. 87). Children use proprioception to explore their world and develop conceptual understandings, a key part of early learning. For example, consider young children's fascinating explorations of water. Through their hands, legs, skin, eyes, ears, tongues and whole-body movements, or however they explore water, they build a sense of water that is the basis of their conceptual understanding of liquid – how it feels and moves, its density and energy against them. Through aesthetic movement, children can express their knowledge and feelings about water. As Dewey suggests, dancing the familiar with imaginative action transforms it into new expressions of ideas (1934/2005). The case study below shows children using dance in these ways.

The Dance of the Firefly

A group of four-year-olds in an early childhood setting, together with their teacher, are creating a dance that tells the story of fireflies and a magic tree that gives them their light each night. One child stands in the centre as the tree. He gets into a stretchy cotton body bag and moves his arms and legs inside it to make a tree trunk shape. The other children choose pieces of gossamer-like coloured fabrics and spread out around the tree. As music starts, the teacher suggests they fly, and the children move around, experimenting with their arms and the fabrics in an improvised dance. As fireflies, they also vocalise different high-pitched sounds. 'Connect!' calls the teacher, and the children move to touch the magical tree, to get their light, in a moment of stillness. The flying-connecting pattern is repeated until the music ends, with the fireflies gathered at the tree. (Adapted from Deans & Wright, 2018, pp. 125–127)

In this dance, the children's movements embodied their imagined versions of fireflies. Their interpretations varied, depending on their ideas, physical preferences, capabilities and interactions with peers. With gentle guidance from their teacher, they used their bodies individually and together to explore a story they'd enjoyed and engage in conceptual learning. Without direct instruction, they were also learning about dance. They explored spatial possibilities around themselves as they moved their arms and travelled around the room, and spatial relationships with peers as they flew, then gathered to connect with the magical tree. They created a range of actions with arms and legs, extending their movement 'vocabulary' and using varying energy to express their imaginative ideas about how fireflies move, inspired by the music *Veronica Takes a Bath*, by Australian composer Peter Mumme.

MOVEMENT, DANCE AND EMOTIONS

Dance can be a powerful tool for cognitive and emotional learning. As well as exploring and developing concepts about the physical world, young children use dance to explore and express feelings. There is great potential for emotional and physical connections with others when dancing together. Physical closeness and creative movement, especially in a collaborative response to music, can foster feelings of self-efficacy and togetherness within a group (Hanna, 2008). Dance can also build respect between children for each other's physical well-being. Richards, reflecting on children's creative movement explorations in a school in Reggio Emilia, Italy, says: 'When children first come to school, a pervasive message (sometimes overt and sometimes covert) exists that the body is something to be kept still and under control. Students are reminded to place their hands in their laps and not touch their peers. With so much emphasis placed on a *no touch* policy in our schools, how can students learn to touch with a sense of care and respect?' (Richard, 2017, p. 79). The case study below, a creative adaptation inspired by Richard's vignettes, illustrates this.

Moving Gently

An early years practitioner has set out soft chiffon scarves for her four and five year old children to explore. Music is playing softly – Tchaikovsky's 'The dance of the sugar-plum fairy'. Scarves are waving above heads, drifting across bodies, being draped over heads, or swung forwards and backwards. Some are moved gently over the bodies of others, in a form of social interaction. Marina rubs her scarf energetically on her friend Marco's arm, leading to a cry of protest. Gianni (practitioner) intervenes, letting his scarf drift slowly and softly down Marco's face and arms, 'Gently like this', Gianni says. Marina begins to mirror Gianni's movements with the scarf, and Marco soon follows. An improvised dance trio develops, gradually synchronising with the mood and tempo of the lilting music.

Perhaps one of many inclusive aspects of dance is shown here, where touch, albeit with scarves, and moving together, led to affirming interactions between children. Few words were spoken, yet important communication and understanding developed. It seems that dance can provide many opportunities for fostering respect and empathy. Movement and touch are valuable 'languages' and a 'no touch' classroom may lock some children who are non-speaking communicators and tactile learners out of important aspects of their ways of being in the world.

MOVEMENT AND DANCE IN EARLY YEARS SETTINGS

Dance has been defined as 'an artistic form that provides participants an opportunity to learn through use of the body in motion' (Zitomer & Reid, 2011, p. 139). For young children, dance can be seen as 'thinking with the body' (Schiller & Meiners, 2012, p. 88), a playful way to explore the world. When approached as play, dance provides valuable opportunities for embodied exploration and learning (Deans & Wright, 2018). When early years practitioners let children set the 'agenda' and choose the role that dance plays for them, children will feel ownership of dance as a means of expressing their ideas – one of the 'hundred languages of children' in Malaguzzi's famous poem (in Edwards et al., 1993).

In the wider world, dance takes many forms and functions, as participant or performance art, and has served different social and cultural functions across the world and throughout history. It is only relatively recently that dance as an elite performance art, requiring bodies that look and move a certain way, has become influential in general dance education. Using dance as a creative, playful communication that is accessible to and includes all bodies and movements can counter this exclusionary thinking. Some dance scholars and educators believe that dance should play a role in challenging the status quo about dance itself and about important local and global issues such as the need for action against climate change (Foster & Turkki, 2021). Reflection on the functions of dance beyond elite performance – such as recreation, community socialising, celebration or therapy – can open up possibilities for early years practitioners to approach dance inclusively, as an embodiment of the anti-bias principles (see Chapter 2). However, perhaps because many forms of dance involve the dancers in synchronised movement to pre-choreographed steps, normative thinking about movement can still be pervasive. This can lead to a view that for people experiencing disability, dance is only therapeutic or recreational, rather than performative or 'artistic'. It then becomes unintentionally ableist, setting up barriers to participation by implying that disability equals inability to fit the physical norms expected of a dancer. As Zitomer and Reid insightfully ask: 'When able-bodied children attend dance classes, no one considers their programme dance therapy. Why should it be different for children with disabilities?' (2011, p. 137).

To move beyond the potential for exclusion that arises from normative visual aesthetics and emphasis on particular body types, early years practitioners can shift their focus towards the sensory aesthetic experience and artistic expression of dancers themselves. The joy of dance for participants is how it feels and what stories or emotions you can express with it. When dancing, we experience a heightened aesthetic sense of how our bodies work more consciously than elsewhere in our lives. When children play, this can bring sensory enjoyment and often involves imagination. Dance play also provides creative opportunities for motor skill development that are collaborative and process-oriented.

Each art form has its own unique physical and aesthetic features. Dance has movement through space. Within this, four specific elements, summarised in the table below, give dance its kinaesthetic and expressive characteristics.

Table 5.1 The elements of dance

Body	What movement are we doing?
	• Which body parts are we using?
Space	Where are we moving?
	• Are we travelling or staying in one place?
	• How much space are we using? (our personal space and the general space)
	• Are we moving through horizontal and/or vertical space?
Dynamics	How are we moving?
	• What energy and weight are we using?
	• Are our movements sustained or short-lived?
Relationships	With whom or what are we moving?
	• How are we relating to other dancers?
	• Objects?

Source: Adapted from Schiller and Meiners (2012).

All dance, including young children's dance play, is created from four elements: body, space, dynamics and relationships. When interacting with or guiding children during creative dance, awareness of these elements will enable early years practitioners to use them to enrich possibilities for creative, aesthetic expression through movement. The simple questions in Table 5.1 can be discussed with children, bringing their awareness to what their bodies are doing. Thus, children can become choreographers as well as dancers, as they play with dance.

MOVEMENT AND DANCE AS CULTURAL AND SOCIAL NARRATIVES

Dance is a unique language of childhood that enables the young child to communicate with others, become part of a cultural group and express personal thoughts, feelings and inner worlds. (Deans & Wright, 2018, pp. 7–8)

Our moving bodies can provide a role in expressing who we are and the communities we identify ourselves with. All art forms are part of social cultures, and the richly diverse cultural heritages of children, families and communities can be explored and celebrated through dance. In many of the world's oldest cultures, such as those of Australia's First Nations people, dance is not a stand-alone art, or simply an expression of music. It is combined with spoken language, song and music to tell stories that communicate cultural knowledge. Dance has functioned as a 'language', along with storytelling, music and visual arts, since the beginnings of human civilisation. For young children, who are discovering themselves and their place in the world, it thus makes sense to focus on dance as communication and play and to integrate it with story and other arts, as children often do in their play.

The arts, including dance, play a central role in disseminating, maintaining and developing culture. This can either support or impede cultural inclusiveness, for example, in countries with a colonial history. Across many former British colonies, British folk dance has long been part of school curricula. Now, however, there is increased incorporation of indigenous cultures in arts curricula in those countries, a practice that early years practitioners can use in their practice. Malaguzzi, the noted educator from Reggio Emilia, Italy recognised the traditional place of dance in establishing a sense of place and belonging in communities (1998). Malaguzzi stressed the importance of children's active participation in dance in community celebrations, as well as the value of revisiting memories of celebrations and dance experiences. Through shared recall, children explore their unfolding life history through the unique physical and emotional experience of moving their bodies in space, with others, accompanied by music.

Dance and Gender

In the dance genres and cultures of many places, in the past and still today, underpinning binary concepts of gender can often be a barrier to equitable participation. In some traditional dance forms, there are gendered male and female roles; in ballet, women go 'en pointe' with blocked shoes and men perform athletic jumps and lift women dancers. While this relates partly to physiological differences, anthropologists argue that dance is a means of transmitting cultural values such as accepted gender role expectations (Fink et al., 2021). In traditional cultures where dance often tells stories, aspects of gender such as strength and speed, and practices such as hunting or war may be a focus of male dancers' roles. Themes of fertility and courtship may also be communicated through dance.

In many contemporary societies, dance for children, particularly ballet, is often seen as an activity for girls. The aesthetic beauty of the female ballet dancer and her ornate costumes are icons of young femininity. Countless little girls love to wear ballet tutus, usually pink, and items such as bed linen featuring ballet dancers (female) adorn many bedrooms. Dance forms from the music hall and cabaret traditions of Europe and North America, along with popular music in the 20th century, focus on celebrating female beauty and sexuality. This gendered thinking has created a barrier to participation in dance by boys, who might not see it as fitting with them. However, approaching dance in early years settings through play and communication, and incorporating a range of different dance traditions and styles, can help to break down exclusive thoughts and beliefs related to gender stereotypes and ideas about what types of bodies, movements or expressions are prioritised.

To think about...

- What have you observed about young children's ideas of dance and gender?
- Think about your dance resources and teaching practices in the light of diverse gender identities and stereotypes. Reflect on your notions with your colleagues.

INCLUSIVE DANCE PLAY IN EVERYDAY EARLY YEARS PRACTICE

In this section, we make suggestions that you can adapt to suit the children and community context of your setting. We hope that these ideas will help with eliminating barriers to engagement and participation, and lead to dance play that fosters social connections and understanding between children, and challenges bias in relation to gender, culture and ability.

Dancing with others has great potential to bring a sense of belonging. As Deans and Wright found in their dance play project, 'the very nature of ensemble improvisation suggests a dialogical relationship, where children are learning about their individual capacities and about how to cooperate with others to achieve shared success' (2018, p. 130). Non-spoken invitations to join in and the sense of community provided by movement in a group are powerful inclusive tools. The integration of other forms of creative expression with dance also adds further possibilities for inclusion, allowing children to choose their ways of engaging.

This sense of community as part of a group is evident in the dance of the firefly (see p. 64). While dance was these children's main creative mode, other arts were also part of their experience. The children moved with the music, responding to it with the flow and energy of their movements. They also added their own vocalisations, exploring pitch and tone colour to create their characters. They used drama to become fireflies and the magic tree and to explore how these roles felt, incorporating dramatic props into their story. After the dance experience, the children gathered to discuss the experience, revisiting and sharing their movement interpretations – the dance 'vocabulary' of their story. Many chose to draw parts of the dance and used their drawings to retell the firefly story from their own perspective. Deans calls this 'drawing telling' (2018), seeing it as a way for children to extend the storytelling aspect of their dance play, and to revisit and reflect on their thoughts and feelings, as Malaguzzi advocated.

Dance, drawing and conversation made these children's thinking visible (Rinaldi, 2021). Children's creative expressions can be deeply meaningful for early years practitioners, enabling them to gain deeper understanding of each child, form positive relationships and become ever more inclusive. The insights gained also help the children to develop their understanding of and relationships with each other. Dance is especially valuable for connecting children because they are moving in the same general space. During dance play such as the dance of the firefly, the children's physical and spatial relationships with each other change, giving them moments to relate to each other through touch, vision, perhaps mirroring or 'answering' others' movements. Observations of children's ways of being during these moments may reveal things about them that would not have been discovered in any other situation. Sometimes too, practitioners may join in with children, becoming part of the experience and building their own empathic understanding of the children's perspectives. By positioning themselves within the dance, practitioners can gain new insights into themselves as early years professionals and creative people.

Dance Activities Enabling Everyone to Participate

We encourage all early years practitioners to include dance in their practice, given its rich potential for social connection, emotional expression, creativity and embodied learning. We propose three key principles for dance activities:

1 Every participant in movement and dance feels accepted and respected. All participation choices – movement, stillness or observation – are honoured.
2 Movement possibilities allow each participant to contribute in their own ways, as suited to their bodily expression styles, preferences and capabilities.
3 Intended outcomes are experiential and open-ended, and movements interpreted or explained by the child, rather than judged by peers or adults. Even a well-meaning 'good' from observers might change the position from a subject to an object (see Langenhove & Harré, 1999). There is a world of difference in being an agent of your creative movement or trying to meet the expectations of others.

When these cornerstones underpin dance activities, all participants are welcomed equitably, which could potentially change young children's attitudes towards physical differences and break down barriers to inclusion. Zitomer and Reid, who set up an integrated dance group for 16 children aged from six to nine years, with and without physical disabilities, found exactly that. They conducted research to investigate the children's understandings of dance in relation to disability and the potential of integrated dance to change understandings and attitudes. In initial discussions with the children about who can and can't dance, ableist assumptions about the capabilities of children who used walkers were almost universal amongst the children who did not. All except one believed that children who could not walk could not dance. However, after the dance programme, during which the children worked in groups that included children of diverse physical abilities, attitudes changed, and most children recognised that all children *can* dance, but differently. The children's initial understandings of dance seemed to centre on their feet, but after participating in the dance programme, they showed an understanding of dance being about moving their bodies in space in a greater variety of ways. The statements of two children – one who does and another who does not experience disability – indicate the impact of their inclusive dance experience: Child A: 'I learned that when you dance, you can use all kinds of parts of your body and also, that when you dance, you can use the low level, the middle level, and the high level'. Child B: 'I learned about making letters and shapes with our bodies. Also, we can dance with many parts of the body and breakdance' (Zitomer & Reid, 2011, p. 147). The findings of this study after a ten-week dance programme were that while children's understandings of who can dance quite clearly changed, less obvious changes occurred in their perceptions of disability in general. The experiences of these children provide support for one of the key messages of this book: the potential of inclusive arts practice for transforming thinking and practices, thus fostering more inclusive communities.

Enabling Dance Play Strategies

Below we offer some practical strategies that align with the three key principles above. These can be applied to planned activities, spontaneous dance play moments and everyday interactions whenever possible. Even daily routine transitions can be moments for spontaneous creative movement!

Moving and Dancing Together

Moving together with some synchronisation brings a wonderful sense of connection and togetherness, ensuring that the types and tempo of movements are suitable for all in the group who choose to participate.

Incorporating Multiple Modes of Expression

Movement can be part of story experiences, including dramatic play, readers' theatre or other group drama. Children can also express their ideas about dance through drawing or painting – perhaps to map out their movements, or to represent their dance after the experience.

Non-spoken Approaches to Inviting Children's Participation

Using ways other than spoken invitations or instructions, can free participants' imagination and be more interesting. Bodily movements, sign language, photos, drawings or sound cues (percussion instruments) provide wide resources for this.

Promoting Creative Expression Through Improvisatory Approaches

While choreographed movement sequences are sometimes appropriate, as in traditional dances, free movement, improvisation or choreography based on children's ideas are important. These can allow all children to contribute to shaping the dance play. The more you encourage children to share their ideas, the more those ideas flow. All contributions should be encouraged and valued, including those of children who show their ideas through sign or communication other than speech.

Using Varied Sounds and Music, Including Silence

Many different sound possibilities can inspire dance – vocal sounds, everyday objects, body percussion, musical instruments, recorded music from many cultures. Imagination can be sparked by new or surprising music. As well as using a variety of styles and tone colours, you can find music that creates different moods/emotions and incorporates varied tempo and dynamics. Dance music doesn't always have to be loud and fast!

Observing and Reflecting on Children's Movement Preferences, Strengths and Challenges

Gathering information on each child's movement will enable you to develop movements that encourage equitable participation by all. Deeper understanding of each child's strengths and interests can also be used to develop peer-to-peer learning.

To think about...

- How do these strategies resonate with you when you think about your practice: where could you apply them?
- How do you see the possibilities for the use of movement as non-spoken communication during learning experiences or routines?
- What kinds of dance activities can you develop that focus on interests and strengths?

ENJOYING MOVING AND DANCING

Inclusive bodily movements need to be approached as unique languages (Bannerman, 2014) through which we learn from others, as well as share something from ourselves. As with all communication, this non-spoken dialogue can be facilitated and learned. While dance will often happen spontaneously as part of children's play, we hope that regular time can be set aside for planned group dance play. Along with the over-arching key principles and strategies for dance activities above, the suggestions we share here can help you to develop enjoyable, inclusive dance sessions in your early years setting. Here are some planning tips (with thanks to Deans & Wright, 2018):

- Space – an open area, indoors or outdoors. Create the mood for dance, perhaps with soft lighting or fabrics.
- Materials – sound system for recordings, camera, scarves, fabrics and wall mirror.
- A gathering place – a mat or clearly designated place to start and end sessions and gather on at any time. Useful for inclusiveness as it gives children participation options – they can choose moments to observe.
- A welcoming ritual – to create a sense of safe familiarity, set expectations and mood, focus attention, spark imagination or wonder. Welcome each child by name using movement.

- Warm up – physical preparation flowing from the welcoming ritual, encouraging 'body awareness' and focus.
- Plan for opportunities for creative initiatives and expression – encourage children to contribute ideas and make decisions.
- Explore – use some of the time to practice particular movement skills.
- Stillness – moments for observing or showing others, reflecting or relaxing.
- Adaptations and choices – to include all children's physical strengths and preferences.
- Balance – between skill exploration and creativity/play.

Below are some examples of inclusive dance play experiences. While there is a suggested procedure for each experience, they are open-ended, and intended for adaptation to be responsive to your context and children's interests and needs.

Listening With Your Body

Imagine our bodies as large 'ears': they receive vibrations and feel our movements through many senses. We can learn to listen to our bodies and interpret music through our movements (Kivijärvi et al., 2017).

Sample Experience 1

Begin by sitting on the floor or standing, spread around to allow everyone their individual space. The most important thing is that everyone feels safe, appreciated and able to move in ways best suited to them.

First, playing any music, ask: *What part of you would like to move?*

Participants can 'listen' to their body and respond by moving a part of their body as they wish. It is also good to communicate that we do not always want to move.

Further 'listening' can be encouraged by asking: *Is there another part of your body that would like to try?*

Then, with music, ask: *What part of you would like to move to this music?*

- You can also explore how different parts of your body move and enjoy moving with the music.
- Now all hands/legs/heads that want to dance can dance together!

For a child who prefers to or can only make a small number of movements, an adult or peer can move with that child, following their ideas. Breath, to move very light, transparent fabric, ribbons or streamers could also be incorporated.

After these movement explorations, reflect together, by asking: *How did it feel?*

- Discuss differences and similarities of the 'dancers' (hands, legs etc.)
- With children who may prefer to communicate in ways other than spoken language, make key word signing, drawing and painting available for use as reflection tools. Photography could also be used – children may enjoy recreating their favourite or most important movements for you or their peers to photograph.

Sharing Our Languages – Creating a Dance Together

As mentioned earlier, a lovely way of creating dance choreography is to collect movements from the group through improvisation. For this, it is often important that you give some ideas or 'limit the possibilities' – not to stifle creativity, but to focus, stimulate or scaffold children's ideas. Simply asking participants to move as they choose can prevent rather than encourage improvisation. Below is an example of how pictures or objects can assist when creating a dance together.

Showing symbol cards to the children, asking 'What kind of dancing could go with this card?', allows the children to 'read' the image and translate it into another mode – movement. This activity can be made accessible to all by creating symbols that are tactile as well as visual, for example, by using string glued onto cardboard. Once familiar with this way of reading, children could also create their own dance cards.

Sample Experience 2

In a small- or medium-sized group, invite the children to:

- Listen to the music and pick a postcard, picture or object
- Look at the picture/feel the object they chose and invent a movement to the picture
- Dance their movements with the music
- Share their movements and pictures/objects with others – show or teach them the movement, let them explore 'your language'
- Put all the pictures/objects on the floor for everyone to see/touch, and ask: *Can we remember which movement belonged to which picture?* (It may be helpful to describe in spoken language all the pictures/objects to make this activity accessible)
- Explore by showing a picture and letting participants memorise with movement

Ask the children: *How can we use your movements to create a dance?*

- Select approximately six cards/objects to form a dance (Use more or less, depending on group size, length of the session and the children's interest)
- Discuss and decide the order of the cards/objects and movements: *'Which movement should we do first?'*
- Dance together, 'reading' the pictures
- You can work with a few pictures at first, adding more depending on interest
- Consider videoing or photographing the movement sequence to revisit and extend in future sessions
- Display the pictures so that the children may use them to dance whenever they wish

How Does My Movement Sound to You?

Creating a dance which begins with movements that the children respond to with sound can form a beautiful dialogue, and a new way for children to interact with each other. Below is an example of an activity that uses this approach to enhance feelings of sharing and acceptance through non-spoken communication.

Sample Experience 3

Half of the group are dancers and half musicians who have instruments with different sounds. Rather than the dancers respond to sound with movement, the musicians will respond to the movements with sound.

To begin, it may be helpful for an adult to be the first dancer while all children 'play' in response to the movements. This will show the children that there are no rights or wrongs. It is important to approach this activity with curiosity about different interpretations! This also provides an opportunity for the adult to model describing their movements to make the experience inclusive of all.

- Organise the group to work in pairs – a dancer and a musician who one selects an instrument to accompany the movement.
- Dancers start to move and musicians make the dancers' movements audible.
- Change roles.

CONCLUSION

Movement and dance offer children rich possibilities for communication, connection with others, creative expression and embodied learning. Our bodies and their movements are central to who we are. They are all different and equally unique. When we recognise that everyone is a dancer, accepting and valuing all ways of moving and being, creative dance becomes a powerful form of inclusion in action. Inclusive dance that challenges ableist or sexist stereotyped views of diverse bodies can also help early years practitioners to work towards anti-bias goals (Derman-Sparks & Edwards, 2019), such as those of justice and activism (see Chapter 2). Movement and dance bring joy and togetherness in early years settings, as in life, and should be part of children's everyday play and learning.

To think about...

- What role did dance play in your childhood and family life?
- Can you remember how you felt when dancing in your childhood?
- If you took part in dance classes, how did this shape your thoughts about your body and ways of moving?
- How many different types of dance can you think of? Make a list.

REFERENCES

Bannerman, H. (2014). Is dance a language? Movement, meaning and communication. *Dance Research*, *32*(1), 65–80.

Deans, J., & Wright, S. (2018). *Dance-play and drawing-telling as semiotic tools for young children's learning*. Routledge.

Derman-Sparks, L., & Edwards, J. O. (2019). Understanding anti-bias education. *YC Young Children, 74*(5), 6–13.

Dewey, J. (2005). *Art as experience*. Penguin. (original work published 1934)

Edwards, Gandini, L., & Forman, G. E. (1993). *The hundred languages of children: The Reggio Emilia approach to early childhood education*. Ablex Pub. Corp.

Fink, B., Bläsing, B., Ravignani, A., & Shackelford, T. K. (2021). Evolution and functions of human dance. *Evolution and Human Behavior, 42*(4), 351–360.

Foster, R., & Turkki, N. (2021). EcoJustice approach to dance education. *Journal of Dance Education,* 1–11.

Hanna, J. L. (2008). A nonverbal language for imagining and learning: Dance education in K–12 curriculum. *Educational Researcher, 37*(8), 491–506.

Kivijärvi, S., Sutela, K., & Ahokas, R. (2017). A conceptual discussion of embodiment in special music education: Dalcroze Eurhythmics as a case. *Approaches: Music Therapy & Special Music Education, 8*.

Langenhove, L., & Harré, R. (1999). Introducing positioning theory. In R. Harré & L. van Langenhove (Eds.), *Positioning theory. Moral contexts of intentional action* (pp. 14–31). Blackwell.

Malaguzzi, L. (1998). History, ideas and basic philosophy: An interview with Lella Gandini by Loris Malaguzzi. In C. Edwards, L. Gandini, & G. Forman (Eds.), *The hundred languages of children: Advanced reflections*. Ablex.

Merleau-Ponty, M. (1962). *Phenomenology of perception*. Routledge.

Richard, M. (2017). Making learning visible in creative arts. In A. Fleet, C. Patterson, & J. Robertson (Eds.), *Pedagogical documentation in early years practice: Seeing through multiple perspective* (pp. 73–84). SAGE.

Rinaldi, C. (2021). *In dialogue with Reggio Emilia: Listening, researching and learning*. Routledge.

Schiller, W., & Meiners, J. (2012). Dance: Moving beyond steps to ideas. In S. Wright (Ed.), *Children, meaning-making and the arts* (2nd ed., pp. 85–114). Pearson Australia.

Zitomer, M. R., & Reid, G. (2011). To be or not to be–able to dance: Integrated dance and children's perceptions of dance ability and disability. *Research in Dance Education, 12*(2), 137–156.

6

STEPPING INTO MANY WORLDS THROUGH DRAMATIC PLAY AND DRAMA

Amanda Niland

Chapter objectives

This chapter introduces you to these key ideas:

- The importance of dramatic play in the early years
- Drama, imagination and empathy
- Drama as a process
- Drama and diversity
- Inclusive early years drama pedagogy

INTRODUCTION

In drama and its forerunner, dramatic play, children can 'look at the everyday with different eyes' (Gibson & Ewing, 2020, p. 21), through the characters and stories they create. This chapter explores some forms and features of dramatic play and drama, and their value in providing a safe space for exploring diversity and fostering empathy and equitable empowerment. The chapter shares findings from research, examples from early years practice, and suggestions to guide you in developing inclusive drama. Some of the case studies have come from published research, while others are creative adaptations based on professional experiences, as explained in the book's Introduction. There is discussion in this chapter of the ways that the forms and elements of drama enable children to explore ideas, feelings, their inner imaginary worlds and life around them, by stepping outside the everyday into the world of the drama.

THE IMPORTANCE OF DRAMATIC PLAY IN THE EARLY YEARS

Drama, mostly in the form of dramatic play, is important in early years curriculum because it is so meaningful to children. When children engage in dramatic play, they enter 'a shared imaginary world, balanced on the edge of reality and fantasy' (Brown, 2017, p. 167) – an enticing and exciting place, a special part of childhood. When approached inclusively, the drama brings many possibilities for welcoming and celebrating children's diverse backgrounds and ways of being. It also has many benefits for learning and development – nurturing imagination, social and communication skills, agency, 'out-of-the-box' thinking and problem-solving. During dramatic play children explore aspects of identity – their own and others' – and issues such as fairness, power relations and equity. Thus, dramatic play can build confidence, self-efficacy, resilience and empathy. It can also foster a sense of belonging and community in early years settings.

Early years drama is an extension of dramatic play, focused on process and experiences in the moment, rather than on public performance or 'product'. It should be led as much as possible by children and guided only as needed by adults. Large-scale research across the European Union (EU) showed that drama in education has many benefits and an overall positive impact on children's lives and development in key areas of the EU's 2009 Lisbon Treaty shared competences for education – confidence, positive dispositions towards school, empathy, flexible thinking, innovation, citizenship, communication and reading ability (Cooper, 2010).

THE ESSENCE OF DRAMA – STEPPING IN AND OUT OF IMAGINARY WORLDS

As Halloween approaches each year, educator Sam often finds ghosts, witches or vampires in her early years setting. One morning several 'ghosts' came up, moving very slowly under their chiffon fabrics and speaking in low, whispering voices. 'Excu-u-u-use me, we need a new house to haunt, can we live in YOUR house?'

'I'm not sure about that' Sam responded, 'you might scare my dog'.

'Oh, we have a ghost dog too, we only spook people, not dogs. OOOOOOOOOH'

'Well, so long as you don't spook our dog, and keep our attic tidy, you may move in'.

'Thank you', said one of the 'ghosts', 'how much is the rent?'

Children are experts at becoming other beings, using their imaginations, bodies, whatever resources are available, and drawing on their life experiences, as the above case study shows. Drama is part of children's play from an early age. They spontaneously take on roles, weaving stories around their life experiences – perhaps prowling and roaring like a lion or pretending to be a dog or a baby. Often others around them enter the child's imaginary world and respond in character – draw back from the lion in fear, pat the dog or comfort the baby. It seems that drama can be an invitation to interact, an example of the human urge to connect and communicate underpin the arts generally. Children often use it to make meaning from their life experiences, as in the story of Alex in Chapter 3, who after the unpleasant experience of being forced to take a horrible-tasting medicine, took on the parental role and dosed his teddy with imaginary horrible medicine. Drama gives children permission to be different from themselves and to explore how that feels. This can be a powerful tool for inclusion, fostering a creative thinking and playing culture that welcomes and celebrates different ways of being. In drama, we can move beyond generalisations about difference or unconscious 'othering', through the experience of acting 'as if' we were someone else and seeing the world through their eyes.

WALKING IN OTHERS' SHOES - DRAMA AND EMPATHY

As children grow and develop, their dramatic play becomes more complex and collaborative, often with evolving narratives and a range of characters. Children take this play very seriously. As many early years practitioners, parents and carers can attest, children don't just act out other characters, they become them. Entering another world through dramatic play enables children to think as their characters, giving them possibilities for understanding experiences and per-spectives different from their own. Thus, dramatic play and drama support the development of empathy.

Empathy is the ability to sense the feelings of another and respond emotionally to them. It involves focusing on another's needs rather than, or as well as, your own. Empathy is associated with kindness, which some argue is an innate human quality as we are biologically a social species (Malti, 2021). While empathy may be innate (Nakao & Itakura, 2009), it is also a cognitive capacity, thus something that can be further developed. In terms of inclusion, empathy allows us to accept and understand others as different from us but also fellow humans. Although the development of empathy is individual, it occurs through interaction with others. Playing, communicating and creating with peers and adults in an early years setting provides an ideal context for children to build their capacity for empathy. Artforms such as drama provide many possibilities for encouraging empathy, as they involve connecting and imaginatively exploring lives beyond our own. When a child is being 'another' in dramatic play or drama they begin to understand another's needs and wishes and recognise them as different from their own (Omdahl, 2014). Through this experience, children develop an understanding of the connections and relationships between people, and perhaps animals also. Out of this understanding, empathy grows.

WHO'S IN CHARGE? POWER IN EARLY YEARS DRAMA

As well as fostering empathy, drama can give a voice to those experiencing oppression or marginalisation, so that their perspectives and feelings are heard and understood. Dramatic play provides such a voice for young children. Its imaginary worlds can give them opportunities to exercise agency in ways that respect the rights and feelings of others. Through dramatic play children can explore and express their ideas about power, and challenge inequitable or unfair power situations; thus drama can be helpful in working towards the anti-bias goals of justice and activism (see Chapter 2).

Early years practitioners can assist children in recognising unfairness and fostering more inclusive dramatic play. For example, by stepping into an imaginary role in the drama, not to 'save' the child experiencing unfairness, but to work with all children so that they understand others' perspectives and are empowered to find fair solutions. As in many early years situations, open-ended questions and 'I wonder' statements are valuable for provoking children to use their agency and empathy. Ensuring that all children have a 'voice', listening to every child and finding shared languages – spoken and unspoken – are essential aspects of inclusive drama and arts pedagogy.

Children's explorations of power can sometimes lead to dangerous moments, not just because they may communicate non-verbally in physically unsafe ways, but because there can be emotional risk in seeking to exercise power. The support of responsive practitioners is thus needed – not to remove possibilities for agency from children but to ensure physical and emotional safety for all involved. An imaginary world can be a safe place for navigating power issues, as early years drama practitioner and researcher Olivia Karaolis shows in her use of puppetry to provoke an alternate approach to children's dramatisation of superheroes, which had involved unequal power relations and physically dangerous play:

> The boys look sheepish as they form a line on the floor. Harry tells me he is a superhero as he takes a superhero pose. Nick then jumps up to tell me he is a Ninja Turtle. Quickly taking on their ideas, I tell them I have the egg of a superhero dinosaur, Supersauraus and that it is about to hatch. I ask them to help me introduce the baby to the world. The boys sit down, nodding as they animatedly discuss who will be the mommy and the daddy. With the baby dinosaur hatching in my hand, we watch in silence. ...:

Olivia:	What shall we do to welcome this Dino into the world?
Harry:	We say hello... (*corrects himself or rethinking this through*) he needs to know how to say hello.
Olivia:	Will you come and show him? (*the dino pops out*)
Harry:	(*I was expecting he would say he was a Ninja as he always does when I ask his name and instead, he formally says*) My name is Harry James Robes.
Dino:	Hello, (*pops head in* and out of the shell *and then adds*) I like your name... (*then adds wistfully*) I don't have a name yet.
Harry:	(*reaching over and kissing him*).
Olivia:	You are so gentle with this baby dino, thank you.
Dino:	Henry James Robes could you please give me a name? (*At this moment, there is a stillness in the room it is serious business*)
Harry:	Ahh. ...., Olivia.
Olivia:	(*my heart is melting*) Thank you for naming the dino, I like her name.

Karaolis (2020, pp. 166-167).

As Olivia's story shows, drama can foster children's empathy. But can drama also support empathy in early years practitioners? For adults, drama – whether on screen or live – is encountered mostly as an audience member. The experience of stepping into an imaginary role is not generally part of adult life. In early years settings, process drama and 'teacher-in-role' (Dunn, 2016) allow practitioners to participate in drama, potentially providing opportunities to build empathy and hence inclusive pedagogy. Process drama is especially valuable for empathy-building in practitioners, as the 'teacher-in-role' is not the most important character. That role lies with children, who are cast as the 'experts' in the drama (Heathcote & Bolton, 1994). Ewing (2011, p. 41) reminds us that 'sharing power and risk-taking' are at the heart of the drama. In an inclusive classroom, this is as important for practitioners as it is for children.

CHILDREN AS EXPERTS – PROCESS DRAMA IN THE EARLY YEARS

Process drama is an extension of dramatic play often used in the early years. It does not focus on performance for an audience, but on collaborative improvisation to build a story. The educator is a facilitator, using the 'teacher-in-role' technique to guide from within the story, empowering children to be the experts who create and lead the drama experience. The educator uses questions and if needed, suggestions and the children's responses and solutions are the drama.

Brown describes process drama like this: 'children play a range of roles and engage in a variety of reflective out-of-role activities, requiring them to think critically beyond their own points of view and consider the topic from multiple perspectives' (2017, p. 165). In process drama, the story is not pre-written but created in the moment. The usual adult/child power relations are challenged when educators intentionally step back and take minor character parts in the story. Children assume the 'mantle of the expert' (Heathcote & Bolton, 1994) and play a powerful role in shaping the drama. Educators can use their roles to encourage children's exploration of feeling powerful and using their power in fair and empathetic ways.

The value of process drama is clear in its name – children learn and develop through the processes of imagining and collaborating to create and enact characters and stories. The potential for learning is often seen through a developmental/curriculum lens – children are building language and communication skills, problem-solving or knowledge about the world. However, the potential of process drama can also be seen through lenses of dispositions and identity. Collaborating to create and inhabit an imagined world empowers children to explore feelings from different perspectives and gain new insights into their own lives and those of others. They can build confidence, resilience and problem-solving skills through creativity and imagination. With these dispositions in mind, responsive educators, informed by inclusive thinking and critical pedagogy, underpinned by anti-bias goals, can use process drama to ensure that every child can participate, and all contributions are respected.

Advocates of process drama argue that the ability to 'walk in another's shoes' is an important human quality, as valuable in adult life as in childhood. Brown (2017) believes that building this ability in children is important both for their own humanity and for working towards a kinder, more inclusive world. As Yaniv states: 'This process presumably requires the simultaneous activation of two internal representations: one of the "self" and one of the "other"' (2012, p. 73). The unfolding story of a process drama allows children to experience the feelings of their character while still being themselves, and this simultaneous dual representation can be a very powerful tool for building empathy. The case study below is an example of this.

> the children planted an imaginary community garden using fabric. The teacher took on the role of a stranger coming into a town and asking for help. The children held a town meeting to decide what to do about it, eventually offering to share their food with her and give her a blanket. Various children said, "You can have some of our food." "I've got carrots." "I have some cereal too." One child said while handing the stranger a paper towel tube, "Hey, I got some hot dogs." Their dialogue and actions demonstrate their abilities to be effective communicators, collaborators, problem-solvers, and empathetic humanitarians. (Brown, 2017, p. 166)

WHOSE WORDS? WHOSE THINGS? WHOSE CULTURES?

While children's cultural backgrounds will influence their dramatic play (consider the food sharing in the case study above), they should never be assumed to be the same for everyone from a particular ethnic or cultural background. Some aspects of a child's life may have much in common with children from different ethnic or geographical backgrounds, for example, through exposure to TV and popular culture. Dramatic play involving Disney princesses or Marvel superheroes happens in many places across the world. However, children's relationships with families, peers and communities also shape values and practices, which are then reflected in children's play. In the case study below the children adopt some of the adult social roles of their community, in a sense learning some practices of the adult world (Schwartzman, 2012):

> One afternoon, a group of eight girls between seven and twelve years of age set up a cubby house in their self-proclaimed and inherited domain — the dry creek bed out of sight from the residential area. Over several hours, elaborate make-believe play developed that became more and more focused on playing at being mothers: the cool sand from the creek poured through the neck of the t-shirts so that these bulge out, makes for a good pregnancy, and filled into discarded Coke and Sprite bottles, the sand turns into newborn infants. Imaginary bank keycards are collected to purchase food in the "store", after a taxi has been called using the "telephone" perched up in a tree. (Eickelkamp, 2011, p. 506)

This dramatic play was observed in the Australian First Nations community of Ernabella, on Pitjantjatjara country in the north-western region of deserts and mountains in South Australia. People in this remote area maintained a traditional lifestyle until 1937, when a Presbyterian mission was established. The mission at Ernabella was atypical of most in Australia's First Nations communities, as local languages were allowed and respected (typically, missions prevented even the youngest children from using their language, forcing them to learn English).

The children's play shows their imaginative interpretation of parenting roles and cultural knowledge. It reflects their experience of living between two cultures, and the intersection of traditional and 21st-century lifestyles, such as the use of bank cards and taxis. Interestingly, this example shows dramatic play that is based on 'what is', rather than on what children wish 'could be', outside the realms of everyday reality – a difference sometimes noted between the dramatic play scenarios of children in indigenous and non-indigenous communities (Schwartzman, 2012).

Children's dramatic play varies not only because of their cultures and life experiences, as in the above story from an Australian First Nations community but also because of their physical and material contexts and the different opportunities these provide. Consider the enormous range of toys produced by global corporations and common in many parts of the world. These are designed with specific types of dramatic play in mind, representing certain lifestyles, social roles and values. They convey implicit messages about what is important or valued, and what is 'normal' – messages that can become barriers to equitable participation and inclusive thinking. 'Closed' replica toys not only largely fail to represent diversity but also limit possibilities for creativity and imagination. When children have access to open-ended dramatic play resources that resonate with their lives and ways of being, more equitable participation is possible, along with richer potential for imagination and creativity.

To think about...

- Reflect on whose interests you are drawing on as the basis of your planning for drama experiences? Have you tried to incorporate children's diverse 'cultural capital' (see Chapter 1)? Have you consulted with the children?
- To draw on all children's cultural capital over time, find ways to incorporate the interests of a child whose fascinations are not usually drawn on for planning inspiration.
- What are some ideas/objects/stories that you could use as springboards for drama that all children can relate to in some way (adopting the 'mirrors, windows, sliding doors' concept shared in Chapter 8)?

Including Diverse Cultures and Languages in Early Years Drama

Dramatic play has great potential for fostering the relationships that are central to inclusion. However, unless early years environments include representations from all children's backgrounds, and educators actively encourage multimodal and multilingual communication, some children will face barriers that impede their entry into dramatic play (Scrafton & Whitington, 2015). Pedagogy that incorporates shared modes of communication, both spoken and non-spoken, can minimise barriers of difference or power inequities, maximise the potential for agency, and thus facilitate the participation of all children in dramatic play. For example, Scrafton and Whitington, studying the impact of English proficiency on children's inclusion in dramatic play, found children from CALD (culturally and linguistically diverse) backgrounds 'may encounter exclusion in education settings within societies where minority groups' cultural funds of knowledge are marginalised' (2015, p. 216). Scrafton and Whitington recognised the need for pedagogy that values all children's cultural knowledge. They found that while children from diverse language backgrounds played together because of common interests, children for whom English was an additional language seemed to have more confidence and sense of belonging in their early years setting when they could use their home cultural knowledge in their play. Their research highlights the need for cultural representations and modes of expression that are genuinely multicultural, rather than favouring one majority culture.

Scrafton and Whitington stress the central role of practitioners in facilitating inclusive dramatic play, for example, by enacting a character who models play entry strategies or uses multiple modes of communication. Their research showed how the lack of a shared language limited some children's opportunities to equitably engage in dramatic play with their peers. Early years practitioners can support the development of a shared 'language' while 'in role' during dramatic play, by using communication modes such as gesture, key word signing, visuals, objects, dance, music and perhaps digital tools. Where children's first languages are not the majority language of the setting, practitioners can incorporate play-related vocabulary from those first languages into the general life of the setting, as well as into dramatic play.

Multilingual practitioners can lead their colleagues and the children in incorporating multi-lingual vocabulary into routines, songs and play. Building this shared vocabulary of imaginative, play-related words not only facilitates multiple modes of communication but also celebrates children's and practitioners' linguistic heritage.

Drama With a Digital Touch

When approached with inclusive principles, drama can be a wonderful way to create a sense of belonging, as illustrated in the examples shared in this chapter. For children settling in a new country, perhaps experiencing trauma from the disruption to their lives, and learning a new language, the arts can provide a shared language and help them to feel welcome. In earlier chapters, we showed how music and dance can provide shared languages. In this chapter, we have seen how drama, particularly process drama, also creates possibilities for shared communication. The story below outlines collaborative story-building, using process drama techniques to explore and honour the experiences of children newly arrived in a school and country.

A group of Australian researchers and primary school teachers used process drama and digital technology to create a story from the lives of children who were refugees recently resettled in Australia (Dunn et al., 2012). Although the children were aged between 8 and 12 years, this project provides many relevant insights for early years practitioners. Drama, as a way of making sense of past experiences and adjusting to a vastly changed life, can help to build resilience for children who have gone through major life disruptions and trauma, as these children had. Resilience means feeling a sense of belonging, control, positivity and confidence to face challenges (Doron, 2005). For these children, the combination of spoken and non-spoken communication, and opportunities to use visual images (drawing and photography), gave them multimodal communication opportunities. Incorporating digital characters and technology into the unfolding drama introduced the children to the technology that is part of everyday life in most Australian schools and homes. The teachers and researchers planned carefully to facilitate resilience that was not underpinned by deficit ways of thinking about the children because of their past. The process drama was planned with emotional distancing in mind, to provide enjoyment and empowerment through collaborative imagination and problem-solving without triggering disturbing memories. The drama was chosen so that the children would enter a fantasy world and identify with the characters' adventures as, just like them, they moved from a familiar to an unfamiliar place and lifeworld – from a far-off planet to Earth.

The drama, undertaken in a specialist English learning class, centred around Rollo the robot, who didn't speak the Earthlings' language. Positioning the children as experts, their first problem was to find a way to communicate with Rollo. The teacher – Rollo's worried mother – emailed from their distant planet. Emails also came from Sparky, Rollo's robot dog, with photos of himself going about his life. Later in the drama, Rollo's fiancé Blue Ray arrived, wishing to learn about Earth weddings. At one point Sparky (an actual robotic dog toy) came looking for

Rollo and then got lost. Sparky's arrival was an exciting moment for the children. Several who were shy about communicating with their teacher or peers, were more confident about communicating with Sparky. When he became lost, they were very concerned. One wrote: 'I think Sparky is at Kmart. He is looking for Rollo and Keyboard. Sparky is so hungry. Sparky look any food. Sparky is no have many'. (Dunn et al., 2012, p. 495). The teacher and researchers noted this child's empathy for the feelings of someone who is lost, alone and hungry, acknowledging how using imaginary characters in the drama allowed children to draw on their own experiences at a safe distance.

Many aspects of this drama project could be incorporated into early years dramatic play to support the sense of belonging and resilience of children who have experienced displacement or trauma, to honour their backgrounds and cultures, facilitate their communication with others and the learning of a new language. For example, the sharing of knowledge about different cultural practices with an imaginary character can involve reciprocal learning that will contribute to building understanding and empathy between all children about their diverse lives. In an early years setting, puppets, dolls, action figures or soft toys, made by practitioners or children from everyday or natural materials, could be used as characters in the drama, so that emotional distance is created. These characters could be physically present or communicate virtually via video on a digital tablet (to simulate a far-off land or planet). The written text forms used in the research for 'inter-planetary' communication could be replaced with non-written visual text forms such as drawing or photography, including on digital tablets.

To think about...

- How might you seek children's responses using spoken and non-spoken forms of communication? How could you facilitate or encourage multimodal ways for children to participate?
- How might you find ways to acknowledge, value and include all contributions, and be open to the children's creative responses leading the drama in unexpected directions?

IMPLEMENTING INCLUSIVE DRAMA

In the creative arts, as in any other aspect of inclusive pedagogy, action must be preceded by thinking, which is clearly shown in the initial thinking behind the process drama about Rollo. You can begin by establishing principles that will guide and inform your resourcing and interaction strategies. The following list can be adapted to fit your particular context, children and pedagogy:

- Respectful representations of diverse cultures, lifestyles, identities of all kinds (e.g. languages, spoken and non-spoken, genders, family structures, lifestyles and life experiences such as disruption or trauma)

- Equitable opportunities for participation in a range of drama experiences
- Inclusive teaching strategies that suit the identities, learning preferences and strengths of every child
- Maximising children's agency, for example, through process drama and 'teacher-in-role'
- Revisit/recall/reflect on dramatic play and drama experiences with children and educators

Once guiding principles have been established, the next step can be to 'audit' your current approaches and provisions for dramatic play or drama for their inclusivity. To do this, you could, with colleagues, take a 'tour' of the play environment and consider the range of interests, cultural backgrounds, and ways of being that are represented. Here are some possible strategies:

- Lay out all dressing up items. List the possibilities for different types of imaginative role play. What cultures, genders and gender roles are represented?
- Lay out all dolls/soft toys. How many different choices are there for children? How gendered are these toys? How gendered are any clothes available for them? Are there any multicultural clothing items? Do the toys include representation of disability?
- If you have a kitchen or café provisions and set up, consider how many different food preferences are there, and what diverse food customs are represented.
- Do you have photos displayed? If so, what provocations for imaginative role play are conveyed? What messages about role play and identity might also be implicit in these photos?

After this tour, review your findings and brainstorm ways to broaden the diversity of dramatic play possibilities, to be more inclusive of every child's way of being. The anti-bias goals (Chapter 2) provide a helpful guide for this. Goal 1 is especially relevant: 'Children will demonstrate self-awareness, confidence, family pride and positive social identities' and 'Teachers will nurture each child's construction of knowledgeable, confident, individual personal and social identities' (Derman-Sparks & Olsen Edwards, 2019, p. 7).

To think about...

- Drama can be a valuable way to foster social justice thinking in tangible ways for young children. Reflect on how you can develop dramatic play/drama resources and experiences that challenge 'normality' or explore different ways of being
- If some children choose not to watch from nearby, how might they still be included in the dramatic play in some way?
- Reflect on the inclusiveness of your language as you interact with and guide the children during drama experiences – are you unconsciously conveying messages about more or less 'appropriate' ways of thinking or responding?

CONCLUSION

In dramatic play and drama, young children explore different perspectives on life, using their imaginations to see the world through the eyes of the characters they play. This makes drama particularly powerful in giving children experiences of empathy, as the examples in this chapter have shown. When approached inclusively, the various forms of drama hold many possibilities for building children's and adults' understanding of, and respect for diverse ways of being. Inclusive play and drama pedagogy, incorporating things such as puppetry or mime, give children opportunities to participate according to their preferences, so that every child can have a voice. Child-led, spontaneous dramatic play, and adult-guided approaches such as process drama provide spaces where complex, challenging or unfair situations can be explored. Thus drama experiences offer many possibilities for working towards the anti-bias goals, including those of justice and activism – working towards positive change on journeys towards inclusion. We hope the discussion and ideas in this chapter will inspire you to try out some new possibilities for fostering inclusion through dramatic play and drama.

FURTHER READING AND RESOURCES

http://www.dramanetwork.eu/
The report from a large European study on the impact of drama on learning.

REFERENCES

Brown, V. (2017). Drama as a valuable learning medium in early childhood. *Arts Education Policy Review, 118*(3), 164–171.

Cooper, C. (2010). *Making a world of difference, A DICE resource for practitioners on educational theatre and drama.* DICE–Drama Improves Lisbon Key Competences in Education. DICE Consortium.

Derman-Sparks, L., & Edwards, J. O. (2019). Understanding anti-bias education. *YC Young Children, 74*(5), 6–13.

Doron, E. (2005). Working with Lebanese refugees in a community resilience model. *Community Development Journal, 40*(2), 182–191.

Dunn, J. (2016). Demystifying process drama: Exploring the why, what, and how. *Nj Drama Australia Journal, 40*(2), 127–140.

Dunn, J., Bundy, P., & Woodrow, N. (2012). Combining drama pedagogy with digital technologies to support the language learning needs of newly arrived refugee children: A classroom case study. *Research in Drama Education: The Journal of Applied Theatre and Performance, 17*(4), 477–499.

Eickelkamp, U. (2011). Agency and structure in the life-world of Aboriginal children in Central Australia. *Children and Youth Services Review, 33*(4), 502–508.

Ewing, R. (2011). *The arts and Australian education: Realising potential.* ACER.

Gibson, R., & Ewing, R. (2020). *Transforming the curriculum through the arts.* Springer International Publishing.

Heathcote, D., & Bolton, G. (1994). *Drama for learning: Dorothy Heathcote's Mantle of the Expert approach to education*. Dimensions of Drama Series. Heinemann.

Karaolis, O. (2020). *Everybody in! Drama as a pedagogy for inclusion*. Doctoral dissertation. University of Sydney.

Malti, T. (2021). Kindness: A perspective from developmental psychology. *European Journal of Developmental Psychology, 18*(5), 629–657.

Nakao, H., & Itakura, S. (2009). An integrated view of empathy: Psychology, philosophy, and neuroscience. *Integrative Psychological and Behavioural Science, 43*(1), 42–52.

Omdahl, B. L. (2014). *Cognitive appraisal, emotion, and empathy*. Psychology Press.

Schwartzman, H. (Ed.). (2012) *Transformations: The anthropology of children's play*. Springer Science & Business Media.

Scrafton, E., & Whitington, V. (2015). The accessibility of socio-dramatic play to culturally and linguistically diverse Australian preschoolers. *European Early Childhood Education Research Journal, 23*(2), 213–228.

Yaniv, D. (2012). Dynamics of creativity and empathy in role reversal: Contributions from neuroscience. *Review of General Psychology, 16*(1), 70–77.

7

CREATING AND SHARING STORIES IN THE EARLY YEARS

Amanda Niland, Kathy Cologon and Laura Huhtinen-Hildén

--- Chapter objectives ---

This chapter introduces you to these key ideas:

- Meaning-making about life through story
- Storytelling across time and cultures
- Storytelling in early years settings: children's diverse voices and generative listening
- Storytelling with puppets
- 21st-century childhoods and digital storytelling
- Developing your inclusive storytelling skills

INTRODUCTION

From childhood, we are all natural creators and tellers of stories. This chapter explores a range of storying roles and forms that can be relevant for young children and practitioners in early years settings. These forms are traditional and contemporary, pre-planned and improvised, multimodal and interactive, and sometimes virtual. We regard storytelling more holistically than as simply a spoken art form. As inclusive practitioners, we share ways for you to 'tell' stories using multiple modes of expression, modelling for children and encouraging them to do the same. That way, your stories can be accessible to everyone. Tuning in and listening out for children's stories is also important (and fascinating!). As we explore in this chapter and in the book overall, every child every child has stories to tell and artistic expression to share if we attend and are responsive to their diverse voices.

STORYING ACROSS TIME AND CULTURES - MAKING MEANING OF OUR WORLDS

Through stories, children can express and reflect on their experiences, hopes and ideas as connected to the past, present and future... (Byman et al., 2022, p. 18)

In a way our lives are stories, and we are the central characters. Storying is an art form that has existed throughout history. In many ancient and continuing cultures, stories are regarded as key ways of imparting knowledge – as central to learning about ourselves, our culture and the wider world. Storying the events of our own lives or those of others is like an intricate dance in which we share aspects of our lives with each other through many modes of communication. Each aspect and element can have multiple potential interpretations, and each shared encounter is a story with many potential tellings. In storytelling with children, we need to recognise and embrace what Malaguzzi and Gandini (1993) refers to as the 'Hundred Languages' of children. This calls for carving out space and opportunities for storying through a myriad of possible methods.

Stories provide us with a way to share the human story across time, space and culture. As the late Australian Aboriginal Elder Bill Neidjie 'Kakadu Man', the elder of the Gaagudji people and poet Bill Neidjie (Neidjie et al., 1985, p. 58) puts it:

This story is for all people.

Everybody should be listening.

Same story for everyone,

just a different language.

Traditionally, storytelling of any kind involves teller and listener being in the same space, so that the communication can be immediate and reciprocal. The story is shaped by both the teller and listener, often including opportunities for the listener to engage in the storying process.

Thus, storytelling is interactive, improvisatory and spontaneous. In its simplest form, oral storytelling is commonly from person to person. While spoken words are most often the mode of communication, some storytelling traditions involve other modes such as drawing, song, dance or puppets as well as words, as we explore within this chapter.

As expressed in Bill Neidjie's poem below, above all – well beyond actual words – storytelling and stories are about the feelings they evoke and express.

I feel it with my body,

with my blood.

Feeling all these trees,

all this country.

When this wind blow you can feel it.

Same for country....

You feel it.

You can look,

but feeling....

that make you.

Feeling make you Bill Neidjie et al. (1985, p. 51)

Facer (2019, p. 3), echoing Biesta (see Chapter 1), argues that, 'To be an educator today is to be confronted with an urgent question: How is what and how I am teaching adequate to the times we are living in?' Facer (2019, p. 10) goes on to explore storytelling as a generative process within which it may be possible to recognise and engage with 'the co-emergence of child and world', as a process through which children and educators can work together to make meaning of the world.

Stories are one of the ways in which cultural practices, values and beliefs are transmitted and maintained. Making meaning through storying is also influenced by the social cultures of communities. This is important to consider in developing inclusive early years pedagogy. Being responsive to the diverse ways of being, interests and backgrounds of every child requires attention to both what is being expressed and how it is communicated. As McKeough et al. argue: 'Through narrative, we develop a deeper understanding of the social world – of how others think, why they behave the way they do, and the implications people's actions hold for others' (2008, p. 150). Storying is one way to work towards developing empathy, shared understandings, and embracing diversity, ultimately fostering a sense of belonging. Storying therefore has rich possibilities for building inclusive early years pedagogy.

Storytelling Traditions

There are many storytelling traditions across the world with long histories that can inspire early years practitioners. Researching these, ideally with the families in your early years communities, and using aspects most relevant to your context and community, in ways that respect the families' cultures, can add multimodal, culturally responsive elements to inclusive arts pedagogy. Below we share one of these traditions and encourage you to search for more. Drawing on the stories and storying styles of the cultures of children and families in your setting can be part of your inclusive pedagogy. In the many nations of the world with histories of colonisation, the incorporation of ways of being and knowing from First Nations peoples is an important element in an inclusive arts curriculum. As two of the authors of this book are Australian, here, we share a storytelling tradition from our First Nations cultures that presents rich possibilities for multimodal storying with young children.

Sand Stories From Central Australia

The Arrernte people, whose country is in Central Australia, near Alice Springs, have an ancient tradition of telling stories visually and orally through drawing in the sand (Green, 2014). They use speech, drawing and gesture, sometimes also singing and iconic symbols, as well as objects that happen to be nearby. Sand stories are a significant cultural tradition of this part of Australia, because 'there is ample inscribable ground' (Green, 2014, p. 2) and 'reading' the ground through close observation is an ancient practice. The sand stories might involve recounting everyday events or telling dreaming stories.

To tell a sand story, the storyteller first creates a framed area in front of them, using sticks, leaves or similar to mark the story frame and sometimes to represent objects in the story. The story generally begins with clearing, smoothing and delineating the space. Drawings may be done with a sharp stick or piece of wire. The story unfolds on the ground, as well as through speech, gesture and signs in a multimodal layering process. The ending is marked by clearing and smoothing the story area on the ground. This form of storytelling, in some ways not unlike children's play, is both process and product, a dynamic, 'in-the-moment' phenomenon.

HUMOUR AND STORYING

Through stories, cultural knowledge and values are passed from generation to generation. Some stories are serious, involving danger, disaster or sadness, while others use humour. Humour, a human instinct from infancy onwards, is also regarded as important for emotional well-being (Crawford & Caltabiano, 2011). Some forms of humour help us feel connected with others – sharing a moment of laughter can lead to feelings of togetherness and belonging, providing of course that the humour does not involve teasing or making fun of others.

For young children, making others laugh can lead to feelings of achievement and power. Developing understanding of the social 'rules' of humour is something children learn in the early years and is important to their explorations of the world (Bergen, 2021). While humour is deeply rooted in cultures and languages, there are also more personal aspects at play – after all, we don't all find the same things funny. Thus, recognising that all children have a sense of humour, while being observant about and responsive towards similarities and differences in each individual child's sense of humour, is part of inclusive practice, particularly when telling or facilitating stories.

CHILDREN AS STORYTELLERS - TELLING STORIES THROUGH PLAY

How children reveal their identity texts through multimodal engagements reflects the significance of being able to understand, communicate, and think in alternative ways. (Binder & Kotsopoulos, 2011, p. 339)

Storying may be realistic, imaginative, or a combination of both. As an exploration and sharing of our lives, storying can encompass the full range of emotions and experiences – including not only humour but also tragic experiences. This is evident in children's own stories as well as those of adults. A story that embedded itself firmly in Kathy's mind when she was researching children's experiences in emergency situations many years back was that of a little girl, Janie, whose father died in the September 11 terrorist attacks in the United States.

> Janie was 2.5 years old, and her mother had explained: "There was a fire in Daddy's building; the firemen came, but they did not have tall enough ladders to save Daddy and the other people" (Gaffney, 2006, p. 1006). Gaffney explains that Janie arrived at playgroup in the aftermath of the September 11 attacks. She raced to the dollhouse where she collected a miniature ladder and a toy resembling a coil of rope, which she then carried with her everywhere for weeks on end. Gaffney writes that "Janie clung to the miniature ladder and rope. In her young mind, she knew she would be able to rescue her father with her own safety equipment: the wooden ladder and coiled rope".
> (Gaffney, 2006, p. 1006)

Janie's story brings to light two further important considerations about storying: Counter-storying and relational-listening. Through her play, Janie storied – or, rather, provided a counter-story – her alternative version of the tragic event in which her father was rescued. Through relational-listening, the adults around her could come to understand what Janie was expressing through her storying.

Children's storying may be inspired by anything they encounter – from everyday experiences with books, oral tales or videos to deeply significant life events, as Janie's story was. Their stories are often told through the characters and worlds they create in pretend play. They may use words, but often gestures, movements or manipulation of 'small world' toys are the primary modes of communication.

3 year old Qwami, who is passionate about water and both fascinated and concerned by boats, had recently been on a driving holiday that also involved a trip in a car ferry. To prepare him for the journey, his family had borrowed books from the library about boats that included photos and information about car ferries. One of Qwami's favourite play experiences in his early years settings was water play, where he had extensively explored floating and sinking. Before the holiday, he began asking for boats in the water play trough, were provided. Noting Qwami's ongoing interest as well as his anxiety about boats sinking, the educators made sure the water play, with boats and cars, was available when he returned from his holiday. They noted how the story of Qwami's voyage on the car ferry unfolded through his play with the cars and boats in the water. "Boats float," he says, then adds a few cars to the largest boat. "Which one is your car?" asks an educator. "Mummy car" says Qwami, pointing. Then he points to an upper deck on the boat: "Look at water. We got ice cream". "Did you have fun?" the educator asks, and Qwami replies "Boat floating".

Using the play resources provided by responsive and inclusive early years practitioners, Qwami was able to engage in multimodal storytelling about an important life event. Recognising Qwami's re-enactment of his journey as storying, rather than only as pretend play, offers insights into how we all, including children, use stories to recall, reflect on and share our life experiences. The play resources his educators provided empowered Qwami with communication tools to effectively tell his story with actions, gesture and spoken language. Similarly to the sand stories of Central Australia and many other forms of storytelling, Qwami's story was both process and product, dynamic and ephemeral – existing only 'in the moment' but engaging and meaningful for teller and audience. For Qwami's educators, the sharing of the story that was so important to him at that time contributed to the building of the 'secure, respectful and reciprocal relationships' (AGDE, 2022, p. 14), which lie at the heart of inclusive early years communities.

Storying helps to connect us, through the immediacy of sharing in a story as it unfolds, and the directness of the communicative interaction between storyteller and 'listeners'. Even when the story being told is ancient and traditional, any oral and/or embodied telling is also an in-the-moment creation of the storyteller. There may be elements of improvisation, play and shared creation involving the audience. Thus, each particular version of the story is in a sense new, and unique to that time and place. Storying may also involve the teller using elements of drama such as focus and tension – the incorporation of vocal qualities, gesture and movement to bring characters to life and create the mood that fits the events and emotions in the story. Thus, as with drama, the audience, through their imaginations, may enter another world and step into the shoes of its inhabitants. These experiences, in families and early years settings, can provide opportunities for children to experience and develop empathy (see Chapter 6).

STORYTELLING AS A BASIS FOR GENERATIVE LISTENING

Writing in the aftermath of the 2019 bushfires that engulfed so much of Australia, Renshaw (2021) explored the potentialities of *placestories* of living justice – storying about and within place. Responding to the silencing felt by children, Renshaw (2021) shares stories of children engaging with the natural world and the creatures that inhabit it, as they connected with sacred Karawatha Country. In engaging with peers and educators through storytelling, these children were able to create space to be changemakers, contributing towards living justice, as their perspectives on caring for our world were no longer ignored.

This chimes powerfully with the words of Bill Neidjie et al. (1985, p. 47):

Our story is in the land...

it is written in those sacred places.

My children will look after those places,

that's the law.

Cologon et al. (2019, p. 60) write that '"generative listening" emerges from the cyclical combination of (a) listening to, (b) meaning-making with and (c) engaging in praxis for, transformation against oppression', praxis being reflection and action towards positive change. The story below, of a five-year-old who was learning about Darkinjung land, advocating for the safety of a spider, illustrates the activist power that can be present through storytelling:

"No, no, no, don't hurt it!" 5-year-old Narul says to the adult who was about to squash a spider they had just encountered on the cubby house door. The spider paused momentarily. Perhaps sensing that the adult was not yet convinced, Narul continued "it isn't hurting us. It needs home too". Narul then, seemingly storytelling on the go, began to explain "This is Abu. Abu likes the tree over there. It is a long, long way for Abu to get there. We can fly Abu". Pausing and looking around, Narul picked up a long, thick piece of bark that had fallen from a nearby tree. "Abu's spaceship" Narul offered, holding up the bark to show the adult how the spider could be safely moved to a new location.

The Storycrafting method created by Riihelä also focuses on giving children extended tools for participative and democratic dialogue with adults (Backman-Nord et al., 2023). It was developed by scholars and educators (Backman-Nord et al., 2023; Karlsson, 2013; Riihelä, 2002) as part of research and educational practice and has been used in Finland since 1991. Storycrafting offers an approach to empowering children through facilitating the shaping and telling of stories that are completely their own. Children create the story they want to share and shape it exactly as they wish to. The adult's role is merely to record as needed and be in dialogue to support storytelling. Storycrafting highlights the child's power to decide, and the important role of the adult as an active, generative listener. As Karlsson (2013, p. 1112) elaborates:

> The adult writes the story down word for word, exactly as it has been told with no adult's corrections. The story is written down using the words, sentence structures and the phonetic form the teller uses and that he or she wants to have in the story. The adult doesn't ask questions, or demand further explanations, or suggest improvements. The adult does not evaluate the child or his or her abilities. The narrator's own tale is fine and interesting just as it is.

Storytelling in which we create spaces for children to genuinely express themselves and contribute meaningfully, using an approach such as Storycrafting, can form a basis for generative listening. Through this, the arts can be the basis of transformative action, and processes for illuminating children's perspectives whereby we acknowledge and engage with children's agency towards social justice (Cologon et al., 2019).

To think about...

- Can you recall examples of children sharing stories about their lives and feelings in your early years settings?
- What modes of communication and tools for expression did they use?
- What stories about their lives have you observed children telling through their pretend play?

STORYING WITH PUPPETS

Storytelling can be visual, oral, embodied and/or multimodal. Further, the relationship between storyteller and listener is always central. Puppetry is one example of these features of storying. Puppets inspire us to use our imaginations to bring them to life. They are a form of fantasy – we know they are objects, yet we pretend they are alive, relating to them as living beings. Puppets have unique power to inspire our empathy, although towards 'someone' we know to be a 'thing'. Perhaps it is the distance between a puppet and the other beings, interactions and relationships in our everyday life that makes us feel that a puppet is safe and non-threatening to relate to. Perhaps too, the imagination needed to respond to a puppet opens our minds and emotions to different perspectives. While puppetry is also a form of drama, we include it as storying because of the potential for interactivity and relationship-building between puppet and audience. Inclusive arts educator and puppetry researcher, Karaolis (2021) states: 'I firmly believe in the power of the puppet to foster relationships, build connections ...., and develop a community of learners'.

Puppetry, like other forms of storying, involves a 'suspension of disbelief' by the child as they enter an imaginary world. In drama, actors adopt the personality of their characters, whereas puppetry involves the 'transmission of personality' (Majaron, 2012, p. 13) from puppeteer to puppet. Children's belief in this 'magical transformation' is similar to the way they relate to their toys. In these imaginative play worlds, children have power to exercise agency, in contrast with their lack of power over other parts of their lives – 'the child dictates the rules and searches for possible solutions to his unsolved problems' (Majaron, 2012, p. 13).

The power of puppetry also seems to lie in its indirectness because puppets are not actually people. As Hamre says, 'the special ability of an animated figure to communicate rests in this ambiguity' (p. 21). For some children, relating to a puppet can feel safer and easier to navigate and control than interacting with a person (Majaron). A responsive, inclusive early years practitioner can contribute to these safe interactions by following the child's lead and respecting the puppet's ways of communicating. For example, adults might encourage the puppet to communicate through gesture and action as well as, or instead of words. They might also model these modes of communication in interacting with the puppet.

Almost any object can become a puppet through the actions of a puppeteer and the imaginations of everyone involved – a sock, a wooden spoon with a face drawn on it or a hand-carved traditional marionette. Children often use their toys as puppets, manipulating them or 'speaking' for them. The unique thing about many puppets is some moving body parts. These might be a mouth, as in sock or glove puppets, or movable limbs operated via strings, rods or direct manipulation. Basically, anything given a personality and 'voice' – spoken or non-spoken – can be a puppet.

Puppetry, Creativity and Story Play in Early Years Settings

Early years practitioners can use puppets in a range of different ways in the life of their setting. Sometimes children will be the puppeteers, using purchased or home-made puppets. Puppets bring many possibilities for children to use as they create and tell their own stories. Children often bring toy figures to life as they play, moving and voicing them, in ways akin to puppetry. Bringing puppets into your early years setting, or making them with children, is an extension of this play.

Making puppets with children opens up many possibilities for exploring ideas about identities and ways of being, for example, in relation to personality and physical traits. For inclusive practitioners, observing, listening and responding with sensitivity and open-ended questions – such as 'I wonder …' or 'Tell me/show me …' – can lead to important opportunities to explore and show respect for diversity. And of course, making puppets and inventing their characters and stories is a wonderful form of creative expression.

STORIES AND EVERYDAY CULTURAL SHARING IN EARLY YEARS SETTINGS

With or without puppets, spontaneous, informal storytelling is part of everyday life, including in early years settings, as shown in the stories already shared in this chapter. The stories about their lives and families that are regularly told by children and adults are examples of children's cultures made visible (Theobald et al., 2022). Sharing these stories contributes to building a community culture in which the diversity of everyone's lives is acknowledged and celebrated. Theobald et al. refer to these as 'small stories', which are often shared spontaneously in early years settings, perhaps while children are playing or during routines such as mealtimes. This type of storytelling often happens in families, where parents, grandparents or other family members share stories of their childhoods, or other parts of family history. Bringing the practice of sharing 'small stories' into an early years setting, with conversations or collaborations with families about home story practices, is a valuable approach to using story sharing as a way of exploring and valuing diversity through this ancient art form that in various ways is part of all our lives (Theobald et al., 2022).

To think about...

- Thinking back to your childhood do you have memories of family storytelling?
- Who told those stories? How did you feel about family and life during those storytelling moments?

Contemporary Learning Through Storying Traditions

While storying is often spontaneous, practitioners can incorporate specific times in the routine for story sharing during group gatherings. In some Australian settings, these may take the form of 'yarning circles' – safe spaces to gather, sit and share conversation and stories. Yarning circles are a First Nations cultural practice and central to traditional ways of learning and being. Similar practices exist in many First Nations cultures, such as those of North America. They are a place to listen, learn and take turns to contribute. Traditional practices related to storying are increasingly acknowledged as having significant value in culturally responsive, inclusive education, in the early years and beyond. In Australia, where education is recognised as central to the processes of reconciliation and healing from the past wrongs done to our First Nations people, traditional ways of learning, including yarning circles and a focus on story, are being incorporated into curriculum and pedagogy, including in the early years (AGDE, 2022). Here, we share one pedagogical model that centres around storying, the *8 Ways of Learning* Framework (Yunkaporta & McGinty, 2009).

The 'Eight-Way' framework belongs to a place, rather than a person or organisation. The Baakindji, Ngiyampaa, Yuwaalaraay, Gamilaraay, Wiradjuri, Wangkumarra peoples and other nations of Western NSW own the knowledges that this framework originated from. 'It is all about relational responsiveness, a protocol of attending to relational obligations to the field you're working in, relating and responding holistically to people, land, culture, language, spirit and the relationships between these with integrity and intellectual rigour' (8 ways online, nd). The Aboriginal *8 Ways of Learning* model is expressed as 8 interconnected pedagogies that each provide a point of entry into Aboriginal ways of knowing. They likewise provide an avenue for developing ways to work with local Aboriginal communities. The framework reflects acknowledgement of the link between culture, place and how people, including children, learn. It is thus an inclusive framework, with links to the arts, as storying is at its heart. In the visual representation of the Framework (see Figure 7.1), the joining lines are as important as the pedagogies themselves. They represent values, protocols, systems and processes, and refer to the ways of valuing, being, knowing and doing. The lines also show how the different pedagogies are inter-related. While it is a framework that can be, and is, used in schools and early childhood settings attended by Aboriginal children, it can be used for all children, of all cultures and in all places. In early childhood, the *8-Way* framework is also in alignment with the concepts of *Belonging, Being and Becoming* that underpin the national curriculum, the Early Years Learning Framework (AGDE, 2022).

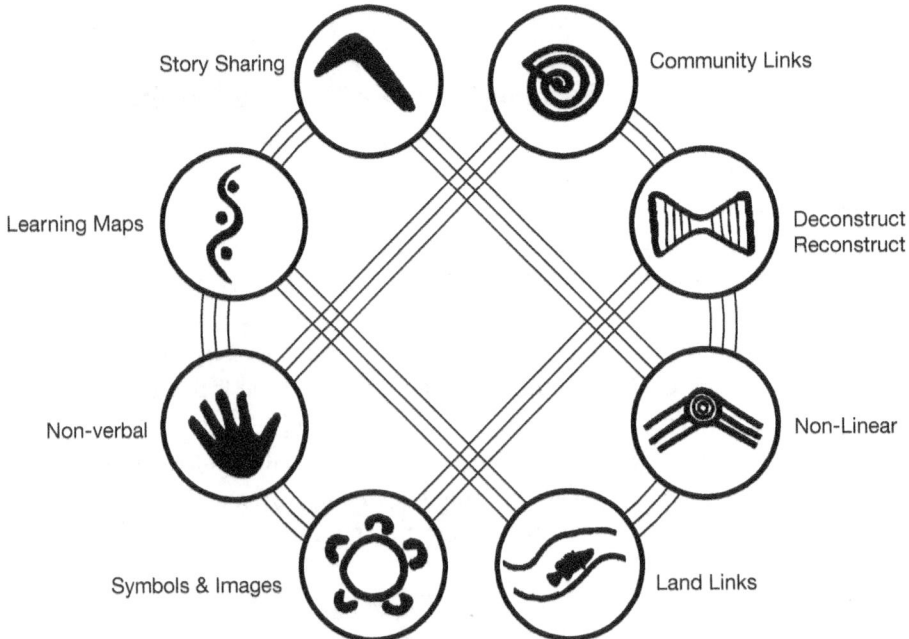

Figure 7.1 8 ways of knowing framework

21ST-CENTURY CHILDHOODS AND DIGITAL STORYING

As storying has such ancient and diverse roots that have been shaped by cultures and human creativity through the ages, its multimodal possibilities have of course widened to embrace digital technology and the cultures that it has led to in the 21st century. Now, in homes and education settings in many parts of the world, digital devices and apps, on smartphones, tablets and computers, have transformed the creation and communication of stories. Indeed, storying by adults and older children is a large part of social media. In early years settings, children often collaboratively create stories in their socio-dramatic play. Digital storying can become an extension of these play processes. When facilitated by a responsive, inclusive educator in the context of respectful, trusting relationships, there is great potential for peer-to-peer learning during story-making processes (community of practice). Thus, digital storying has rich potential for building inclusive early years communities.

Digital technology offers multimodal expressions of diverse voices, making it ideal for implementing Universal Design for Learning (see Chapter 10). Digital tools such as tablet apps can be used to photograph, draw or manipulate images, to make them move, and make sound, with music, synthesised sounds or recorded voices. Various visual symbols, including photographs, other visual images, verbal text, emojis and so on, can all be part of digital storying.

In the thick of coronavirus disease 2019 (COVID-19) lockdowns in many places around the world, digital storytelling became a site of connection explored in new ways in early years settings. For example, educator storytelling was shared with children who were at home with their families. Drawing together play, traditional storytelling, puppetry and a wide range of art engagement including drawing, painting, and sculpting, shared online storytelling became a regular part of the daily lives of many children.

> In Australia, in response to the isolation of many children within high-rise towers. Including refugee children, Leah Vandenberg – a presenter on popular children's educational television show Play School developed an online play group targeted particularly at isolated children and children who are refugees within Australia and in Australian detention centres. This online play group, called The Cubby House engaged children through shared storytelling with a range of art activities aimed at connecting children together in a time where human connection was much needed (https://www.abc.net.au/news/2021-09-16/biloela-girls-loving-online-sessions-with-play-school-presenter-/100463184).

For many children, digital applications became places for connection – whether simultaneous (as for *The Cubby House*) or over time. Byman et al. (2022, p. 18) explore the potentialities for digital storytelling to engage with children's 'emotional experiences in and about nature' understanding children's digital storying as incorporating 'storycrafting and storytelling… emerging through relational entanglements'. While extending beyond the focus on nature, below is an example of creating a new mode of connection between young cousins who were separated during lengthy lockdowns.

Three and four-year-old cousins Lee and Aisha spoke regularly using video calls as they missed each other during lockdown. As fast friends, they were accustomed to playing regularly and their play was long, complex and very important to them both. Video calls were an important form of ongoing contact, and they would often experience companionship as they independently played side by side with the video call running. However, over time they expressed a need to engage more in activities with each other – as they would in face-to-face contact. With support from two of their older cousins (aged 6 and 7 years), Lee and Aisha collected photos, drawings, artefacts from around their homes including leaves, rocks and sticks, and began to co-construct stories online together. Using a simple animation app, they worked little-by-little over time to create a fully animated video, complete with songs, drawings (digital and photographed pencil drawings), photos of themselves and their families, and animated versions of themselves. The end result was a genuinely co-constructed artwork, made across the distance using digital applications to facilitate shared storytelling about what was important to these children. More importantly, digital storytelling enabled connection and shared expression within an isolated situation.

CONCLUSION

Relationships and belonging, imagining and sharing, are at the heart of inclusive early years pedagogy. Stories and storying provide ways of sharing our lives, histories and interests with others. Through stories we connect with and learn about the past, and imagine the future. In early years settings, recognising that children's communications are often forms of storying presents rich possibilities for generative listening. This helps us get to know children, and fosters their sense of identity and belonging in the early years community. Creating or stepping into the worlds of stories also contributes to building empathy, as do all forms of arts, in varying ways (see Chapter 6). In this chapter, we have shared a tiny sample of the myriad of form of storying that humans engage in. Storytelling, by children and adults, involving diverse modes of communication beyond the verbal, offer rich possibilities for inclusive arts practice. It can support all four anti-bias goals – allowing children to feel pride in their identity, connect with others, explore challenging or unfair aspects of life and pose equitable solutions. Storytelling has been part of life throughout human history, and in the 21st century the urge to tell our stories is as strong as ever. While the direct, immediate interaction between teller and listener is not always part of storying in the digital world, the continuing development of new virtual tools is a testament to human creativity and the need to tell our stories.

--- To think about... ---

- How might you use storying in your work with young children, to learn with and from each other?
- What strategies and resources could you use, so that storying provides possibilities for all to listen and share their stories?

RESOURCES

On Australian Aboriginal storying practices:

https://www.qcaa.qld.edu.au/about/k-12-policies/aboriginal-torres-strait-islander-perspectives/
resources/yarning-circles

https://www.cambridge.org/core/books/abs/drawn-from-the-ground/sand-stories-as-social-and-
cultural-practice/AA8CEF7F93C2D2B4D28056268D9846C3

8 ways of learning framework https://www.8ways.online/about

On puppetry:

http://thespoke.earlychildhoodaustralia.org.au/give-hand-using-puppets-classroom/

https://www.edutopia.org/article/no-strings-attached-supporting-social-and-emotional-
learning-puppets

On inclusive arts:

Fox, A., & Macpherson, H. (2015). *Inclusive arts practice and research: A critical manifesto.* Routledge./http://arts.brighton.ac.uk/__data/assets/pdf_file/0003/195717/Chapter-1-Inclusive-Arts-
Practice-and-Research.pdf

REFERENCES

Australian Government Department of Education [AGDE] (2022). *Belonging, being and becoming:
The early years learning Framework for Australia (V2.0).*

Backman-Nord, P., Staffan, E. & Nyback, M.-H. (2023).The storycrafting method: A systematic
review. *Journal of Early Childhood Education Research, 12*(2), 34–50. https://journal.fi/jecer

Bergen, D. (2021). Humour as a resource for children. In E. Vandelheiden & C. Mayer (Eds.), *The
Palgrave handbook of humour research* (pp. 311–323). Springer International Publishing AG.
https://doi.org/10.1007/978-3-030-78280-1

Binder, M., & Kotsopoulos, S. (2011). Multimodal literacy narratives: Weaving the threads of
young children's identity through the arts. *Journal of Research in Childhood Education, 25*(4),
339–363.

Byman, J., Kumpulainen, K., Wong, C. C., & Renlund, J. (2022). Children's emotional experiences
in and about nature across temporal–spatial entanglements during digital storying. *Literacy,
56*(1), 18–28.

Cologon, K., Cologon, T., Mevawalla, Z., & Niland, A. (2019). Generative listening: Using
arts-based inquiry to investigate young children's perspectives of inclusion, exclusion and
disability. *Journal of Early Childhood Research, 17*(1), 54–69.

Crawford, S. A., & Caltabiano, N. J. (2011). Promoting emotional well-being through the use of
humour. *The Journal of Positive Psychology, 6*(3), 237–252.

Facer, K. (2019). Storytelling in troubled times: What is the role for educators in the deep crises of the 21st century? *Literacy, 53*(1), 3–13. https://doi.org/10.1111/lit.12176

Gaffney, D. A. (2006). The aftermath of disaster: Children in crisis. *Journal of Clinical Psychology: In Session, 62*(8), 1001–1016.

Green, J. (2014). *Drawn from the ground: Sound, sign and inscription in Central Australian sand stories.* Cambridge University Press.

Karaolis, O. (2021, August 19). *No strings attached: Supporting social and emotional learning with puppets.* Edutopia. https://www.edutopia.org/article/no-strings-attached-supporting-social-and-emotional-learning-puppets/

Karlsson, L. (2013). Storycrafting method–to share, participate, tell and listen in practice and research. *European Journal of Social & Behavioural Sciences, 6*(3), 1109–1117.

Majaron, E. (2012). Art as a pathway to the child. In L. Kroflin (Ed.), *The power of the puppet* (pp. 11–17). The UNIMA Puppets in Education, Development and Therapy Commission.

Malaguzzi, L., & Gandini, L. (1993). For an education based on relationships. *Young Children, 49*(1), 9–12.

McKeough, A., Bird, S., Tourigny, E., Romaine, A., Graham, S., Ottmann, J., & Jeary, J. (2008). Storytelling as a foundation to literacy development for Aboriginal children: Culturally and developmentally appropriate practices. *Canadian Psychology, 49*(2), 148–154.

Neidjie, B., Davis, S., & Fox, A. (1985). *Kakadu man–Bill Neidjie.* Mybrood P/L Incorporated.

Renshaw, P. (2021). Feeling for the Anthropocene: Placestories of living justice. *Australian Educational Researcher, 48*, 1–21. https://doi.org/10.1007/s13384-021-00433-z

Riihelä, M. (2002). Children's play is the origin of social activity. *European Early Childhood Education Research Journal, 10*(1), 39–53. https://doi.org/10.1080/13502930285208831

Theobald, M., Busch, G., Mushin, I., O'Gorman, L., Nielson, C., Watts, J., & Danby, S. (2022). Making culture visible: Telling small stories in busy classrooms. In *Storytelling practices in home and educational contexts: Perspectives from conversation analysis* (pp. 123–148). Springer Nature.

Yunkaporta, T., & McGinty, S. (2009). Reclaiming aboriginal knowledge at the cultural interface. *Australian Educational Researcher, 36*(2), 55–72.

8

EXPLORING THE WORLD THROUGH THE CREATIVE ARTISTRY OF PICTURE BOOKS

Amanda Niland and Kathy Cologon

Chapter objectives

This chapter introduces you to these key ideas:

- Young children and picturebook artistry
- Picturebook portrayals of diversity – 'mirrors, windows and sliding doors'
- How picture books convey values and attitudes
- Taking a slow look at picturebooks
- Sparking children's creative responses to picture books

INTRODUCTION

Enjoyment of stories is part of being human, as explored in the previous chapter. One form of story that is particularly loved by young children is the picturebook. As well as being an enchanting part of childhood, books and stories are important parts of early years curriculum. They provide enjoyment, inspire creativity, support language and emergent literacy development, can affirm identity, and perhaps most importantly provide rich opportunities for relational experiences, shared understandings and feelings of empathy. Thus picturebooks are invaluable resources for fostering inclusion in early years settings. In this chapter we explore the ways in which possibilities for meaning-making are created in picturebooks for young children, and how this unique form of artistic expression (Nodelman, 2008) can stimulate children's imagination and inspire creative responses through drama, storytelling, visual arts, music, dance and imaginative play.

YOUNG CHILDREN AND THE ARTISTRY OF PICTUREBOOKS

We begin with a glimpse into *Patricia*, by Stephen Michael King (1997):

> Patricia's head was filled with thoughts – wonderful, amazing thoughts. It was so full she needed to find someone to share them with. . . .

The magic of books like *Patricia* lies in the way they invite children to identify with a character's inner imaginative world. In this book, King creates a magical climax where, in two wordless double page spreads 'in one gigantic burst. . . . all of her thoughts came tumbling out' (King, 1997). Children often place themselves in stories like this one or compare it to their own experiences; for example, Patricia's need to share her thoughts with a world of adults who don't always pay attention strikes a chord for many children.

To think about. . .

- What are your earliest memories of books or stories?
- What were your favourites?
- How did you relate to the characters?

The encounters children have with diverse lives and representations of the world within books can help them build positive self-identities, as well as respect and empathy for others. Through picturebooks, children can be inspired to advocate for the rights of everyone to participate equitably and experience belonging. Sitting comfortably with a trusted adult to share a favourite picturebook is one of the ways that relationships grow between children and early years practitioners. Just as music creates a metaphorical 'lap' in which children and adults can come together (see Introduction chapter), so too do picturebooks. Many authors have written about shared reading as an act of caring and love (e.g. Berg, 1977; Fox, 2008). Shared reading enables children and adults to get to know each other and experience moments of togetherness and belonging. These experiences can be powerful in creating an inclusive early years community. However, we also know from research that children's literature does not always adequately portray human diversity (Boyd et al., 2015; Koss, 2015), and that existing portrayals may be stereotypical, inaccurate, or 'othering' (Yoo-Lee et al., 2014). Therefore, thinking about which books we choose for children, carefully considering how humans in all our diversities are portrayed, is important and complex (Yoo-Lee et al., 2014).

Which Books?

Sharing a book with children is often used as a way of fostering a sense of calm – hence the reading of bedtime stories, or a quiet story time after lunch in an early years setting. Perhaps this is why many adults choose books that are light-hearted, whether about everyday life or flights of fantasy. Books are often seen as 'quieting texts' (Whitelaw, 2017, p. 33) that present 'knowledge as a thing known' (p. 33). But life is not always happy, fair, certain or easy to understand for children; their creation of knowledge is ongoing and requires questioning, curiosity and encounters with the unknown. The 'easy' books may not offer children the chance to connect with experiences and issues that reflect the actuality of life. As part of your inclusive practice, you may like to consider books that are 'disquieting' (Whitelaw) as well as those that are light-hearted or calming. Just as children are diverse in their ways of being and knowing, so too are their motivations, interests, and ways of exploring. and making meaning from books.

We can reflect on the role of 'disquieting' books in light of the many difficult experiences children may encounter – directly or through the media, as in the following examples:

> In grappling with the death of his baby brother, Deci's mother searched high and low for children's books that might help him to explore and feel less alone in his confusion and complex feelings.

> Following a highly publicised boat disaster in which several children who were seeking asylum with their families died, Ana – an early childhood teacher – responded to the children's graphic illustrations of the disaster within their drawings by searching for children's books such as 'Ziba Came on a Boat'.

> When her brother was diagnosed with a terminal illness and the family were working towards saying goodbye, Lyla's Auntie borrowed 'Jenny Angel' and the two of them read and cried and hugged and read more.

As the brief case studies above show, the value of shared reading lies in the experience of closeness, and in the books themselves. Books can foster not only children's imagination, learning and development, but also their perspective-taking and empathy (McCallum & Stephens, 2011), and hence inclusion. Choosing books that encompass the rich diversity of life with respect, and are aesthetically interesting and creative, is central. Given the lack of diverse representations of ways of being in the world, while books can be a catalyst for fostering inclusion, they may also create barriers. Consider the ubiquity of monocultural representations in picture books for young children (Adam et al., 2019), including those published in braille form (Coleman & Harrison, 2022). Consider also the mostly heteronormative and binary constructions of gender and the stereotypical portrayal of the nuclear family structure (Lo, 2019), the absence of representations of houselessness (Terrile, 2022), as well as either the absence of disability or ableist portrayals of characters when they experience disability (Hayden & Prince, 2020). When educators choose books that go beyond portraying or implying narrow concepts of 'normality' and also select those that incorporate and value diversity, as well as books that 'challenge ableist discourses' around disability (Kleekamp & Zapata, 2019, p. 589), then children's literature can be a powerful inclusive tool.

Shared reading can stimulate rich and meaningful discussions with children about diversity and belonging and about others' ways of being and living. Books about some of the more complex, confusing or challenging aspects of life can open up spaces for dialogue about or exploration of, children's feelings and experiences. 'As a medium intended to be shared, the picturebook offers a generative site for meaning-making to be negotiated relationally among children and adults and within a larger community in the context of the classroom' (Whitelaw, 2017, p. 36). Thus the role of the educator is highly significant in selecting, and engaging inclusively with available books.

PICTUREBOOKS AND DIVERSITY

> children need to see their faces and situations reflected through the pages of books, to learn who they are, and to learn that they matter. (Johnson, 2016, p. 53)

In picturebooks, children explore a range of characters, contexts and worlds, giving them opportunities to use their imaginations to reflect on their own world and experience the worlds of others.

> Daniel read 'Susan Laughs' for the first time. Listening and sharing in the story, he smiled and commented on different aspects of the story he could relate to. As the final page showed that Susan uses a wheelchair, he exclaimed in surprise and delight "She has a wheelchair like me!" Beaming all over, he asked to read the book again and again.

Through exposure to a rich range of quality literature children can encounter varied perspectives, building their understanding of the diversity of life and creating empathy with other characters and situations (Leahy & Foley, 2018). As we all bring our own identities, experiences and perspectives to any text we meet, and interpret them through our own 'lenses', we simultaneously look outwards and inwards, wondering about where we fit in, or how the imaginary world of a book relates to us. This means that books function as metaphorical windows, mirrors and/or sliding doors (Bishop, 1990), positioning children as outsiders looking in, or as insiders in the world of the book. Books that are windows allow children to encounter and imagine worlds other than their own, enabling them to build empathy and understanding of diversity. However, if all or most books position some children as outsiders, then those children can never experience books as mirrors or go through those metaphorical sliding doors to feel a sense of connection, identification or belonging in the fictional worlds they encounter. Books can therefore be facilitators of, or barriers to, inclusion. Ivy, a final year preservice early childhood teacher of Taiwanese background living in Australia, reflecting back on the books encountered during her early years education, shared this:

> I started school in Los Angeles, California when I only knew how to say 'hello' and 'thank you' in English. It was difficult and confusing to be in a foreign country where everyone looked different from me and did not eat the same food or speak the same language as I did. I remember every single picture book read in the classroom had a Caucasian character, whether the hair colour was blonde or brunette. One day, while walking home from school with my mother, I excitedly told her that in a few weeks, my eyes would turn blue and my hair would turn blonde. I truly believed this would happen as I thought there must be a reason why every character in books, movies, and cartoons were Caucasian. My mother found this amusing and told the story to friends and family for years after. However, when I look back on this memory, I realised that even as a child, I quickly saw my own cultural identity as something to be disregarded or changed because it was not something of value. I believe this was due to the utter lack of representation of characters that looked like me when I was a child. (Ivy, preservice early childhood teacher, University of Sydney, 2020, with permission)

The representations of life and messages in picturebooks are communicated not only through the topic or story, but through how verbal text and images create discourses that convey values both implicitly and explicitly. We explore this below.

HOW PICTURE BOOKS WORK

Picturebooks for young children often appear deceptively simple, however a closer look can reveal layers of possibilities for children's meaning-making. This is because they are multi-modal texts – meaning is created by language, image, and the interaction between the two (Callow, 2018). 'The picturebook slows down our awareness, and it holds ideas up to the light in words and pictures in suspended moments' (Whitelaw, 2017, p. 35). Through the artful combination of words and images, picturebooks create an imaginative, multimodal space that sparks curiosity, questioning, imagination and empathy in the process of making meaning. Words and images work together to evoke an aesthetic response that neither could do as completely without the other. The language of the best picturebooks is often simple, with a succinctness and attention to sounds and rhythms that is akin to poetry, except that the imagery which is an essential ingredient of poetry is created through the combination of words and pictures.

Multimodality

In the 21st-century world, picturebooks are just one of many types of 'text' – any produced piece of communication or artefact that potentially conveys meaning. The immense diversity of text forms available today means that children and adults engage in many types of literacies, in the texts they encounter every day.

Multimodality is like weaving – each type of strand has an essential function that contributes to the single, finished artwork (Kress, 2003), but needs to work with the other strands to do its job. In picturebooks, author and illustrator weave together different strands of meaning created by each mode (words, images, layout) and its elements, so that the full meaning is only conveyed by the whole. The reading encounter then completes the multimodal experience – just as in an art gallery the way works are displayed contributes to how they are experienced, so the reading of a picturebook is part of the child's experience of multimodality, particularly when being read to.

Knowledge about multimodality enables early years practitioners to understand the creativity and meaning-making potential of picturebooks and other texts. This also opens up possibilities for practitioners to provide inclusive opportunities for children to respond creatively to those texts in a variety of modes, depending on their interests and strengths. Multimodality is a feature of Universal Design for Learning (UDL), which provides children with multiple means of engagement, representation and expression/action (Kleinfeld, 2019) (see also Chapter 10). Martens et al. advocate for the potential of multimodality for all learners: 'constructing meaning multimodally broadens learners' avenues for gathering and expressing meaning, making their meanings richer and more complex and allowing them to triangulate their knowing within and between modes' (Harste et al., 1984, as cited in Martens et al., 2012, p. 291).

The multimodal artistry of picturebooks means they can convey complex ideas in seemingly simple ways – with very few words, and in 32 pages or less! Nodelman writes 'picture books …. convey "simple delight" by surprisingly complex means' (2008, p. 131). He highlights the prerequisite knowledge children need to make sense of what they meet in a book. For example, to understand the representation of something on the page, children must first have encountered it in their lives. They are not just holding, looking at or listening to a book, but – in different ways depending on sensory preferences and capabilities – at the same time engaging in complex perceptual, intellectual and emotional processes to 'see', hear, and make meaning of visual and verbal texts, mediated for young children by someone reading aloud, and perhaps signing.

Below we offer some examples of how illustrations and written language work individually and in combination to provide children with potential for meaning-making. You may like to explore these books yourself (in print if available, or perhaps via YouTube read-alouds). As you explore these books or others, and look for the ways the various features analysed below are used, take time to reflect on how they work to convey implicit and explicit layers of meaning, and note any feelings that arise for you as a result.

'Reading' the Visual - Illustrations and Meaning-Making

Colour may often dominate children's first sensory engagement and initial impressions of a picture book. It can therefore be a useful entry point for exploring and building awareness of the multimodal creativity of books. Here are examples of how colour, its textures and tones, can play a role in creating the worlds of characters, their emotions and the general mood of a story.

> In 'Patricia' (King, 1997), the swirling blue skies bring a feeling of freedom and excitement about the world of Patricia's "wonderful, amazing thoughts".
>
> In 'Amy and Louis', (Gleeson & Blackwood, 2006) the richly textured clouds that form imaginary creatures bring to life the feelings of togetherness of these two friends playing together. When Louis' family moves far away and the children are missing each other, illustrator Freya Blackwood uses more sombre shades to reflect their sadness and loneliness.
>
> In 'Little Beauty' (Browne, 2008), the gorilla's deep anger at the 'baddie' portrayal of one of his kind in a TV programme climaxes in a page that is completely red.

Perspective is another visual feature that conveys meaning in picturebooks; illustrators often manipulate perspective and size to highlight what is or isn't important. In *Patricia*, when Patricia tries to share some of her 'wonderful, amazing thoughts' with her mother, who 'didn't seem to hear a single word Patricia said', we see Patricia as so tiny that only her mother's legs and the lower torso are visible. Readers can sense how unacknowledged and powerless Patricia feels without any words being used.

Many illustrators use perspective at important moments in the narrative. Anthony Browne uses it to convey especially strong emotions in *Little Beauty* (Browne, 2008):

> Early in the story, when the gorilla is lonely and very sad, we see his face close up and nearly front on. He is frowning, with eyes sadly staring and mouth turned down. Later, his happiest moment is shown with a side view, in a double page spread of the gorilla and his kitten friend Beauty. The text states: "They were happy for a long time...". The illustration shows the gorilla lying on his back, eyes closed, smiling, arms and legs in the air balancing the kitten, who gazes fondly down at him.

Framing can also contribute to meaning. A notable example of this is in Maurice Sendak's *Where the Wild Things Are* (1963), one of the most beloved picturebooks in the English language.

> In the real life situation of Max being sent to his bedroom for being what his mother called a 'wild thing', illustrations are small and wide frames are created by the white pages. Once Max enters his imagined world and "sailed off through night and day and in and out of weeks and almost over a year", the illustrations take up gradually more of the page - the frames become smaller, then disappear, until full double page spreads with no borders celebrate Max's adventures in the wonderful world of the wild things.

Picturebook illustrators also use techniques such as line, angle, positioning and size to create **vectors** that guide readers as they scan the page. Vectors combine with written text to create point of view – our experiencing of the story from one character's perspective. We may be invited to view characters from above – a 'bird's-eye' view – or view characters from below – a 'worm's-eye view'.

An interesting example of how vectors convey point of view is the double page spread mentioned earlier, in which Patricia (King, 1997) unsuccessfully tries to get her mother's attention.

> King uses lines, angles and colour contrasts to guide our looking. Patricia, only a little taller than her mother's knee, faces away from us, looking up at her mother. Her arm reaches up to tug her mother's skirt and the line of Patricia's arm is repeated in the angle of the floor. The wooden floor has lines that also angle upwards, and the wall above it is white, to highlight the vectors.

This visual technique draws us into Patricia's perspective, helping us to empathise with her feelings in this situation, making a potentially 'mirror' moment for some children (Bishop, 1990).

Early years practitioners can use their understanding of the visual features of picturebooks to encourage children's slow looking and exploration of the situations, characters and ideas in the books. Knowledge of how picture books work can thus enrich shared reading, supporting practitioners to engage with children in open-ended discussions, listen and respond sensitively to their ideas and questions, hence developing children's empathy and perspective taking (Wee et al., 2022). When books contain inclusive portrayals of human diversity, we can support children in celebrating that diversity (Erwin et al., 2021), challenging prejudice and stereotypes (Bow, 2019), and engaging with complex concepts such as social oppression (Nguyen, 2022).

To think about...

- Find one of the books discussed (see list below), taking time to explore and appreciate the images and design as well as the words
- Consider the most important character(s) and make a few notes on what you learn about them - their personality, challenges, interests, feelings
- Go through the book carefully and note how you learnt these things - from words, images, design?
- Consider how line, shape, colour, size and positioning have been used to highlight things of importance, add information or create mood?
- Reflect on how the multiples modes of the book, through the artistry of author and illustrator, worked together to enable you to make meaning about character and story

---

You can use this reflective task for many picture books in your collection. As part of your inclusive pedagogy, you may find it valuable to do this together with colleagues in a staff meeting or professional learning session.

Here are a few useful examples for exploring the multimodal creation of discourse in picturebooks:

- *Where the Wild Things Are* (Maurice Sendak)
- *Amy and Louis* (Libby Gleeson & Freya Blackwood)
- *Patricia* (Stephen Michael King)
- *The Snowy Day* (Ezra Jack Keats)
- *Changes* (Anthony Browne)
- *Little Beauty* (Anthony Browne)
- *The Black Book of Colours* (Menena Cottin & Rosana Faría)

Many of the elements of children's books are directed at visual engagement. But what about children who are blind? How can inclusive early years practitioners find and use books with possibilities for multi-sensory engagement for children who have low vision or are blind? One interesting example is *The Black Book of Colours* (Cottin & Faría, 2008). It can be read using touching and listening, as illustrations and textured and verbal text is printed in written alphabet and braille. For children who are sighted, images can be seen, and change in their visibility depending on the angle of light. The written text portrays one child's multi-sensory ideas and feelings about colours in his life. This book can stimulate rich conversations about all the sensory explorations that children engage in every day, and prompt new ways of thinking about colour. Its imaginative multimodal exploration of colour from the perspective of someone who sees through touch, hearing and smell presents possibilities for children's creative thinking and art-making, as well as for experiencing the world in another child's shoes.

Amelie moved her fingers lightly over the cover of the book, quickly and gently exploring the page with her hands. "I found the words!" she said, a smile spreading across her face. Together she and her big brother began to read the story 'The Black Book of Colours'. Each page is black with raised black images illustrating the colours, such as strawberries for red. The children felt the pictures with their hands. Amelie felt the words with her fingers and her big brother read the typed text aloud. Amelie is blind, her brother is not. As they read the story they chatted together about the colours as the story protagonist experienced colour through senses other than sight. Each of them thinking of other possibilities for the colours from their shared experiences and giggling together about what is brown that 'stinks'.

Tactile books provide opportunities for multimodal exploration that doesn't depend on vision. For example, in Australia, the *Felix Library*, created by Vision Australia, provides tactile books to accompany braille books, audio books, and objects that relate to the story. Early years practitioners can build on these ideas. For example, by adding tactile elements and relevant objects that illustrate key concepts when exploring children's books. The use of clear braille overlays added to books makes the text accessible to users of braille. The image below shows a child exploring a tactile display at an exhibition of children's books entitled *Imagine, The Wonder of Picture Books* at the State Library of NSW (https://www.sl.nsw.gov.au/exhibitions/imagine-the-wonder-picture-books). This exhibition showcased the work of authors and illustrators and included tactile elements and braille translations of books (Figure 8.1).

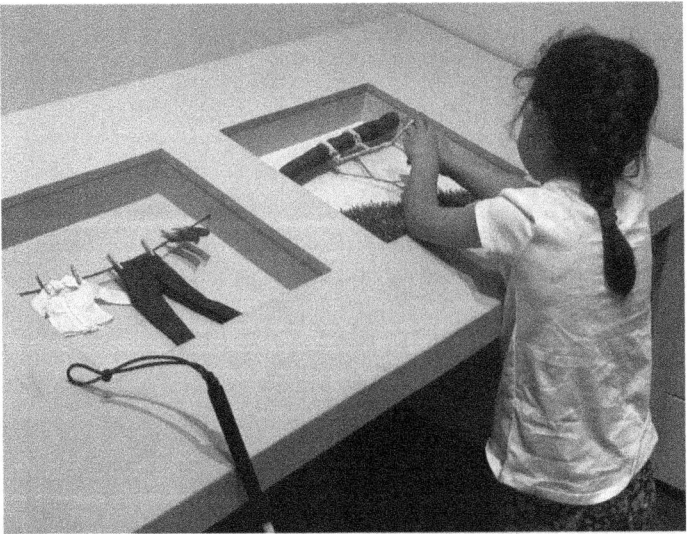

Figure 8.1 Tactile versions of picture book illustrations

> **To think about...**
>
> - What adaptations to your shared reading approaches would you make so that all children can engage in exploring and enjoying books?
> - How might you choose books for shared reading that are imaginative and interesting for children with children who have low vision or are blind?

DISCOURSE AND IDEOLOGY AND VERBAL TEXT IN CHILDREN'S PICTUREBOOKS

Now we turn our attention to the verbal aspect of picture books. Language is a socially constructed semiotic (meaning-making) system that underpins discourse, both shaping and reflecting social attitudes, values and actions (Ainsworth, 2017). In picturebooks for young children, values, social structures and roles, power relations or positioning, are all represented, perhaps clearly conveyed in words or images or implied by what is not stated or visually evident (McCallum & Stephens, 2011). Added to this, each reader uses their own life experiences and identities to make meaning from texts. For young children, this is often also mediated by an adult reading the story. So, the embedding of children's literature into inclusive pedagogy necessitates intentional strategies that build critical literacy – for practitioners and children. Critical literacy involves analytical reflection on the messages conveyed in texts 'from the perspective of social equity and justice for positive transformation of unequal practices' (Sun, 2021, p. 234). A central question to ask is thus: *Whose voices are privileged in this text?* (Sun).

TAKING A SLOW LOOK AT PICTURE BOOKS

Young children can develop critical literacy when given the knowledge and opportunities to explore how picturebooks work, by engaging in 'slow looking' and exploration over time. Pantaleo found that where teachers take time and provide scaffolds and provocations, children are capable of being insightful analysts of how texts work and discourse is created (Pantaleo, 2015, 2016). In a class of 6 and 7 year olds of diverse linguistic and cultural backgrounds and abilities in Canada, Pantaleo and the class teacher shared knowledge of key visual elements of a few picturebooks with the children. They then provided prompts to guide their oral and written analytical responses. The children showed understanding of how colour, line, point of view, perspective, typography and framing were used to convey meaning. The example of one child's analysis of the use of framing in *This is a Moose* (Morris, 2014) show how much meaning children can gain from a book when given knowledge and ways to use it (Pantaleo, 2018, p. 162):

> I notice the chipmunk is breaking the frame with his head. This shows that the frame is too small for him. He feels important because he's a superhero and he is going to save the moose. (Leena)

Leena's response shows her ability to interpret the characters' feelings and motivations, although these were not described in words. The project ended with the children using their insights into how the visual elements of picturebooks work to create their own books, allowing them agency to be creative and to express their interests, thoughts and feelings in words and pictures.

Sparking Children's Creative Responses to Picturebooks

Creative arts explorations provide rich possibilities for children to express their responses to books – to delve into the layers of meaning and discourse conveyed multimodally. Early years practitioners can use their understanding of the creative, multimodal techniques authors and illustrators use to inspire children's slow looking and awareness of the creativity of picturebooks. As part of their inclusive arts pedagogy, practitioners can provide children with multiple means of communication and expression – such as dramatic play, puppets, construction with varied play and mark-making materials, musical instruments, digital story apps – so that every child can respond to books in their own ways. The metaphorical mirrors, windows or sliding doors that children encounter through picturebooks can be extended or varied through their creative responses to them. Children may choose to replicate a story, take the characters on adventures beyond those in the picturebook, or bring new characters into the story. Some children may wish to create a 'product' such as their own book or digital text, or they may focus on the processes of developing worlds and characters from a picturebook in their spontaneous dramatic play with peers. Through picturebooks, children can dive into the 'sea of creativity' described by Laura in Chapter 3, and make it as infinitely varied as their imaginations wish it to be.

The two-year-olds in the case study below spent months embarking on imaginary bear hunts in their play and requested that educators read the book *We're going on a bear hunt* (Rosen & Oxenbury, 1989) many times every day. Their 'sea of creativity' eventually extended to collaborative art that encompassed sensory exploration, mark-making, sound, and movement (Figures 8.2 and 8.3).

Today we had an art experience that extended from "Going on a Bear Hunt". As we were reading our bear hunt book, we came to the snowstorm page and made the 'oooOOOOooooOOOooo' sounds. Starting with frozen white paint on cardboard, we gathered around a large flat card to feel, touch, and manipulate frozen cubes of cold white paint, feeling it with our hands and feet, breaking it apart, noticing it melt away. We then went and washed our hands so that when we came back, we could play with the materials without them sticking to our bodies. Swirling and whirling around with the tissue paper was great fun and added lots of dynamic energy. We laughed and expressed surprise ripping and scrunching the paper (displaying active agency). Tearing the paper, we felt the tension of the paper rip and hear the sound. Cotton buds were added to the cardboard, sticking only on the glue and not the tissue paper; some of us chose to continue to swirl and whirl through the snowstorm. Some of us worked out where it was sticky and lined up cotton buds and paper neatly. Some of us started throwing cotton buds, mid swirl, aiming them for the sticky patches on the cardboard. We created a snowstorm of paper, cotton buds, and our friends whirling and swirling through the air of our classroom. (Pedagogical documentation by visual artist, early childhood teacher and art therapist, Georgia Freebody, 2023, with permission)

Figures 8.2 and 8.3 Toddlers' art-making about *We're going on a bear hunt*
Source: Photos Georgia Freebody, with permission.

CONCLUSION

In this chapter we have outlined how picturebooks work to convey meaning and create discourse, reflecting attitudes, values and knowledge that shape children's understanding of their world, themselves and each other. Given the wonderful creativity that picturebooks embody, the enjoyment children find in them, and the creative responses they can inspire, picturebooks play an important role in early years settings. Their value in fostering children's language and literacy development is widely recognised. However, the role they can play in either facilitating inclusion, or unwittingly contributing to marginalisation or discrimination, is perhaps less recognised, although equally important.

RESOURCES

Some examples of picture books that explore diversity through stories and characters:
The Black Book of Colours (Menena Cottin & Rosana Faría, 2008); Groundwood Books.
Two Mates (Melanie Prewett & Maggie Prewett, 2012); Magabala Books.

Susan Laughs (Jeanne Willis & Tony Ross, 2000); Macmillan.
Pearl Barley and Charlie Parsley (Aaron Blabey, 2008); Front Street Press.
Some Brains (Nelly Thomas, 2020); Piccolo Nero.

Culture-affirming picture books for babies and toddlers:
Hush a Thai Lullaby (Minfong Ho/Holly Meade, 1996); Orchard Books.
Baby Business (Jasmine Seymour, 2019); Magabala Books.

Picture books that deal with challenging emotions and life situations:
The Heart and the Bottle (Oliver Jeffers, 2010); Harper Collins.
Jenny Angel (Margaret Wild & Anne Spudvilas, 1999); Viking.
Ziba Came on a Boat (Liz Lofthouse & Robert Inkpen, 2012); Penguin.

REFERENCES

Adam, H., Barratt-Pugh, C., & Haig, Y. (2019). 'Portray cultures other than ours': How children's literature is being used to support the diversity goals of the Australian Early Years Learning Framework. *Australian Educational Researcher, 46*(3), 549–563. https://doi.org/10.1007/s13384-019-00302-wRefstyled

Ainsworth, S. (2017). Discourse analysis/methods. *The International Encyclopaedia of Organizational Communication*, 1–14.

Berg, L. (1977). *Reading and loving* (1st ed.). Routledge. https://doi.org/10.4324/9781351237062

Bishop, R. S. (1990). Mirrors, windows, and sliding glass doors. *Perspectives, 6*(3), ix–xi.

Bow, L. (2019). Racial abstraction and species difference: Anthropomorphic animals in "multicultural" children's literature. *American Literature, 91*(2), 323–356. https://doi.org/10.1215/00029831-7529167

Boyd, F. B., Causey, L. L., & Galda, L. (2015). Culturally diverse literature: Enriching variety in an era of Common Core State Standards. *The Reading Teacher, 68*(5), 378–387. https://doi.org/10.1002/trtr.1326Refstyled

Browne, A. (2008). *Little beauty*. Candlewick Press.

Callow, J. (2018). Classroom assessment and picture books: Strategies for assessing how students interpret multimodal texts. *Australian Journal of Language and Literacy, 41*(1), 5–20. https://doi.org/10.1007/BF03652002

Coleman, M. A., & Harrison, J. (2022). Cultural diversity in children's braille books. *Journal of Visual Impairment & Blindness, 116*(2), 127–140. https://doi.org/10.1177/0145482X2210902Refstyled

Cottin, M., & Faría, R. (2008). *The black book of colours*. Groundwood.

Erwin, E. J., Bacon, J. K., & Lalvani, P. (2021). It's about time! Advancing justice through joyful inquiry with young children. *Topics in Early Childhood Special Education, 43*(1). https://doi.org/10.1177/0271121420988890Refstyled

Fox, M. (2008). *Reading magic*. Harcourt.

Gleeson, L., & Blackwood, F. (2006). *Amy and Louis*. Scholastic Australia.

Hayden, H. E., & Prince, A. M. (2020). Disrupting ableism: Strengths-based representations of disability in children's picture books. *Journal of Early Childhood Literacy, 23*(2), 236–261. https://doi.org/10.1177/1468798420981751Refstyled

Johnson, D. D. (2016). Diversity in children's literature: 1 year later. *Journal of Children's Literature, 42*(1), 53.

King, S. (1997). *Patricia*. Scholastic Australia.

Kleekamp, M. C., & Zapata, A. (2019). Interrogating depictions of disability in children's picturebooks. *The Reading Teacher, 72*(5), 589–597. https://doi.org/10.1002/trtr.1766

Kleinfeld, E. (2019). Reimagining multimodality through UDL. In S. Khadka & J. Lee (Eds.), *Bridging the multimodal gap: From theory to practice* (pp. 20–42). Utah State University Press.

Koss, M. D. (2015). Diversity in contemporary picturebooks: A content analysis. *Journal of Children's Literature, 41*(1), 32–42.

Kress, G. (2003). *Literacy in the new media age*. Routledge.

Lo, R. S. (2019). Resisting gentle bias: A critical content analysis of family diversity in picturebooks. *Journal of Children's Literature, 45*(2), 1–30.

Martens, P., Martens, R., Doyle, M. H., Loomis, J., & Aghalarov, S. (2012). Learning from picturebooks: Reading and writing multimodally in first grade. *The Reading Teacher, 66*(4), 285–294. https://doi.org/10.1002/TRTR.01099

McCallum, R., & Stephens, J. (2011). Ideology and children's books. In S. Wolf, K. Coats, P. Enciso, & C. Jenkins (Eds.), *Handbook of research on children's and young adult literature* (pp. 359–371). Routledge.

Morris, R. (2014). *This is a moose*. Little Brown Books.

Nguyen, A. (2022). "Children have the fairest things to say": Young children's engagement with anti-bias picture books. *Early Childhood Education Journal, 50*(5), 743–759.

Nodelman, P. (2008). *The hidden adult: Defining children's literature*. JHU Press.

Pantaleo, S. (2015). Language, literacy and visual texts. *English in Education, 49*(2), 113–129. https://doi.org/10.1111/17548845.2015.11912532

Pantaleo, S. (2016). Primary students' understanding and appreciation of the artwork in picturebooks. *Journal of Early Childhood Literacy, 16*(2), 228–255. https://doi.org/10.1177/1468798415569816Refstyled

Pantaleo, S. (2018). Learning about and through picturebook artwork. *The Reading Teacher, 71*(5), 557–567. https://doi.org/10.1002/trtr.1653

Rosen, M., & Oxenbury, H. (1989). *We're going on a bear hunt*. Walker Books.

Sun, L. (2021). Children of 'A Dream Come True': A critical content analysis of the representations of transracial Chinese adoption in picturebooks. *Children's Literature in Education, 52*, 231–252.

Terrile, V. C. (2022). Scenes from the class struggle in picture books: Depictions of housing and home in books for young children. *Children's Literature in Education, 53*(4), 526–546.

Wee, S. J., Kim, S. J., Chung, K., & Kim, M. (2022). Development of children's perspective-taking and empathy through bullying-themed books and role-playing. *Journal of Research in Childhood Education, 36*(1), 96–111. https://doi.org/10.1080/02568543.2020.1864523

Whitelaw, J. (2017). Beyond the bedtime story: In search of epistemic possibilities and the innovative potential of disquieting picturebooks. *Bookbird: A Journal of International Children's Literature, 55*(1), 33–41. https://doi.org/10.1353/bkb.2017.0004

Yoo-Lee, E., Fowler, L., Adkins, D., Kim, K. S., & Davis, H. N. (2014). Evaluating cultural authenticity in multicultural picture books: A collaborative analysis for diversity education. *The Library Quarterly, 84*(3), 324–347. https://doi.org/10.1086/676490

9

SEEING, FEELING AND CREATING 'FUTURE IMAGINARIES' WITHIN AND THROUGH THE VISUAL ARTS

Kathy Cologon

Chapter objectives

This chapter introduces you to these key ideas:

- The rich possibilities for inclusion through visual arts
- Exploring and challenging gender constructions within and through visual arts
- Recognising and valuing family diversity within visual arts
- Culturally sustaining visual arts pedagogy
- Taking anti-ableist approaches to visual arts
- Communicating with and through the arts

INTRODUCTION

I make my thinking in my paint. (Wynn, 4 years old)

Visual arts are rich with the possibility for expression about everyday life and exploring imaginaries beyond the lived experience. The potential and delights of art-making are endless, beautiful and magical. As well as the processes of making art, which are so powerful and important in and of themselves, appreciating artworks of our own and others, and exploring and revisiting art has so many possibilities for all children in learning, sharing, and further developing artistic creativity and beyond.

The visual art includes a myriad of different art forms such as painting, drawing, sculpture, photography and digital arts. This chapter explores art-making and appreciation with an emphasis on the many ways in which we can approach visual art to make it inclusive and relevant for children in all their diversities. I also consider some of the powerful possibilities for communicating within and through visual arts. As Diment and Hobbs (2014) argue, visual art is important in developing children's communication, problem-solving, social and emotional skills, as well as motor control, creativity and self-expression.

POSSIBILITIES FOR INCLUSION THROUGH THE VISUAL ARTS

Hickey-Moody (2017, p. 9) contends that inclusive education is a process of 'making culture' and 'making cultural imaginaries', with art playing a powerful role in the creation of such imaginaries. Fairclough (2003, p. 445) in exploring the powerful role that language (discourse) plays in our social worlds explains that creating imaginaries involves 'not only representations of how things are, they can also be representations of how things could be'. These representations and explorations *through* language enable us to develop 'future imaginaries' (Fairclough, 2003, p. 445) from which the world (and our everyday practices as educators) do not need to remain as they are now. This way of thinking opens spaces for future possibilities that are more inclusive of all our students with endless, wonderful, potentialities.

> Alex, Frankie, and Jordan are working together at the play dough table making and remaking sculptures, deep in an imaginary game as they work together. "It's a portal that will take us to the future!" Alex exclaims, showing it to Jordan and offering it to Frankie to feel and see with her hands. "A portal! Wow, where does it go?" asks Jordan. "I'm making a hovercraft. Is that a flying car?". "Zoom" responds Frankie, making a piece of play dough fly through the air. The play continues for an extended period as the three children continue to explore future imaginaries together through sculpture.

Penketh, in applying Fairclough's work to a consideration of ableism in arts education, argues that if we rely on traditional – therefore 'normative' – approaches to arts education, 'then those who experience the world in ways other than visual, those who do not rely on fine motor skills and those who remain dependent are purged from our consciousness. It becomes difficult to recognise how non-normative bodies might participate in art education because they are alien to 'future imaginaries' (2017, pp. 122–123). In this chapter, we ponder and build further on Penketh's problematisation of traditional approaches to art education in considering some ways we can ensure that *all* children are included in our planning and practice within visual arts.

Throughout this chapter, and this book, we focus on anti-bias and anti-oppressive pedagogies in which we actively seek to examine, uncover, reflect on and take actions to address the often 'hidden', subtle and unnoticed or unconscious biases that can make the arts inaccessible or less relevant for some children. When we consider inclusive approaches to the visual arts, we can see the direct relevance to the four anti-bias goals addressing identity, diversity, justice and activism (see Chapter 2) (Derman-Sparks & Edwards, 2021). While there are probably endless potential examples of unconscious bias in every aspect of education – including the visual arts – this chapter focuses on:

- removing gendered assumptions in our language or framing of visual art.
- everyday visual art experiences that address family diversity.
- taking culturally aware approaches to visual arts.
- addressing ableism within visual arts.
- making visual arts accessible to children who are blind or have low vision.
- being conscious of the sensory aspects of visual art-making and appreciation and addressing diversity in the way children experience sensory input.
- engaging in activism within and through visual arts.

Cappelen and Andersson (2018, p. 635) write that art is:

> breathing space in our society, a free voice, an alternative world that challenges imagination …shakes our prejudices …connects with us and challenges our mind and will, and helps communities grow.

In taking up this invitation, one key consideration is how to make arts experiences – in this instance, visual arts – inclusive for everyone. To do this, we need to think about our own perceptions of visual art and art-making. We need to value process and diverse ways of making and sharing art.

PINK IS FOR EVERYONE!

It is mostly far too blunt to suggest that as early years practitioners we assign colours by gender within art. However, our notions of art-making and appreciation are often heavily (albeit subconsciously) gendered. Consider any mainstream online or physical art store and think about the marketing and packaging of 'art-kits' and even basic art materials along gendered lines. Over time, research has led to increasing awareness of the impact of the early years, and early years settings, on the ways in which gender is understood and performed and how this influences children's perceptions about themselves and others (Black Delfin, 2021). This includes the potential to use art to disrupt stereotyped gender constructions with children (Hickey-Moody, 2013). When we think about children and art, it is important that we reflect on our own assumptions and consciously remove gendered notions from our approach. When we (often unintentionally) gender our art experiences or our interpretations of children's artistic engagement we impact who children feel they can be and how they feel about themselves. Yes, pink IS for everyone, as are dinosaurs, unicorns, trucks, butterflies, superheroes and fairies! We do not need to prescribe art focus or materials based on gender – when we actively make visual arts open-ended without these assumptions we allow children the space to be and explore who they are and the world around them together and individually. This freedom can make the arts such an important and powerful part of life.

To think about...

- In our own practices, do we hold any gendered notions about visual arts?
- Are there any gender-related elements to what we consider to be appropriate approaches, activities, or materials for particular children?
- Are there any materials, approaches, or activities that we engage children in that portray prescriptive and/or limiting gender notions?

VALUING FAMILY DIVERSITY IN VISUAL ART EXPERIENCES

Reflecting further on gender and visual art can create space for us to consider family diversity. Depictions of family are frequent in early years imagery and create a wonderful starting point to consider how to represent family diversity positively and inclusively. This may encompass representation of LGBTQIA+ families, representation of cultural diversity within families and different family make-up. In our conversations with children and our planning for early years visual arts experiences, we need to consciously consider *who* and *what* we view and value as family, and *how* we perceive families come together (e.g. birth, extended family, out-of-home-care, adoption etc). There are many 'typical' early years activities that we can rethink to increase inclusivity. For example: How do we think inclusively about cultural celebrations such as Mother's and Father's Day? How do we include families with two mums, two dads, single-parent families and so forth? Families are the core of children's belonging, inclusive approaches to family diversity are crucial, as shown here:

It is Mother's Day and the centre is abuzz with excitement as the children draw pictures of their families, sing songs about mothers, and talk about what is special to them about their mum or mums. With many a swipe or splatter of paint visible on the children's clothes, hands and arms, three of the children, two of whom had baby siblings, were sitting together talking.

Ashley: "We got born out of mummy's tummy. Like my baby"

Davi: "Yeah. I got a baby too"

Ashley: "Mummy's tummy was big" (making a shape in front of her stomach to show)

Rylan: "Not my mummy, I got [a]dopted"

This conversation reminds us that there are many diverse ways in which families form. It is easy to inadvertently layer our own unconscious bias in the ways we represent and talk about families. For example, we may unintentionally infer negativity around out-of-home care if we display sympathy. An open but 'matter of fact' approach can enable us to create space for important conversations through art without 'accidentally' introducing bias.

CULTURALLY SUSTAINING VISUAL ARTS PEDAGOGY: MORE THAN 'DOT PAINTING'

Culturally sustaining pedagogy is a concept developed by Django Paris (2012). Culturally sustaining pedagogies proactively seek to value and uphold multi-ethnic and multicultural practices and communities (Paris, 2012). Culturally sustaining pedagogy goes beyond culturally relevant and culturally responsive teaching, requiring educators to support children '... in sustaining the cultural and linguistic competence of their communities while simultaneously offering access to dominant cultural competence' (Paris, 2012, p. 95). This includes learning about, being open to, and incorporating community languages, histories (including oppressive histories and colonisation and their individual and collective legacies), 'valued practices and knowledges, student and community agency and input' (Paris & Alim, 2017, p. 14).

Engaging in culturally sustaining pedagogy involves being 'committed to envisioning and enacting pedagogies that are not filtered through a lens of contempt and pity (e.g. the "achievement gap") but, rather, are centred on contending in complex ways with the rich and innovative linguistic, literate and cultural practices' (Paris & Alim, 2014, p. 86). One piece of this process is recognising privilege and positioning ourselves within the colonising histories of the places and spaces that we occupy. I am a disabled white woman living and working on unceded Australian Aboriginal land. I acknowledge my white privilege and sit uncomfortably in my role in the colonising and racist history of Australia. I bring this awareness to my work and although, as a consequence of my own identity, I feel inadequate to address culturally sustaining pedagogy, I also seek not to shirk away from the shared work needed from *all* of us in addressing the oppressions and injustices still rife in our education settings, systems and broader societies. I take up Stevenson's (1993) challenge – as relevant now as the several decades from whence it was issued – to take a 'hands-on' approach rather than placing the burden of such work on those of us who face ongoing racism, for fear of 'messing up' (Figure 9.1).

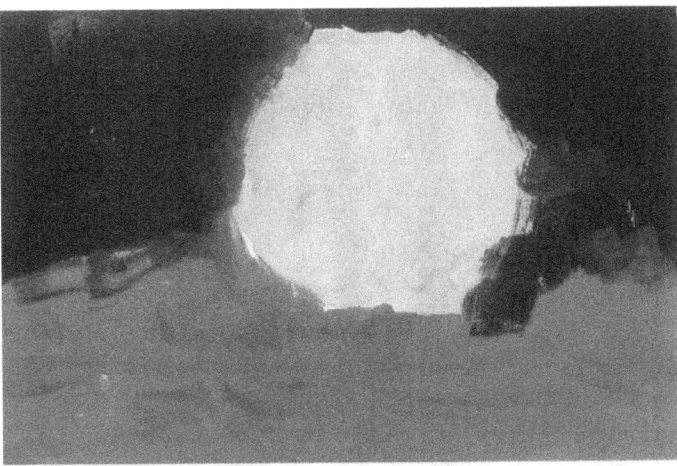

Figure 9.1   What country are we on? Painted by Connor, age 3

In engaging in culturally sustaining pedagogies in the visual arts in the early years, we might begin by considering whether we are taking a mono-cultural or culturally sustaining approach to visual arts. We can increase our awareness of the multi-ethnic and multilingual influences on art in our local and broader communities. Through connecting children with local artists and visiting art galleries and museums, we can readily find examples from which to begin to build our culturally sustaining visual arts pedagogies. This involves going beyond tokenism, which would lead to the pity and contempt that Paris and Alim (2014) warn of. One element of avoiding tokenism is to recognise that culture and art are always intertwined and cannot be separated without risking imposing a colonising (and often Euro-centric) view on our engagement with the art (Bishop et al., 2021).

To achieve culturally sustaining visual arts pedagogies, we must be aware of the risks of contributing to cultural oppression (Bishop et al., 2021). However, we should not let our fears prevent us from working proactively towards culturally sustaining practice. Let's explore some challenges in the story below.

Getting Started: Towards Culturally Sustaining Pedagogy at Stringybark

Stringybark is a community early years setting in an increasingly multicultural and multilingual local community. This community has a proud First Nations history, but colonisation has led to the loss of much knowledge regarding the traditional custodians and languages of the area. Consequently, the identification of the traditional owners is contested. However, there is a strong group of First Nations custodians working to protect and increase awareness of First Nations cultures and languages within the community.

Visual art by a local Aboriginal artist is central to the Stringybark early years environment and the children engage in a shared Acknowledgement of Country every day. The educators at Stringybark are strongly committed to working towards culturally sustaining pedagogies. However, they are quite new to the concept and building their understanding of what it means in practice for their work with the children and families and their connections within the community. One focus area is a recognition of the need to connect culture and visual art in the practices at the preschool.

In developing initial ideas for a 'way in' to increasing the connections with Aboriginal Australia, the educators began to discuss ideas. The suggestion was made to engage in an Aboriginal dot painting workshop with the children. This led to a challenging and important discussion, provoked by the query from one team member regarding whether dot painting is a cultural practice of this area. This question came as a surprise to some of the team as they held the assumption that dot painting was universal. The team then worked together to develop their understanding, including building their knowledge of culturally appropriate and sustaining visual art practices.

To begin, the team contacted a local Aboriginal Elder to gather advice. Upon sharing and reflection, the decision was made to start with a series of workshops from a local Aboriginal group, guided by an Elder. This was accompanied by the Elder coming to the preschool to share stories with the children. An important part of the plan was to engage in ongoing conversations with the children at the setting and be responsive to these discussions. The team made an ongoing commitment to reflection, discussion, and action in working together, in community, towards developing culturally sustaining pedagogy across all of the practices within the early years setting.

TAKING AN ANTI-ABLEIST APPROACH TO VISUAL ARTS

In Chapter 2, we explore ableism and anti-ableism. In this chapter, as we continue to explore inclusive approaches and key areas of addressing oppression within the arts, I take an anti-ableist approach to visual arts. In acknowledging that ableism permeates every aspect of human society, we of course recognise that this too is the case within visual arts education. As Clare Penketh (2017, p. 113) writes, 'Art education as part of the "ableist landscape" of educational practice determines the extent to which the lives and experiences of disabled children and young people are valued'. However, this does not necessarily need to be the case. Early years practitioners can play a key role in undoing this ableism. Brewer et al. (2012, p. 7) write that 'If disability is seen, written about, and represented artistically, it becomes one location on a continuum that includes all humans, and can no longer be understood as deviance'.

Taking a child's perspective, I would like to share an image drawn by a six-year-old.

In this image, the child, who is using a wheelchair for mobility, approaches a door only to find it inaccessible due to stairs. Returning to the notion of future imaginaries, the child imagines having a flying carpet on which the child could float up and through the doorway. This image shows a person using a wheelchair, encountering an inaccessible entrance to a building, and imagining an alternative world (Figure 9.2).

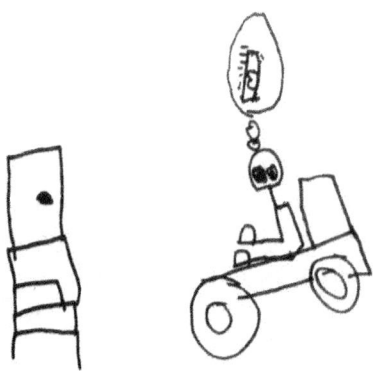

Figure 9.2 A child's imagined world

The child who shared this illustration and story was quite excited by this idea and went on to draw this follow-up image in which there are a diverse array of people all of whom have or are waiting for a turn to use a magic carpet to fly around (Figure 9.3).

Figure 9.3 A future imaginary

The possibilities in our imaginations are endless. Through art, this child could explore some of these possibilities and – in doing so – imagine a more accessible, inclusive and wonderful world! This art also provides communication regarding this child's perspective on the current situation in which we live. While the art communicates a message about disability and ableist structures more broadly – not only within arts education – it shows that there are many possibilities for making art accessible and for addressing ableism through art. Below, to explore such possibilities, I have chosen to 'flip' the notion of 'visual arts' and consider how it can be 'visible' beyond sight. I also consider possibilities for inclusive sensory exploration within visual art. The chapter concludes with some key questions to consider in embarking on inclusive approaches to visual arts in early years settings.

Making Visual Art 'Visible' Beyond Sight

In the image below, a young child explores paint with her hands. Finger painting is not an uncommon early years visual arts experience. What is different here is that the child in this photo can feel, but does not see, the paint. As the child paints, the adult comments on the colours – red like the strawberries from morning tea, yellow like the warm sun on our skin, blue like the big wet ocean and green like the leaves on the tree branch they found this morning. The adult asks questions about how the paint feels, sharing descriptive words such as smooth, cold and wet; and comments on the movements that the child is making – 'I can see you moving your hands up and down on the paper' or 'I can see you making dots with your fingers, dot, dot, dot' and so forth. Through this process, the art-making process becomes somewhat more accessible to the child. The child shows enjoyment through smiles, sustained voluntary engagement in the experience and excited verbal responses (Figure 9.4).

Figure 9.4 Art beyond the visible

This is a starting point that can be extrapolated endlessly to other materials and visual arts experiences. However, the educator in this setting, wanting to give the child more agency and autonomy, sought to make visual art 'more visible' to this child who is blind. The educator spent considerable time reflecting, thinking and reading. Through this process, the educator learnt of an upcoming art exhibition, *Sea, Space and Beyond* in which Vision Australia was partnering with Newcastle Museum (Australia) to present an exhibition of artworks by artists who are blind. Visitors to the exhibition were invited to explore the artworks through touch, creating a further layer of opportunity for engaging children in anti-ableist, inclusive visual arts experiences. The educator took a small group of children on an excursion to visit the museum, where they had the opportunity to explore the artworks in this tactile exhibition.

Following this excursion, the educator and children explored how they might engage in tactile art. They were particularly captured by an artwork entitled *Deep Sea Dive* by artist Samantha Ogilvie. The artwork included sand, shells, glass beads representing water drops, rope, metal chain, coral and driftwood all overlaid onto a painted background. Immersing themselves in exploring the artwork provoked much discussion of the beach, as well as the artist's art-making process. One child recognised the glass beads as being the same as some already present in the early years setting. This prompted the children to explore and identify further the artefacts included in the artwork and discuss similar items they had found at the beach. Being located by the sea, the educators arranged a beach excursion. This created an opportunity to further 'bring to life' the artwork and explore and discuss its elements and what was being represented. At the beach, the children collected some small items and talked about how they felt, and smelt, and how they were similar and different from artefacts in Samantha Ogilvie's *Deep Sea Dive* (this process also created a valuable opportunity to discuss sustainability and the need to leave the beach intact).

Following the beach visit, the children were offered the opportunity to make their own tactile artworks. They explored the grounds of the early years setting and collected sand, sticks, leaves and rocks. The educators also provided shells, glass beads, seed pods, paint, glue and canvas for the children to use. They had already discussed and experimented with different ways to make materials stick to various surfaces and concluded that paint and glue were needed.

Throughout the process, educators and children discussed and described aloud what they were encountering and doing. The educators consistently sought to describe the visual elements of the experiences and activities to ensure that the child who saw with her hands and hearing, but not with her eyes, had greater access to what was happening. Through this ongoing modelling, the children who see with their eyes gradually began to describe things around them and what they were doing. Together the children experimented, made and remade tactile artworks inspired by *Deep Sea Dive*, feeling the materials individually and together as they changed through the process of adding them together and with paint and glue. After the artworks were dried the children shared and explored each other's tactile artworks, further building on their experience at the *Sea, Space and Beyond* exhibition (Figure 9.5).

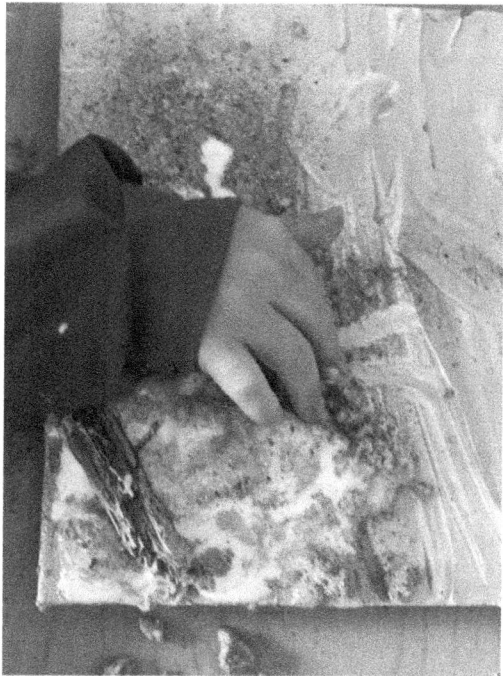

Figure 9.5   Children's tactile art-making

Art Play in the Kitchen!

The case study above, exploring tactile approaches to visual art, engages many senses in the process of art appreciation and art-making in the early years. The sensory aspects of the visual arts provide many wonderful avenues for exploration and experiential learning. Being conscious of these aspects of visual art-making and appreciation and addressing diversity in the way children experience sensory input is an important aspect of engaging inclusively with the visual arts. There are many considerations for the sensory processes of art-making and viewing, as shown in the case study below.

Art play in the kitchen is a community group in the New South Wales Central Coast where families with young children come together to engage in art play with food materials. In these early years experiences the focus is not on creating an 'end product' but rather on the processes of art-making, often including forming and reforming many times over. All the materials used in this art experience are edible, and – without pressure – the children taste as they wish. The children are invited to use their hands but are also provided with a range of tools including paint-brushes, kitchen tools and gloves. The children are offered many different items throughout and encouraged to join in and build their sensory engagement at their own pace and within boundaries that are comfortable for them individually. An important focus is on ensuring all opportunities are made accessible and available to all children every time, even if they have been disinclined to participate in aspects of the same activities or the same materials previously but without any pressure or obligation. Common activities include edible slime, dough, flour drawing, edible sculptures, edible 'shaving cream' and edible paint.

> The children have just finished drawing in flour on the table. Some children use their fingers, others paintbrushes; one child wore gloves and used gloved fingers. The children and adults formed shapes and images in the flour, changing and remaking as they experimented, commenting on the feeling of the flour as it moved around the table. As the children are ready to move on to a new activity, the floury table creates an ideal surface for edible dough sculpting. The children work together with the adults taking turns to identify the ingredients and measure and mix together the eggless biscuit dough. When the dough is ready, the facilitator divides it and shares it out, engaging the children in counting how many as part of the process. Borrowing a song from a local playgroup, the facilitator begins and is soon joined in song by children and adults alike singing:
>
> "Roll it, and knead it, and roll it again
>
> Until the dough is ready, and then,
>
> Flip it over"
>
> The final line is greeted by excited squeals as the children flip over their piece of dough. Some use their hands, others a spoon, and others still use tongs or an egg flip. This element of the process is repeated several more times before the children begin to explore the dough further, shaping, poking, pressing and creating their own sculptures with the dough. The dough is made and remade again, with the focus firmly on the process of sculpting. As with all aspects of this group, each part of the process is accompanied by song, the children are offered a range of implements to use, all materials are edible and the children are encouraged to taste if and when they wish to.

To think about...

- In reflecting on the snapshot of *Art Play in the Kitchen*, what senses are being used to access the art experiences?
- What can you identify about this experience that is intentionally inclusive in engaging young children with visual art?
- What further strategies could you employ to increase the inclusivity of this experience, being mindful of different sensory engagement preferences?

COMMUNICATING WITH AND THROUGH THE ARTS

The arts can be powerful forms of human communication. They can open otherwise impossible communication and allow us to communicate in ways and across time and context that would not otherwise be possible. The arts can also be avenues through which children who might often be 'silenced' may be able to be 'heard' (Cologon et al., 2019).

I started this chapter with the words of four-year-old Wynn, expressing his perception of communicating within and through visual art, as he painted outside on a beautiful sunny day. These words were shared in a study researching the perspectives of young children on inclusion in education and their everyday lives using Arts Based Research Methods (Cologon & Cologon, 2023). Nutbrown and Clough (2014, p. 402) write:

> Engaging in creative arts experiences is important for the sheer joy it can bring, as well as on account of the self and shared expression that can be enabled through creative processes.

To think about. . .

Recalling a visual arts experience:

- What was accessible about it, and for whom?
- What was *inaccessible* about the experience, and for whom?
- What were the underlying assumptions about who the arts experience was *for?*
- What does this tell us about the inclusivity of the experience?
- Are there possibilities for building further on the inclusive aspects of this arts experience so that it is inclusive of and for all children?

Whether it is our intention or not, children often communicate with us through visual art. Creating the space for children to communicate and share through visual art is valuable and can also enable them to engage in their own activism. The image below was painted, unprompted, by a seven-year-old shortly after the conclusion of one of the many 'lockdowns' that occurred across the world because of the coronavirus disease 2019 (COVID-19) global pandemic. The child, without comment or question, painted this with sustained concentration. When the painting was complete the child shared the artwork, explaining that everyone needed to be vaccinated so that they could be safe (Figure 9.6).

Figure 9.6   'Everyone needs to be safe' by Quinn, aged 7

CONCLUSION

Through visual arts, we can be intentionally inclusive in art-making and viewing processes as explored in this chapter. We can also engage with art as a modality through which to be inclusive through 'listening' to children. In reflecting on the power of being listened to, we have written elsewhere:

> What does it feel like to be truly 'heard'? Is it when one experiences empathy and compassion in a communication exchange? Is it feeling a sense of connection, inclusion or belonging? Is it not feeling judged? Or not feeling alone? Is it the relief, joy, or peace, of being truly understood? Does it give a sense of power? Few could argue against the notion that the desire to be truly 'heard' is universal, even if the feeling of being 'heard' is unique to each person, context, culture, society and situation. (Cologon et al., 2019, p. 55)

There is so much to consider in taking an inclusive approach to visual arts in the early years. The provocations and questions shared in this chapter are only starting points, but hopefully they are useful in supporting inclusive thinking within the diverse settings in which we engage with young children.

To think about...

In carrying forward this thinking and engaging in inclusive pedagogies in the visual arts in the early years, we offer the following:

- How do we *approach* art-making in the visual arts?
- *Who* is 'visible' in our approaches to visual arts?
- What *words and languages* do we use?
- What *materials* do we use and what reflections of diversity might these hold?
- Where do our *examples of visual art* come from and how are they situated?
- *Who* are we appreciating in our visual arts?
- *How* are we sharing visual art with and within the community?

REFERENCES

Bishop, M., Vass, G., & Thompson, K. (2021). Decolonising schooling practices through relationality and reciprocity: Embedding local Aboriginal perspectives in the classroom. *Pedagogy, Culture & Society, 29*(2), 193–211.

Black Delfin, A. (2021). The discursive and the material in early childhood play: Co-constitution of gender in open and subversive spaces. *Gender and Education, 33*(5), 594–609.

Brewer, E., Brueggemann, B., Hetrick, N., & Yergeau, M. (2012). Introduction, background, and history. In *Arts and humanities* (pp. 1–62). SAGE. https://doi.org/10.4135/9781452218335

Cappelen, B., & Andersson, A. (2018). *Cultural artefacts with virtual capabilities enhance self-expression possibilities for children with special needs.* IOS Press.

Cologon, K., & Cologon, T. (2023). Children as changemakers. In K. Cologon, & Z. Mevawalla (Eds.), *Inclusive education in the early years: Right from the start* (pp. 36–45). Oxford University Press

Cologon, K., Cologon, T., Mevawalla, Z., & Niland, A. (2019). Generative listening: Using arts-based inquiry to investigate young children's perspectives of inclusion, exclusion and disability. *Journal of Early Childhood Research, 17*(1), 54–69

Derman-Sparks, L., & Edwards, J. O. (2021). Teaching about identity, racism, and fairness: Engaging young children in anti-bias education. *American Educator, 44*(4), 35–40. https://www.aft.org/ae/winter2020-2021/derman-sparks_edwards_goins

Diment, L., & Hobbs, D. (2014). A gesture-based virtual art program for children with severe motor impairments – Development and pilot study. *Journal of Assistive, Rehabilitative & Therapeutic Technologies, 2*(1), 23206. https://doi.org/10.3402/jartt.v2.23206

Fairclough, N. (2003). *Analysing discourse: Textual analysis for social research.* Routledge.

Hickey-Moody, A. (2013). Do you want to battle with me? Schooling masculinity. In A. Hickey-Moody (Ed.), *Youth, arts, and education: Reassembling subjectivity through affect* (pp. 93–118). Routledge.

Hickey-Moody, A. (2017). Integrated dance as a public pedagogy of the body. *Social Alternatives*, *36*(4), 5–13.

Nutbrown, C., & Clough, P. (2014). Engaging all children through the arts. In K. Cologon (Ed.), *Inclusive education in the early years: Right from the start* (pp. 401–421). Oxford University Press

Paris, D. (2012). Culturally sustaining pedagogy: A needed change in stance, terminology, and practice. *Educational Researcher*, *41*(3), 93–97.

Paris, D., & Alim, H. S. (2014). What are we seeking to sustain through culturally sustaining pedagogy?: A loving critique forward. *Harvard Educational Review*, *84*(1), 85–100.

Paris, D., & Alim, H. S. (Eds.). (2017). *Culturally sustaining pedagogies: Teaching and learning for justice in a changing world*. Teachers College Press.

Penketh, C. (2017). Children see before they speak: An exploration of ableism in art education. *Disability & Society*, *32*(1), 110–127. https://doi.org/10.1080/09687599.2016.1270819

INTRODUCTION TO PART III

Part Three completes the book's exploration of inclusion through the creative arts by widening the focus to survey the pedagogical framing of inclusive arts in early years settings. It draws on the key principles of inclusive education, anti-bias goals and positive understandings of diversity explored in Part One and the individual art forms explored in Part Two, and applies these to considerations of pedagogical framing and the role of inclusive practitioners.

Chapter 10 explores Universal Design for Learning as central to inclusive arts pedagogy, applying its principles to provide all children with opportunities to engage with the arts according to their ways of being and doing.

Chapter 11 focuses on the role of the educator or other early years practitioners, providing a critical rationale for embracing inclusive pedagogy and establishing the importance of self-reflection. This chapter also provides practical, arts-based tools for professional reflection.

Chapter 12 weaves together the key themes that have been explored throughout the book, to consider holistically what inclusive, arts-based early years pedagogy might look like in practice.

10

CREATING ACCESSIBLE ARTS EXPERIENCES THROUGH UNIVERSAL DESIGN FOR LEARNING

Kathy Cologon

Chapter objectives

This chapter introduces you to these key ideas:

- The importance of accessibility in all arts experiences
- The framework of Universal Design for Learning
- Applying UDL in the arts
- Implications for early years educators

INTRODUCTION

How can we make the arts accessible to children in all their diversities? Can we really create arts experiences that everyone can participate in? If this sounds a tad impossible, then this chapter is for you! Throughout this book we have engaged with the broad notions of accessible approaches to the arts, the importance of the arts for all children, and the potentialities of the arts for inclusive education. In this chapter I invite you to explore a framework of Universal Design for Learning (UDL) as a way to plan for accessibility within and through the arts in the early years.

ACCESSIBILITY WITHIN AND THROUGH THE ARTS

Participation in the arts is the right of every child, as outlined in Article 31, of the United Nations Convention on the Rights of the Child (United Nations, 1989). However, underpinning this right (and so many others) is the need for access. The fundamental need for accessibility is outlined in a range of international covenants and treaties. For example, in the Universal Declaration of Human Rights (United Nations, 1948), the International Covenant on Civil and Political Rights (United Nations, 1966), and more recently as a core principle underpinning the United Nations Convention on the Rights of Persons with Disabilities (CRPD) (United Nations, 2006). This principle is directly applied to inclusive education in General Comment 4 on the CRPD (United Nations, 2016). UDL is fundamentally about accessibility within all aspects of education, and is therefore strongly intertwined with a rights-based approach to the arts in the early years.

The chapter begins by unpacking Universal Design for Learning (UDL) as a framework for creating accessible arts experiences in the early years. At the core of applying a UDL framework is the need to consider the question of *who* we are planning for and with. Clare Penketh, whose work was explored in Chapter 9, argues for 'the creative potential of diverse minds and bodies' and the reciprocal relationship between what humans, in our diversities, bring to the arts and for the arts as a powerful site for 'critical social practice emphasising the relationship between powerful pedagogies and social and political change' (2017, p. 111). However, the arts and arts education have also been criticised for being exclusionary and inaccessible to a diverse range of people (Penketh, 2017).

In this chapter, and throughout this book, we are engaging with fundamental considerations for inclusive practice in the early years. I invite you to apply an anti-bias lens to inclusive education and the arts with children across all aspects of human diversity. This includes taking an anti-ableist approach building on Penketh's work and considering children in *all* our human diversities.

There is much to be said about the arts as critical social practice, and the possibilities that the arts, therefore, hold for inclusion. Penketh (2017) acknowledges the power of the arts in addressing community, local and global issues, thus developing awareness of equality and diversity. However, Penketh critiques that disability is not included in these practices, so that 'disability is therefore reinforced as an individual problem rather than a social concern'. This is a fundamental concern for inclusive education and for the arts, if the arts are to achieve the potentialities they hold. Inclusive approaches within and through the arts need consideration of who is present and who is missing in all aspects – art making, art viewing, and arts education.

When the arts are inclusive, we are all welcomed and valued for what we bring. However, as Penketh (2017, p. 123) reflects, too often 'non-normative' bodies/minds are eliminated and alienated in arts education. She argues that 'When bodies/minds depart from the norms established, they are brought explicitly to our attention via special pedagogic interventions, which place them on the periphery of art education with therapeutic and compensatory approaches dominating the creative dimensions of their education'. From this, differences become viewed as 'problems' or 'difficulties' within individual children that need to be 'fixed' or 'overcome', rather than as necessary questions for pedagogical approaches, materials, and the planning cycle. Applying a framework of UDL flips this and 'involves examining who is considered in the design of our world, who is missing in these considerations, why, and how this can be addressed in order to make design universal – as in, for all of us' (Cologon, 2022).

The Sound and Colour Symphony

Ms. Martinez was keen on introducing her students to the world of abstract art. Using the Universal Design for Learning (UDL) principles, she structured a multi-faceted project to cater to a variety of learners.

1. Representation: Ms. Martinez began with an interactive presentation. She showed videos of artists creating abstract art, played songs that were inspired by visual arts, and had tactile examples of textured abstract paintings for students to feel. There was also a scent station, where different fragrances were paired with abstract images, encouraging students to connect visuals with aromas.

2. Action & Expression: Students were then given a choice of how they wanted to express their understanding of abstract art. Some painted, others crafted music compositions, a few created tactile art with mixed media, and some chose to write poems or stories inspired by abstract visuals.

3. Engagement: To keep motivation high, Ms. Martinez introduced an "Artistic Mystery Box". Each week, a new abstract art-related item was placed inside, be it a textured painting sample, a musical note sequence, or a fragrance. Students could explore the box and then discuss or create something inspired by it. Furthermore, she set up a collaborative corner where students could combine different art forms, like adding music to a painting, thereby creating a shared art experience.

By weaving UDL principles into her abstract art project, Ms. Martinez not only introduced her students to the world of abstract art but also ensured they had various avenues to understand, express, and engage with it.

What Is Universal Design for Learning?

UDL grew out of the broader concept of Universal Design, which developed within architecture. The United Nations defines Universal Design as 'the design of products, environments, programs and services to be useable by all people, to the greatest extent possible, without the need for adaptation or specialized design' (United Nations, 2006, Article 2). For example, kerb cuts; automatic doors; ramps; lifts with visual, audio and braille information; wide doorways; closed captioning; and in-built screen readers (CAST, 2018).

A common misunderstanding of Universal Design, and UDL is the notion that universality is about creating a 'one-size-fits-all' approach. Rather, it is about ensuring that design is accessible to all people across all aspects of human diversity. Thus, the United Nations articulates the importance of incorporating assistive devices where relevant and needed to facilitate access and genuine universality (United Nations, 2006).

UDL is a framework developed to support educators in taking an inclusive approach to the planning cycle that creates accessible educational opportunities for all. At the core of UDL is the understanding that education is flexible and responsive and there is more than one way to engage in, represent, and express all aspects of learning and teaching. While the outcomes of UDL are intended to benefit learners, the process of implementing UDL is really about educators – our willingness and capacity to 'think outside the square', be responsive to and valuing of diversity, and our approach to the planning cycle underpinned by a commitment to inclusive thinking.

In applying UDL to the creation of accessible and meaningful arts experiences in the early years, there are many different factors to consider. These include:

- **Planning** for accessible arts experiences;
- **Materials, resources and repertoire** which can be used to create inclusive and accessible opportunities for meaningful engagement with and through the arts;
- Taking an accessible approach to **implementing** creative arts **curricula** with all children;
- **Applying and evaluating effective strategies** to make arts experiences accessible to children in all their diversities.

Glass et al., two key scholars in UDL and with an arts educator, have explored the specific application of UDL to the arts (2013, pp. 99–100, emphasis original). They state:

> UDL is organized around three principles, each of which is based on the learning sciences, that guide the design and development of a curriculum that is effective and inclusive for all learners:

1. To support affective learning, provide multiple means of **engagement** by offering options for generating and sustaining motivation, the *why* of learning

2. To support recognition learning, provide multiple means of **representation** by offering flexible ways to present *what* we teach and learn

3. To support strategic learning, provide multiple means of **action** and **expression** by offering flexible options for *how* we learn and express what we know.

Within UDL, the considerations of why, what and how we learn is underpinned by consideration of *who* is learning – as in, recognising the diversity of learners and starting from the premise of planning for children in all of their diversities. When we are 'in the thick' of teaching we plan actively for the children in our settings at the time. UDL is a framework that we can apply from the outset in any early years setting – even when we are yet to build relationships with the children we will be teaching. We can intentionally plan for children across as many aspects of human diversity as we can identify. This will provide us with planning that is far more likely to be responsive to diverse groups of children than if we simply plan for an arts experience without considering the question of *who* the children may be. When we embed multiple means of engagement, representation, action and expression in all aspects of our practice – our environment, curriculum, pedagogy and assessment – we create more accessible and inclusive arts experiences for all children. The same can be said when we consider ways in which we use the arts to facilitate inclusion in other aspects of early years education. For example, consider how the arts may form a core aspect of the multiple means of engagement, representation, action and expression in an endless array of early years experiences.

To unpack this a little further, in valuing diversity, a seemingly obvious but often 'forgotten' aspect of inclusive planning is that when we plan educational experiences – within and beyond the arts – we need to be developing experiences that 'fit' the children we are teaching, rather than expecting the children to 'fit' the experience (Darragh, 2007; Edyburn, 2010). A benefit to educators as we develop our skills in implementing UDL is that this process necessarily reduces the number of individual adjustments that we need to make in order to include the children with whom we work. While it can take time initially to develop our practice of UDL, once we shift our thinking into this mindset, this approach will save considerable time and frustration as our planning will 'fit' better to all the children we teach.

A core underpinning of UDL is recognition of the contextual realities of children's abilities. As in, what a child can do in any given situation or setting is dependent on interactions between the child and the environment – including the people around the child (Rose et al., 2018). This subtle but important shift in thinking enables us, as educators, to recognise that if a child is not finding positive success within a particular activity or situation we can reflect on the design of the experience in light of the core principles of UDL. Perhaps the accessibility of the resources or of the experience itself within the broader context of the setting (including the interactions between people and space) may need further consideration. You may find the following questions helpful as a starting point.

To think about...

- How does the principle of UDL challenge traditional notions of education and the one-size-fits-all mentality?
- Reflect on a recent teaching experience. By implementing UDL, what would you change in your approach to better accommodate the diversity of learners?
- In what ways do you think UDL principles can encourage a more inclusive and responsive teaching environment, especially in the context of arts education?
- How might the arts provide unique opportunities to address the diverse needs and preferences of early learners, ensuring each child can access and benefit from the curriculum?

IMPLEMENTING UDL IN EARLY YEARS ARTS

Implementing UDL creates early years environments and experiences that are inclusive and explicitly value the full breadth of human diversity (Hall et al., 2012). Implementing UDL involves processes of increasing access through reducing barriers that would otherwise prevent or reduce participation and outcomes for children or that may positively or negatively impact on who or what a child believes they can be and do (Glass et al., 2013; Ok et al., 2017; Quaglia, 2015). UDL offers a flexible framework to be responsive to children in all of their diversities and support each child to flourish (Basham et al., 2010). Applying the processes of UDL also involves addressing a seemingly subtle but important distinction between access to information and access to opportunities for learning. When we implement UDL we are considering all aspects of the learning experience, not only the information we are sharing (Edyburn, 2005).

Implementing UDL involves holding high expectations hand in hand with appropriate and accessible support (Edyburn, 2010; Katz, 2015). Reflecting on Vygotsky's (1978) notion of the Zone of Proximal Development (ZPD) is helpful in bringing together high expectations and support. As explored more deeply in Chapter 2 of this book, the ZPD is the space between what a child can do independently today, and what they can do when supported or scaffolded. Vygotsky (1978) theorised that what a child can do with support now, they will be able to learn to do independently next.

In their exploration of a UDL framework and its implications for arts education, Glass et al. (2013, p. 99) delve into the potential intersections between the arts and UDL, emphasising the necessity of catering to the unique learning experiences of each student for a more inclusive arts-centred curriculum. Glass et al. (2013, p. 99) raise the questions of:

- What can the UDL framework add to the design of arts curriculum?
- How might the arts provide rich learning options for a curriculum that is universally designed?
- How might considering the arts and UDL together foster better curriculum design and learning for everyone?

Glass et al. (2013) argue that in order to make the arts more inclusive, particularly as the arts takes its rightful place at the centre of the curriculum, it is important for teachers to respond to individual differences and acknowledge the individuality of their students. Glass et al. (2013) propose that UDL is a valuable framework in addressing this individuality, particularly in the way that it recognises learning as being unique and individual to each person.

Planning for accessibility in the arts in the early years in line with UDL means attending to the varied ways that children learn and participate, moving beyond a one-size-fits-all approach to arts learning and recognising the many varied and different ways that children learn, engage, and demonstrate their understandings. As Glass et al. (2013) argue, 'The hoped-for result is that more individuals can understand art, more can create it, and more can value it'. This accessibility can shift the way that we engage in, approach, and view art. When engaging children in the arts in this way, we change our understanding of what art is. This not only enables acceptance of different ways of doing and being, but also celebrates this diversity as opening up possibilities to creating and engaging in the arts in unique and interesting ways. As Glass et al. (2013, p. 107) suggest:

> The advantage of UDL in the arts is a more inclusive art – expanding the options for representation, expression, and engagement. The benefit is that we will have to expand our view of who can be an artist and what we mean by art.

These considerations are essential in considering how we facilitate access to arts education in the early years. They are equally essential in addressing inclusive education through the arts in that access to the arts is fundamental to this process. In their exploration of a UDL framework and its implications for arts education, Glass et al. (2013, p. 99) delve into the potential intersections between the arts and UDL, underscoring the philosophy and practicality of striving for inclusive arts education. This focus on inclusivity is further echoed by Coleman and Cramer (2015, p. 6) who write that:

> The art classroom is a place where students of all learning levels come together to create artwork. A greater understanding of working with diverse populations comes through inclusion of teaching diverse groups of children of various abilities. The openness of art instruction (many solutions, not single answers) naturally allows the expressions or voices of multiple learners. But how can all students participate successfully?

UDL and Visual Arts

Coleman and Cramer (2015) provide a series of suggestions that may be helpful in considering possibilities for multiple means for engagement, representation, action and expression. This includes considerations for incorporating assistive technology (AT) to assist with participation. This is divided into AT for positioning to enhance access to art activities (gross motor solutions) and AT to enhance access to art activities focused on fine motor activity demands.

Coleman and Cramer (2015) argue for careful planning for positioning to facilitate access within visual arts experiences. For example, this includes:

- the positions of furniture within the room (spacing),
- the heights of individual items such as tables,
- using a slantboard/table top easel,
- placing materials closer to the student's dominant side,
- using non-slip materials for stabilisation of art resources,
- using rolls or wedges to stabilise students (such as a rolled-up towel under the arm when playing a ukulele).

Coleman and Cramer also recommend adaptive art tools being standard equipment in the art room for all children to use to maximise participation.

Where support is required to facilitate fine motor engagement, Coleman and Cramer (2015) outline a range of AT that can facilitate access. For example,

- using alternative body parts to hold tools such as holding a paintbrush or percussion instrument in the mouth or with the foot,
- providing hand-under-hand support to guide and explore the materials but with the child still maintaining autonomy in the experience,
- larger materials such as large handled maracas or paintbrushes or larger and softer surfaces to increase grip and control,
- adaptive scissors or pre-cut materials,
- the child creating part of a sculpture project and directing a peer or teacher to put together the pieces,
- or using adaptive tools instead of hands to shape clay.

For children who are blind or have a visual impairment, Coleman and Cramer (2015) offer suggestions of:

- providing tactile materials (for example, different textures rather than different colours),
- the use of a light box to provide visual contrast and,
- where relevant, using large text, magnification, or voice output to make text accessible.
- Contrasting sounds (for example high and low or fast and slow) and 'big movements' are also examples that can facilitate accessibility for children who are blind or have a visual impairment.

In supporting successful shared communication through diverse approaches, Coleman and Cramer (2015) recommend using signing, pictures, communication boards, and computerised communications devices as relevant.

UDL and the ORIM-Arts Framework

UDL is a framework that can be applied to create accessible and inclusive approaches within the early years and beyond. There are many different ways of thinking through the implementation of this framework. In this section, we will explore how we might draw on the ORIM-Arts framework in thinking through the application of UDL.

The ORIM-Arts framework, developed in the UK by Cathy Nutbrown (2013, pp. 248–249), stands for providing **opportunities, recognition, interaction** and a **model** for engaging in the arts:

- Opportunities: 'permissions' to do things. This may include offering events, materials, toys, equipment, space and time
- Recognition: acknowledging children's achievements, through e.g. 'praising efforts, telling others what the child has done, celebrating their successes, taking photographs, taking an interest in and displaying their work'
- Interaction: adults spending time with children. This may involve adults 'supporting, explaining, endorsing, talking about what they are doing and challenging them to move on from what they know about to do more'... 'demonstrating, tutoring, involving children in real tasks and projects and playing games'
- Adults acting as powerful models: Children learning from adults through modelling

The ORIM-Arts framework was adapted from a literacy framework to focus on arts education, which incorporated **'materials and experiences'**, **'imagination'**, **'skills'** and **'talk about the arts'**. To use the framework, each strand – **opportunities**, **recognition**, **interaction** and a **model** – is considered in relation to **'materials and experiences'**, **'imagination'**, **'skills' and 'talk about the arts'** (see Resources).

Reflecting on the ORIM-Arts framework, alongside UDL, we can see a strong alignment between the two. Exploring this further, consider an example of the ORIM framework in practice, used to facilitate accessible approaches to music education.

ORIM has been used in a variety of contexts for working with young children. For example, Niland (2017), used it to develop a community music programme for children who experience disability and their families, as well as for analysing and evaluating this programme. As Niland outlines, the ORIM-Arts framework intends to respect 'a child's competence and right to learn in the arts through child-led play and exploration, while also allowing for specific focus on skill development' (p. 278). This means that the ORIM-Arts framework allows for open-ended, child-led play, as well as intentional teaching.

The structure of the framework is valuable for detailed observation and documentation allowing practitioners to explore children's learning in and through arts experiences. The ORIM framework focuses on interaction, communication, language and physical/sensory exploration and requires reciprocal partnerships between children, peers and adults.

In applying the framework to music education, Niland proposes:

- *Engagement with a diverse range of materials and experiences*
- *Skill development in using instruments, voices and bodies in musical ways*
- *Imaginative exploration and musical creativity*
- *Spoken and non-spoken communication*

Niland explores the application of the ORIM framework in terms of **materials and experiences'**, **'imagination'**, **'skills' and 'talk about the arts'**. This includes addressing: Materials and experiences:

- Examples of resources used in the music groups included percussion instruments, sound-making toys, balls, puppets, beanbags, scarves, ribbons, pictures, recordings of instrumental music and a ukulele. The variety of materials also motivated cooperation and social connections.

Skill development:

- For example, joint attention, articulation, receptive or expressive language development – these skills can be enhanced through 'observing, listening or physical participation in music experiences, including singing, playing instruments, performing actions. Music provides a reason to interact with others that builds children's motivations and abilities to connect socially'.

Imaginative exploration and musical creativity:

- Children were provided with the freedom to make their own choices
- This led to feelings as belonging as their ideas were shared with the rest of the group

  Verbal and non-verbal communication

- Songs are a form of communication, and engaging in singing can therefore be beneficial for other communication goals such as speech and language development. (Niland, 2017, p. 278)

Uke can Play the Ukulele! Implementing UDL in Early Years Music Experiences

This case study is a retelling based on a series of conversations that I had with a teacher who was exploring the implementation of UDL as a framework for creating accessible and inclusive music arts experiences in an early years setting. This teacher was undertaking a Masters programme with me to further develop her inclusive practice, alongside her work as a teacher.

'It's our time to sing together' sang the teacher, gently inviting the children to join her with voices, percussion instruments, or dancing ribbons. The children were seated in a circle and in the middle was a collection of untuned percussion instruments, including rhythm sticks, egg shakers, tambourines, bells with Velcro around wrist, in a basket nearby was a collection of scarves attached to scrunchies for over the wrist, ribbons on thick sticks intended to be easy to hold. As the children joined in, they chose an action or body percussion and gradually the group transformed as they began tapping, spinning, jumping, dancing, twirling and singing. The singing morphed into a range of actions as the teacher continued to lead the song incorporating a range of possible and suggested ways to participate 'It's our time to clap together'. The children visibly relaxed as they settled into this familiar and joyful experience. At the end of the song the teacher began to introduce the new focus on learning the ukulele. The teacher had prepared a ukulele for each child, some tuned for the left hand, some tuned with strings changed to make a C chord with open strumming and no left hand needed to press down on strings), and some ready for students to try a C chord with two hands, with puff paint creating raised dots to feel the placement of the hands. Along with the thoughtfully tuned ukuleles were a range of rubber and felt picks of different sizes for ease of strumming and grip on the edge and rubber door stoppers to be used as large grip picks. Another basket held towels rolled up to support ukuleles under arms, coloured red dots, and red nail polish. Behind the towels sat a set of paper communication boards with actions, and songs for children to choose and point to. The children watched and/or listened together to a two-minute video about the Ukulele and then the teacher handed out the instruments for exploration. As the children explored the ukuleles with their hands, gentle sounds from the strings or tapping on the body of the instruments formed the backdrop as the teacher described the parts of the ukulele, gently guiding the children to find each part, some through spoken prompts and some with hand-under-hand guidance. Taking turns the group worked together to make a game of 'Simon says' naming and finding each part of the ukulele ('Simon says put your hands on the ukulele's neck' etc). Giggles ensued as the children worked to find the parts of the instrument and play the game. Seamlessly, the teacher led the children into a variation of the Song 'Heads and Shoulders, Knees and Toes' but with the parts of the ukulele "head and neck and frets and body, frets and body, frets and body..." changing bit by bit to other parts of the ukulele including tuning pegs, frets, sound hole and bridge. The children spent some time individually or in pairs exploring the ukulele further before coming back together to listen/watch another brief video, this time a video showing a range of different ways to play the ukulele, including using adaptive materials such as those the teacher had prepared. The teacher then modelled playing a C Chord on the ukulele, firstly as open strumming and then showing the children the red dot painted on her fingernail and how it could be match to the red dot sticker on her ukulele.

The children then had the opportunity to choose if they wanted to use red dots or open strumming and the teacher supported each child in the small group to get set up with their ukulele. The teacher supported the children to experiment and choose a pick for strumming and propped towels and non-slip rubber mats as needed to make sure each child was best set up to participate. Considerable thought and preparation had gone into making this possible, but within the experience it was just a brief moment connecting with each child. The children experimented with strumming and playing before the teacher invited them to join in a familiar song with a C Chord, encouraging each child to make an attempt and scaffolding through spoken and hand-under-hand support as they went. Sound filled the air as the children experimented and explored the instruments together in a collaborative song.

To think about...

- What aspects of UDL can you identify in practice in the case study above?
- How might the tools of the UDL framework and the ORIM-Arts framework be used to support the planning for the experience above?
- How might you develop this arts experience to include further means of engagement, representation and expression?
- Using this case study as a starting point for connecting your understanding of UDL with your own practice, write down three ideas to explore in your own work.

IMPLICATIONS FOR PRACTITIONERS

In reflecting on what this all means for planning for accessible and inclusive early years arts education, there are multiple implications. This includes recognition that engaging in the arts in the early years requires a revision of deficit-based perspectives on children and their 'needs'. Penketh (2017, p. 111) writes that engaging children with the arts

> ...has the potential to shift the boundaries of limited realisations of inclusive education to pedagogies that recognise and work with diversity in generative and creative ways... However, art education has also been criticised for its adherence to outmoded and archaic practices which can result in the exclusion of those for whom art education is inaccessible or alienating

In working towards the realisation of the powerful potentiality of the arts in the early years, we first need to be open to identifying where we need to reconsider our approaches to create space for inclusivity. This is both philosophical and practical – it is about what we think and what we do. UDL is one framework from which we can draw these threads together to develop arts experiences and opportunities in the early years that are genuinely accessible to all.

Genuinely engaging with notions of arts for *all involves* challenging ourselves to think about our own conceptions of art, of ourselves as artists, and of arts education in the early years. Reflecting on our own experiences, perhaps we can recognise elements of the potentiality of arts education for inclusion – and thus embracing of human diversity. At the same time we may also recognise elements of extremely limiting and exclusionary approaches which are almost startling in their rigidity – counter to any notions of creativity.

CONCLUSION

There is a great deal to think about in creating genuine access to the arts in the early years for all children. In the space of this chapter we can really only offer provocations and suggestions to guide you as you begin this journey – from whatever point you are currently at. UDL provides a valuable tool through which to engage in these processes. In drawing together the many considerations for applying UDL to the arts in the early years, we come back to the key elements of providing multiple means of engagement, representation, action and expression:

- multiple means of engagement: generating and sustaining motivation (the *why* of learning)
- multiple means of representation: offering flexible ways to present *what* we teach and learn
- multiple means of action and expression: offering flexible options for *how* we learn and express what we know

At all times, these processes are underpinned by considering *who* is learning – as in, recognising the diversity of learners and starting from the premise of planning for children in all of their diversities.

And, of course, the diversity of humanity is central to the arts. 'Diversity has the unique ability to refresh, replenish and to stimulate the arts by encouraging new work that challenges, innovates and takes risks. It is not really possible to talk about a modern and relevant arts sector without talking about diversity and equality'. (Arts Council England, 2010, cited in Aujla & Redding, 2013, p. 81). This reflects an important and reciprocal relationship between human diversity and the arts with considerable implications for the early years and beyond.

RESOURCES

ORIM arts framework:
https://sheffield-real-project.sites.sheffield.ac.uk/about/other-ways-of-using-orim

REFERENCES

Basham, J. D., Israel, M., Graden, J., Poth, R., & Winston, M. (2010). A comprehensive approach to RTI: Embedding universal design for learning and technology. *Learning Disability Quarterly, 33,* 243–255.

CAST. (2018). *Universal design for learning guidelines: Version 2.2.* http://udlguidelines.cast.org

Coleman, M., & Cramer, E. (2015). Creating meaningful art experiences with assistive technology for students with physical, visual, severe, and multiple disabilities. *Art Education, 68*(2), 6–13. https://doi.org/10.1080/00043125.2015.11519308

Cologon, K. (2022). Considerations for implementing universal design for learning: Toward anti-oppressive pedagogies. In R. Tierney, F. Rizvi, & K. Ercikan (Eds.), *International encyclopedia of education* (4th ed.). Elsevier Science.

Darragh, J. (2007). Universal design for early childhood education: Ensuring access and equity for all. *Early Childhood Education Journal, 35*(2), 167–171.

Edyburn, D. L. (2005). Universal design for learning. *Special Education Technology Practice, 7*(5), 16–22.

Edyburn, D. L. (2010). Would you recognise universal design for learning if you saw it? Ten propositions for new directions for the second decade of UDL. *Learning Disability Quarterly, 33*, 33–41.

Glass, D., Meyer, A., & Rose, D. (2013). Universal design for learning and the arts. *Harvard Educational Review, 83*, 98–119.

Hall, T. E., Meyer, A., & Rose, D. H. (2012). *Universal design for learning in the classroom: Practical applications.* Guilford Press.

Katz, J. (2015). Implementing the three block model of universal design for learning: Effects on teachers' self-efficacy, stress, and job satisfaction in inclusive classrooms K-12. *International Journal of Inclusive Education, 19*(1), 1–20.

Niland, A. (2017). Singing and playing together: A community music group in an early intervention setting. *International Journal of Community Music, 10*(3), 273–288. https://doi.org/10.1386/ijcm.10.3.273_1

Nutbrown, C. (2013). Conceptualising arts-based learning in the early years. *Research Papers in Education, 28*(2), 239–263. https://doi.org/10.1080/02671522.2011.580365

Ok, M. W., Rao, K., Bryant, B. R., & McDougall, D. (2017). Universal design for learning in pre-K to grade 12 classrooms: A systematic review of research. *Exceptionality, 25*(2), 116–138. https://doi.org/10.1080/09362835.2016.1196450

Penkerh, C. (2017). Children see before they speak: An exploration of ableism in art education. *Disability & Society, 32*(1), 110–127. https://doi.org/10.1080/09687599.2016.1270819

Quaglia, B. (2015). Planning for student variability: Universal design for learning in the music theory classroom and curriculum. *Music Theory Online, 21*(1). https://doi.org/10.30535/mto.21.1.6

Rose, D. H., Robinson, K. H., Hall, T. E., Coyne, P., Jackson, R. M., Stahl, W. M., & Wilcauskas, S. L. (2018). Accurate and informative for all: Universal design for learning (UDL) and the future of assessment. In *Handbook of accessible instruction and testing practices: Issues, innovations, and applications* (pp. 167–180). Springer.

United Nations. (1948). *Universal declaration of human rights.* https://www.un.org/sites/un2.un.org/files/udhr.pdf

United Nations. (1966). *International covenant on civil and political rights.* https://www.ohchr.org/en/professionalinterest/pages/ccpr.aspx

United Nations. (1989). *United Nations convention on the rights of the child.* https://treaties.un.org/pages/viewdetails.aspx?src=treaty&mtdsg_no=iv-11&chapter=4&lang=en-title=UNTC-publisher=.

United Nations. (2006). *Convention on the Rights of Persons with Disabilities.* https://www.un.org/development/desa/disabilities/convention-on-the-rights-of-persons-with-disabilities.html

United Nations. (2016). *General comment No. 4, Article 24: Right to inclusive education.* https://www.refworld.org/docid/57c977e34.html

Vygotsky, L. (1978). *Mind in society.* Harvard University Press.

11

CARING, COMPASSION AND CREATIVITY: REFLECTING ON OUR PROFESSIONAL NARRATIVE

Laura Huhtinen-Hildén

Chapter objectives

This chapter introduces you to these key ideas:

- Developing caring and compassion-infused communities
- Reflecting on our professional narrative
- Activities and examples to be used and reflected on individually or in a group of colleagues

---

INTRODUCTION

This chapter discusses the role that early childhood pedagogy can have in creating possibilities for the future in this uncertain world, with its challenges both between people and related to the future of the whole planet. Navigating this topic, the gaze shifts from children towards ourselves as professionals. It is important to reflect on the pedagogical thinking and professional narratives that are our companions and that set the horizons for our work. Within this landscape, it is possible to develop caring and compassion-infused communities that are essential to equip children for the future and its challenges. It is also important to see ourselves as part of the inclusive community of our early childhood settings, forming the 'we' that consists of all adults and children in the setting. In the latter part of this chapter, there are activities and examples that can be used among practitioners. They offer possibilities to explore the experience of creative activities – individually or in a group of peers such as in a team meeting – and through these, to reflect upon our professional narratives. Sharing experiences of walking along pathways in the professional landscape contributes to our professional learning and also creates a we-culture in early years settings.

FUTURE HOPE UNDERPINNING EARLY YEARS PEDAGOGY

The starting point for exploring the professional landscape could be possible future horizons. The challenges that the future holds are enormous regarding the climate crises facing the planetary boundaries in various ways. As professionals working with children and youth, we are likely to meet new kinds of challenges in our practice. Uncertainty arising from climate change and ecological crises may create anxiety in ourselves. There is a lot that we do not know related to these issues, and yet there is a need to facilitate the younger generations to create a hopeful approach towards the future: Early childhood pedagogy cannot be underpinned by anxiety but by hope for the future instead.

Suggesting creativity and imagination as essential tools for early childhood pedagogy to meet future challenges may come as a surprise. However, digging a bit deeper into this thought reveals that hope for the planet actually relies on the caring and compassionate potential of children and youth. Advancing trust, compassion and equality in increasingly diverse communities creates an inclusive approach in early years settings and beyond. Education that is embedded in fostering imagination, creativity and compassion-infused interaction has the potential to lead to change. It can support the construction of sustainability-oriented values and lifestyles – in other words sustainable well-being. Thus, developing pedagogy that is underpinned by eco-social sustainability is essential (see e.g. Keto & Foster, 2021). Professionals working with children are facing the 'future' every day – children and youth are the ones to face the consequences of the choices and actions of today. In order to deal with these consequences and construct solutions for the future, they need creativity, imagination, hope and each other (see e.g. Kaufman & Glăveanu, 2022; Weckström et al., 2022).

FOSTERING A SENSE OF COMMUNITY AND COMPASSION

A sustainable life orientation and well-being are possible only if we are able to move away from viewing life from just the individual's perspective and enlarge the circle of care outside ourselves. In developing caring and compassion-infused communities and societies, early childhood education has the important role of fostering capabilities to imagine and be empathic towards the lifeworlds of others. And only caring and compassion-infused communities can be inclusive and equal. Therefore, it becomes clear that sustainable well-being, caring, compassion and sensitivity are intertwined. In the earlier chapters of this book, the various ways that arts activities can foster well-being, caring, compassion and relationships have been discussed from many viewpoints. Continuing along those lines, in relation to music, Smith (2021) challenges us to rethink music education so that it can 'provide the necessary interdisciplinary and experiential learning for children to maintain their sense of wonder in nature; to fully develop their sensory capacities; to maintain, and if necessary, repair their mental health; and to attune more carefully to their wild nature and soul's purpose' (Smith, 2021, p. 9). Also, other arts activities can be utilised to explore sensitivity, togetherness and empathy: for example, shared creative movement offers a fruitful environment to attune to each other, visual arts expose our senses to capture the beauty around us, drama and stories make us empathise with the experiences of others.

Empathy and sensitivity in interaction do not appear by themselves, or at least they do not necessarily develop to their full potential without an environment to support them. Researchers Weckström et al. (2022) studied early childhood education and care practice that especially aims to foster being heard, taking initiative, expressing opinions and altering one's practices for all members of the community. Based on their findings, they highlight the 'we-narrative' that underpins a socially sustainable culture of participation. In this kind of operational culture, the sensitive presence of all participants is important. Weckström et al. emphasise that the necessary sensitive presence is not self-evident and needs to be developed and nurtured in practice. Creative activities in a group and shared arts experiences offer possibilities for developing a sense of togetherness and we-narrative.

Developing a we-narrative, equity and dialogic relationships among children and the adults working with them may also be an important aim of professional arts practice beyond the education field. For example, a study by Cedar et al. (2022) focused on child drama therapy in a primary school context and pointed out the need to approach children as active agents and experts in their therapy. These researchers point out the absence of knowledge of children's views related to drama therapy. This may be familiar also in terms of early childhood education: do we see children as competent co-creators and co-artists? And if so, how can this be reflected in our practice? Also drawing from human/child rights, Weckström et al. (2022) highlight jointly constructed, long-lasting narrative play as an approach to achieving pedagogical objectives. In their research, the process of narrative play was co-constructed by children and educators in all its phases from planning to evaluation. In this project, the story-crafting method was utilised (see Karlsson, 2013; also Chapter 7 in this book); however, the importance of narrative playfulness and the importance of co-created projects applies to all forms of creative group activities in early childhood education.

Reflecting on the research findings above encourages us to study our own context and practice in a new light. Developing a caring- and compassion-infused operational culture calls for education that is embedded in fostering imagination, creativity and we-culture. It also has the potential to support the construction of sustainability-oriented values and lifestyles. Creating an environment and pedagogical climate that fosters a collective we-narrative and co-creation may require changes in the values, structures of practice, working culture and professional narrative. It is important to depict the obstacles that might be met on our way towards a co-constructed creative learning environment where pedagogical objectives are set, worked on, achieved and evaluated together.

PROFESSIONAL KNOWLEDGE AND NARRATIVE

How we interpret our daily experiences at work, and what solutions we create in our everyday practice, are rooted in how we view our profession and ourselves as practitioners. This can be referred to as our professional *narrative: 'Narrative identity is a person's internalised and evolving life story, integrating the reconstructed past and imagined future to provide life with some degree of unity and purpose'* (McAdams & McLeigh, 2013, p. 233). Our narrative is interconnected with the knowledge we use and form. Together these construct the professional landscape – a continuous evolving process of narrative and knowledge (see Connelly & Clandinin, 1995; Huhtinen-Hildén, 2012; also Huhtinen-Hildén & Pitt, 2018). With the metaphor of a landscape, it is easy to capture that discovering a new horizon, its emerging new possibilities and experiences change the landscape. Viewing professionalism as a continuous process is not a failure to rethink pedagogical values or reconstruct pedagogical approaches. Quite the opposite: professional thinking and practice need to be responsive and proactive in the current circumstances outlined at the start of this chapter. I suggest also approaching professional narrative as a situated and co-constructed story evolving in the context of our community, culture and society (see McAdams & McLeigh, 2013; McLean et al., 2007). Narrative is often used to refer to a verbal story, but we also share stories of ourselves – personally and professionally – with our creative narratives: at work, we decorate our classrooms and design our practice utilising creative thinking, or at home arrange flowers on the dinner table, select music dear to us for listening together or create paintings for others to see. These are also narratives conveying our life stories. Creative activities hold this potential for reflecting, evolving and sharing our life narratives (see e.g. Huhtinen-Hildén & Isola, 2019a). This explains the importance of experiential learning and reflection in continuous professional learning. Our theoretical knowledge needs to be intertwined with our experiences. Our emotional and creative capacities are important features of our professional selves and therefore should be explored and nurtured.

NAVIGATING CREATIVE PRACTICE

As this chapter, and others in the book have explored, experiences of shared creative activities may advance well-being, but positive, inclusive experiences do not emerge automatically; rather, they need to be carefully facilitated and supported. Creative activities for groups of people, including children, form a pedagogical challenge: to facilitate group activities one needs many possible plans – ways to navigate group situations in dialogue in order to create a safe environment for learning and experiencing for all participants. This is a creative pedagogical journey: to support the unique being of each participant is not an easy task. In Chapter 3 of this book, the delicate elements of shared creative activities are explored using a model of creative group activities as a lens (Huhtinen-Hildén & Isola, 2019b). This model shows that the adult has the biggest responsibility in the journey, to create a safe and meaningful environment for the group experience. At the same time, each participant contributes and connects to the aims and means of the journey. The journey is an adventure, where various options emerge. Gibson (1979, pp. 127–137) named these possibilities for action as affordances. Each choice for acting and being leads to a different turn in the journey. The most important element in this creative, artistic collaboration is the company. The creative activities offer an environment, but the group that is on the journey together makes the difference. Therefore, one cannot emphasise enough the importance of pedagogical sensitivity (Van Manen, 1991, 2008; Huhtinen-Hildén, 2012). Our pedagogical thinking and sensitivity are the essential tools and companions on the journey. In other words, the professional is facilitating the compassionate and inclusive community of practice to develop and flourish (Wenger, 1998).

Navigating in creative practice often happens non-verbally. For example, we communicate with our movements in dance activities, which in turn offer someone else an idea about how to move; or we may accept a dancing invitation to join in. The 'dialogue' is situated within a creative, playful and/or artistic narrative. Isaacs (1999, p. 45) explains the essence of dialogue being 'about exploring the nature of choice', whereas discussion may refer to making a decision. It is easy to understand why dialogue is a more fruitful underpinning for creativity than discussion. In pedagogical reality, in order to facilitate creative, dialogic interactions, one must have solid plans for how to create scaffolds for the group situation. But as important as planning is exercising pedagogical improvisation (see Donmoyer, 1983; Sawyer, 2011; see also Huhtinen-Hildén, 2017; Huhtinen-Hildén & Pitt, 2018) and pedagogical sensitivity, as these allow co-construction.

Facilitating creative group activities in early childhood settings may sometimes feel overwhelming: the excitement and joy burst out from children and the situation may become difficult to understand and handle. This is where I suggest we should free ourselves from unhelpful ideals of what it means to be a professional early years practitioner. We could explore our thinking by asking: is it helping us during those moments or is it adding to the pressure? Thinking differently creates affordances that lead to other kinds of actions. To unravel Isaacs' notions of dialogue in practice, we should explore the nature of choice in our own pedagogy as well as opening these explorations up to those we work with. As professionals, we are quite used to setting aims for learning: Instead, we could direct our energy towards the idea of viewing our tasks as educators in the light of opening possibilities for learning and experiencing (Huhtinen-Hildén, 2017; also Huhtinen-Hildén & Pitt, 2018). This helps us to focus on developing our pedagogical sensitivity, by asking: How could I think, act and be in order to create the environment for creative experiences, we-narratives and dialogue, and through these facilitate compassionate and inclusive cultures? This question turns our gaze towards the activity at hand and helps us to be present in the moment.

Taking a pedagogically sensitive approach allows us to focus on understanding the group and its dynamics (Huhtinen-Hildén, 2017), rather than approaching the group through a concept of group management. Thinking differently has an effect on affordances emerging for the entire community we work with. When working with children, the adults in the creative, collaborative interaction have more responsibility for the psychological safety of the situation and also more possibilities for affecting positioning within a group. Navigating within a creative interaction, one is constantly positioning oneself in relation to others as well as being positioned by others (van Langenhove & Harré, 1999, pp. 16–17). Navigation happens within non-verbal, creative actions as well as through spoken interaction. Navigating different possible positions as an adult calls for sensitivity. For example, it is necessary to find moments to deliberately position oneself as an adult to be in the 'audience' or 'assistance' tasks instead of also sometimes needed 'leading and giving instructions' positions within the creative activities. This gives active examples of interaction and varying tasks needed (Huhtinen-Hildén & Pitt, 2018, p. 50). Adults utilising various positions within group interactions also allows children to explore possibilities of positioning in creative activities, which strengthens the children's experience of their agency.

INTERCONNECTEDNESS OF PROFESSIONAL LANDSCAPE, PEDAGOGICAL PRACTICE AND FUTURE PROSPECTS

Above I have explored navigating creative practice, and have unravelled how the pedagogical thinking and choices are situated in living group interactions. These form a system that is linked to eco-social sustainability (see Keto & Foster, 2021). Figure 11.1 shows the connections between professional narratives, practice and advancing an eco-socially sustainable future in inclusive, creative, arts-infused early years practice. The interconnectedness of experiences of children, inclusive creative activities, the compassion-infused culture of early years settings and an eco-socially sustainable future can also be understood in the light of theories by Vygotsky et al. (1978) and Bronfenbrenner (1979/2009) (see Chapter 2 of this book,).

In Figure 11.1, the interconnected elements of the early years education context are shown as a process: The professional landscape creates the dimensions in which the journey of pedagogical, dialogic practice takes place. Pedagogically sensitive knowledge and narrative enable dialogic practice and open up possibilities for learning and experiencing inclusion and agency. This will facilitate the development of eco-socially sustainable values and cultures.

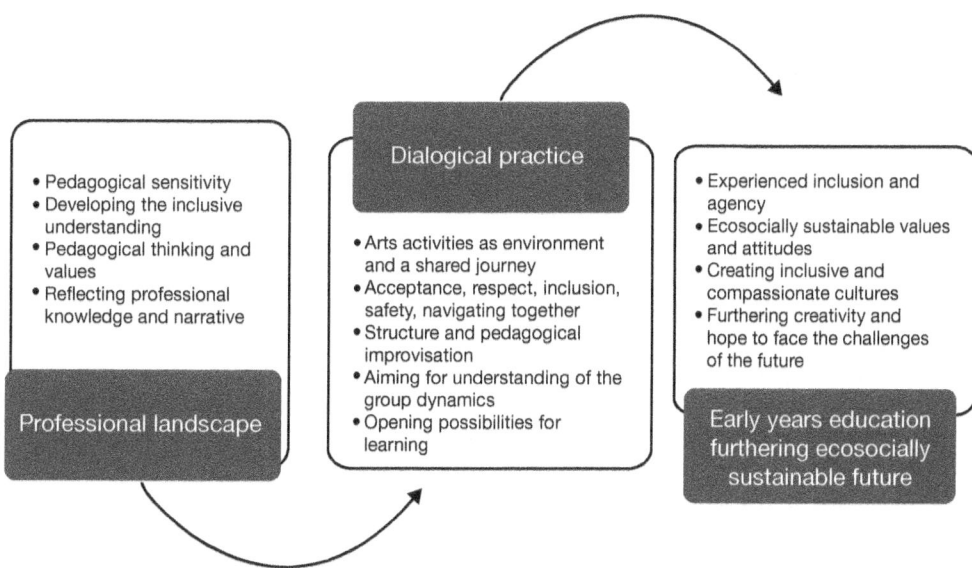

Figure 11.1 Interconnectedness of the professional narrative, practice and advancing eco-socially sustainable future in inclusive, creativity and arts-infused early years practice

To sum up, inclusive and pedagogically sensitive arts education can form an environment to enhance the experience of inclusion, eco-socially sustainable values and future hope (see Keto & Foster, 2021). Shared arts activities, experiences that connect ourselves with emotions and facilitate exploring them, may allow emotions and experiences to open up towards empathy, compassion and inclusive understanding. This applies to early years practitioners as well as children. Experiencing respect, sharing and dialogue in interaction, and directing our agency towards creating compassion-infused communities and operational cultures creates eco-social sustainability. Experiences of being connected with each other and the planet advance the development of eco-social ways of life (Keto & Foster, 2021).

REFLECTIVE WORKSHOP ACTIVITIES

The final part of this chapter is dedicated to practitioners' experiences and reflections. Here you can find activities that can be explored alone, shared with a colleague or used at the beginning of a team meeting. The focus is on discovering the pathways in our professional landscapes, reflecting on our professional narratives, maybe finding completely new terrains, enjoying sharing these notions with your peers and learning from their experiences. Sharing experiences of walking along pathways in our professional landscape also creates a we-culture amongst early years practitioners. Our pedagogical thinking is the professional tool that we utilise and which plays a crucial role in developing a caring and compassion-infused operational culture in early years settings. Let's encourage each other to walk along these creative pathways and maybe together find horizons not yet explored!

Looking at a Picture

This activity can be done individually or in a group.

Choose a picture (postcard, painting etc.) and look at it in a quiet space.

It is important that you do not intentionally direct your thoughts, but rather note where your mind takes you.

Ask yourself: 'When I look at this picture,

- How does it feel in my body?
- What thoughts come to my mind?
- Does that raise images or memories?
- Do I hear sounds?'

After this activity, take a moment to note your mood or experience and the possible changes in them before and after the activity.

If this activity is used in a group situation, the participants can also prepare for it by bringing (selecting) a picture for the group to look at. The group can choose to look at each other's favourite scenery, art paintings or photos taken from a detail noticed on one's way to work in the morning.

Reflect on your experience of the picture(s) and share your impressions with your peers. It is vital that you concentrate on the experiential level first, even if for example the activity brings to your mind ideas about how to apply it with a group of children!

After the discussion you can also revisit the model for creative group activities in Chapter 3 and reflect how the phases of creative group processes shown in the model may be applicable to this activity.

Listening to Music

This activity can be done individually or in a group.

Listen to the selected piece of music in a quiet space and in a comfortable position. In this activity, the piece of music should be instrumental because the lyrics may direct our imagination towards the topic of the verbal text (there is nothing wrong with listening to songs, but it is a different activity). As in previous activity, it is important that you do not intentionally direct your thoughts, but rather note where your mind takes you.

Ask yourself: 'When I listen to the music,

- How does it feel in my body?
- What thoughts come to my mind?
- Does that raise memories?
- Do see colours, images or pictures?'

After this activity, take a moment to reflect the mood and your bodily or emotional sensations and the possible changes in them before and after the activity.

If the participants each bring a piece of music for the group to listen to, it is important to take a moment to 'receive this gift'. What role does this piece of music play in the life of a colleague, and why have they selected this for others to listen to?

As with the previous activity, reflect on your experiences of listening and share your impressions with your peers. It is vital that you concentrate on the experiential level first, even if for example the activity brings your mind ideas how to apply it with the group of children! Revisit the model for creative group activities in Chapter 3 and reflect, based on the shared experiences in this situation.

Forming of a Group

For us as adults, experiential learning is as important as it is for children, but sometimes more difficult. We often intellectually analyse rather than focus on sensory, embodied or imaginative aspects of an experience. This activity may offer a laboratory to explore this type of adult response.

The group stands and passes messages in a circle. Once a message is passed forward, each messenger can sit down.

1 Whispering messages
   ○ The starter whispers two random words to the person on the right.
   ○ This person passes on two words that came to their mind from the received ones.
   ○ The next person continues likewise, whispering words that come to mind from the received ones.
2 Sound messages
   ○ The starter sends a sound made with one's mouth, hands, feet etc. in the circle.
   ○ The second person changes this sound slightly, when passing it further.
   The sound travels around the circle and forms a continuous, modifying soundscape, not stopping on its way.
3 Passing on acceptance
   ○ In this round, the group passes on acceptance as a facial expression such as smile, gaze etc.
   ○ If the group members are familiar with each other and they feel comfortable with it, it is also possible to send a gentle touch on the shoulder or arm.

Reflect on your experiences of these activities with your colleagues. For professionals, this may be a very fruitful way to discuss how the same activity can raise different feelings for each of us.

Being Present Through Body-Listening

As adults, we quite often concentrate on our cognitive side at the cost of the emotional one. This also applies to neglecting our bodily experiences. The example explained in Chapter 5 (p. 73) is also a potential one for starting the team meeting or parents'/family gathering. Listening to music and focusing on the question: What *part of you would like to move?* connects us with ourselves as creative, emotional, bodily beings. Reflecting these experiences may facilitate discussions related to feeling safe, being seen and heard, acceptance and inclusion.

Your Professional Horizons

Draw an outline of a landscape scene you like.

- Think about five important landmarks that tell about your professional thinking (values, approaches in your practice, guiding thoughts, metaphors etc.). Write these words in or near the scene.
- What are the other elements, pathways, hidden treasures in your landscape that you could include? Add these words also in the picture.
- Take a moment to look at the picture with your important words. What does it tell you? Share these reflections.

Draw a copy of the outline of the scene you started with,

- This is a picture about your professional horizons in five years' time. What would you like this scene to look like? What words would you like to add to it, make stronger, or take away? Draw/write as above.
- Take a moment to look at the picture with the words. What does it tell you? Share these reflections. (This activity is modified from Huhtinen-Hildén & Pitt, 2018, p. 197.)

Drawing Ourselves Beyond Reality

This activity invites us as adults to utilise artistic possibilities beyond the reality of our own lives. In the case study in Chapter 3, Tom used drawing to come to terms with his frustration with reality, which did not offer any possibilities for him to be taller and wiser than his dad. We could apply Tom's strategy to our everyday experiences and consider whether they could be eased or changed with the help of drawing as well.

1 Think of a difficult or uncomfortable encounter, situation or task in your week.
2 Make any kind of drawing inspired by thoughts and emotions related to this experience.
3 Now look at the drawing: What could you change in it? Shapes, colours, sizes of objects etc.
4 Make a new drawing or amend the previous one.
5 Look at your new drawing. How do you feel, when looking at it?
6 Reflect your emotions and thoughts in the beginning and now after looking at the second drawing. Has something changed in your feelings and thoughts, while changing the visual picture?
7 Add another layer: Find a sound or a piece of music that is soothing and calming for you.
8 Play this while looking at the picture.
9 How does this affect your feelings about the situation or task illustrated in the picture?

If you explored this in a group, discuss your experiences of this activity together.

OBSERVING CREATIVE GROUP ACTIVITIES

In order to deepen understanding of the group situations in our daily practice, it is sometimes useful to approach creative activities from an analytical point of view. A tool for systematic observation was developed for this purpose and can be found through the website offered in the references (Huhtinen-Hildén & Isola, 2021). The reason why it is useful for all practitioners to study group situations is that experiences of inclusion appear gradually. In the beginning, the changes may be very small, almost invisible – just a look or subtle change in facial expression. In order to support these fragile beginnings, one needs to be aware of them: the model for systematic observation may help to develop our abilities to perceive small changes in human interaction (Huhtinen-Hildén & Isola, 2021).

- Read the article introducing the observation model.
- Observe and document a group situation following the instructions.
- Share this with your colleagues and discuss your impressions.

CONCLUSION

This chapter has discussed early childhood practitioners' professional landscapes: the important landmarks, underpinning values and possible horizons. The focus has been on reflecting on the underpinnings of pedagogical practice, which is vital for our continuous professional development. Early childhood pedagogy has wide possibilities for developing the caring and compassion-infused communities that are essential for the future. Advancing trust, empathy, compassion and equity in increasingly diverse communities creates an inclusive approach in early years settings and beyond.

The chapter has explored creativity and imagination as tools for professional reflection on early childhood pedagogy, because education that fosters imagination, creativity and compassion-infused interactions can support the construction of sustainability-oriented values and lifestyles – in other words sustainable well-being. This chapter has also invited practitioners to embark on a reflective journey through creative activities shared with colleagues. This is a fruitful way to learn and develop shared understanding and practice in early years settings. Our pedagogical thinking is the professional tool that we utilise in our daily practice, our companion in developing creative dialogues and activities in early years contexts. The latter part of the chapter has highlighted the importance of continuous professional learning and reflection on our professional narrative and provided creative activities that can be used for this important process.

REFERENCES

Bronfenbrenner, U. (1979/2009). *The ecology of human development: Experiments by nature and design.* Harvard University Press.

Cedar, L., Coleman, A., Haythorne, D., Jones, P., Mercieca, D., & Ramsden, E. (2022). Child agency and therapy in primary school. *Education 3-13, 50*(4), 452–470. https://doi.org/10.1080/03004279.2022.2052231

Connelly, F. M., & Clandinin, D. J. (1995). Teachers' professional knowledge landscapes: Secret, sacred, and cover stories. In D. J. Clandinin & F. M. Connelly (Eds.), *Teachers' professional knowledge landscapes* (pp. 3–15). Teachers College Press.

Donmoyer, R. (1983). Pedagogical improvisation. *Educational Leadership, 40*, 39–43.

Gibson, J. (1986/1979). *The ecological approach to visual perception.* Laurence Erlbaum Associates.

Huhtinen-Hildén, L., & Isola, A.-M. (2019a). Reconstructing life narratives through creativity in social work. *Cogent Social Sciences, 5*(1). https://doi.org/10.1080/23311886.2019.1606974

Huhtinen-Hildén, L. (2017). Elävänä hetkessä. Suunnitelmallisuus ja pedagoginen improvisointi. Teoksessa. In A. Lindeberg-Piiroinen & I. Ruokonen (toim.) (Eds.), *Musiikki varhaiskasvatuksessa -käsikirja* (pp. 389–411). Classicus.

Huhtinen-Hildén, L. (2012). *Kohti sensitiivistä musiikin opettamista. Ammattitaidon ja opettajuuden rakentumisen polkuja.* Jyväskylä studies in humanities 180. Jyväskylän Yliopisto.

Huhtinen-Hildén, L., & Isola, A.-M. (2019b). *Luova ryhmätoiminta lisää hyvinvointia.* Data Brief. Finnish Institute for Health and Welfare. http://urn.fi/URN:ISBN:978-952-343-329-8

Huhtinen-Hildén, L., & Isola, A.-M. (2021). *From systematic observation to verifying impacts: Observation model for creative group activities.* Data Brief 49/2021. Finnish Institute for Health and Welfare. https://urn.fi/URN:ISBN:978-952-343-729-6

Huhtinen-Hildén, L., & Pitt, J. (2018). Taking a learner-centred approach to music education. In *Pedagogical pathways.* Routledge.

Isaacs, W. (1999). *Dialogue and the art of thinking together.* Currency.

Karlsson, L. (2013). Storycrafting method–to share, participate, tell and listen in practice and research. *European Journal of Social & Behavioural Sciences, 6*(3), 1109–1117.

Kaufman, J. C., & Glăveanu, V. (2022). Positive creativity in a negative world. *Education Sciences, 12*(3), 193. https://doi.org/10.3390/educsci12030193

Keto, S., & Foster, R. (2021). Ecosocialization–an ecological turn in the process of socialization. *International Studies in Sociology of Education, 30*(1–2), 34–52. https://doi.org/10.1080/09620214.2020.1854826

McAdams, D., & McLeigh, K. (2013). Narrative identity. *Current Directions in Psychological Science, 22*(3), 233–239. https://doi.org/10.1177/0963721413475622

McLean, K. C., Pasupathi, M., & Pals, J. L. (2007). Selves creating stories creating selves: A process model of self-development. *Personality and Social Psychology Review, 11*, 262–278.

Sawyer, R. K. (2011). What makes good teachers great? The artful balance of structure and improvisation. In R. K. Sawyer (Ed.), *Structure and improvisation in creative teaching* (pp. 1–24). Cambridge University Press.

Smith, T. (2021). Music education for surviving and thriving: Cultivating children's wonder, senses, emotional, wellbeing, and wild nature as a means to discover and fulfill their life's purpose. *Frontiers in Education, 6*(648799). https://doi.org/10.3389/feduc.2021.648799

van Langenhove, L., & Harré, R. (1999). Introducing positioning theory. In R. Harré & L. van Langenhove (Eds.), *Positioning theory. Moral contexts of intentional action* (pp. 14–31). Blackwell.

Van Manen, M. (1991). *The tact of teaching: The meaning of pedagogical thoughtfulness.* State University of New York Press.

Van Manen, M. (2008). Pedagogical sensitivity and teachers practical knowing-in- action. *Peking University Education Review, 1*(1), 1–23.

Vygotsky, L. S., Cole, M., John-Steiner, V., Scribner, S., & Souberman, E. (1978). *Mind in society: Development of higher psychological processes.* Harvard University Press.

Weckström, E., Lastikka, A.-L., & Havu-Nuutinen, S. (2022). Constructing a socially sustainable culture of participation for caring and inclusive ECEC. *Sustainability, 14,* 3945. https://doi.org/10.3390/su14073945

Wenger, E. (1998). *Communities of practice: Learning, meaning, and identity.* Cambridge University Press.

12

CONNECTING THE THREADS: THE INCLUSIVE POTENTIAL OF THE ARTS

Amanda Niland, Laura Huhtinen-Hildén and Kathy Cologon

--- Chapter objectives ---

This chapter introduces you to these key ideas:

- Revisiting the inclusion potential of each art form
- The centrality of relationships
- Fostering opportunities for manifesting agency through inclusive arts pedagogy
- Inclusive arts in an anti-bias curriculum
- Creating safe spaces for and with the arts

INTRODUCTION

We are all different, but we share a common humanity; as we have explored throughout this book, inclusion is based on the need to value that shared humanity, while also valuing our differences. Inclusion is therefore not a choice but a right of all children, enshrined in international and national laws, and in curricula in many nations, from early years onwards (e.g. AGDE, 2022; Ministry of Education, 2017). Creativity and artistic expression are also central to our shared humanity, making them central to early years' education and care. In this chapter, we draw on the discussions and explorations in previous chapters to explore some practical strategies for fostering inclusion through arts activities. As in previous chapters, some case studies are from our research or teaching experience, as indicated by citations. Others are creative adaptations inspired by our experiences within early years of practice over our careers.

FOSTERING INCLUSION THROUGH ARTS ACTIVITIES

While there are many systemic barriers to the realisation of inclusion and inclusive education, in practice, inclusion often occurs in simple and everyday actions. At the core of enacting inclusion is a strong commitment to making everyone welcome and ensuring that each person can participate meaningfully in the life of their early years' community in ways that value everyone just as they are and foster a sense of belonging for all. The question of how to work towards these commitments can be summed up in this way: While acknowledging and nurturing the bonds of our shared humanity, how can we at the same time respectfully acknowledge, value and respond to difference? Throughout this book, our focus has been on addressing that question with the arts as central to our exploration. As we have brought together the thoughts, ideas, research and experience of others, and shared our own research and experiences in the many case studies, we have discussed and advocated for the importance of processes of reflection as critical to building inclusive pedagogy. Throughout the book, we have provided suggestions and prompts that can be used by early years' practitioners to build reflection and critical thinking into their practice as they work towards developing or extending inclusive arts pedagogy. The previous chapter's exploration of the importance of our professional narrative also includes art activities designed for early years' practitioners to use as tools for professional reflection. Thus, we have sought to show the possibilities that creativity and the arts can open up not only for children but also for practitioners as they reflect on how to honour that common humanity while also respectfully embracing everyone's diverse ways of being and doing.

THE THREADS OF ART AND CREATIVITY

As every person, setting and community is different, there are a myriad of possible pathways to bringing about inclusion in early years' settings. Mapping those pathways or creating the weaving of inclusive early years' education and care cannot be prescribed with any sort of template or recipe. However, the information and ideas in books such as this one can be used to facilitate the development of inclusive approaches to practice in individual settings. In Part Two of the book, we explored the various roles that arts activities and experiences can play in fostering inclusion through the special qualities of the individual art forms. We discussed the potential of each for building connections and relationships, and their value as resources for learning and development. Each art form offers children diverse possibilities to express their thoughts, feelings and creative ideas, and provides important ways for us to listen to, and hear, the voices and perspectives of children. Recalling Part Two, we reflect on some of the unique aspects of each art form below.

Music can be experienced through many senses, and whether participants are hearing, feeling or making it, music may have an effect on one's mood and emotions. Music can foster inter-actions and moments of connection. Similarly, dance, which is often a child's way of responding to music, is a meaningful physical and sensory experience. Dancing and moving together with others, with direct physical contact or by synchronising movement with others, also creates moments of connection. Thus, music and dance can be powerful in fostering a sense of belonging.

Stepping outside of one's usual self into the role of another person or character through drama may be experienced through the body, similarly to music and dance. Becoming someone or something else can also be embodied in other ways, such as through puppets, toys or other items and the use of language, whether spoken, gestured or signed. Drama and puppetry often engage the imagination, inviting us to enter imaginary worlds and create imagined characters. Doing these things with others involves interactions and shared creative thinking, opening possibilities for building relationships in new ways. Stepping into the metaphorical shoes of others encourages empathy, making these experiences valuable for fostering understanding of, and respect for diverse ways of being and doing.

Books and stories also provide ways to enter other worlds and lives and encounter others' feelings and perspectives, for example, through the artistic creativity of authors and illustrators. When children themselves are the storytellers, they can share their thoughts and feelings about their lives and create imagined worlds through their storying. Children tell stories in a variety of playful ways, using spoken and non-spoken languages – speech, gesture, movement, drama, puppetry, mark-making and more. Current digital technology and the internet have enabled the creation and sharing of stories across distance and time. Open-ended apps that are accessible to children can allow these possibilities also and can be supported by assistive technology to enable every child to participate.

The visual arts have rich potential for children as ways to explore, create, wonder at their surroundings, and express their thoughts, feelings and perspectives on the world. In Chapter 9, there are examples of how the visual arts can provide meaningful ways for young children to connect with, and build understanding of diverse cultures.

Each of the art forms and every art activity can be thought of as the rich variety of different coloured and textured threads that together comprise the woven fabric of an early years' setting. The art of weaving these threads together involves a range of tools and techniques, which are discussed in the sections below. Any weaving also requires a frame – a loom or similar support structure. The principles of Universal Design for Learning, discussed in Chapter 10, can provide that frame. As with any artwork, time to act and time to step back, think and reflect are essential parts of the creative process. Often this reflection leads to new thoughts and creative ideas, and the need to adjust the techniques, tools and materials along the way. So it is with the journey of developing early years' pedagogy.

RELATIONSHIPS

The foundational threads in a woven artwork, in this case the first steps on any pathway towards inclusion, are the establishment of responsive, respectful, trusting relationships between early years' practitioners and children, and between children themselves. This involves being open, spending time, getting to know each other and valuing each other just as we are. Arts activities are invaluable for this.

The aim of an inclusive early years' setting is to ensure every child will belong and feel a sense of belonging. This requires building strong and trusting relationships with each child and their family. Arts activities can be at the heart of the processes involved in working towards a universal experience of belonging for everyone in an early years' community. Children's engagement with the arts can be infused throughout the day, from entry in the morning to going home in the afternoon or evening. Each child can for example be welcomed with a favourite song or story, making the transition between home, travel and the early years' setting happen through the metaphorical 'lap' of music and story. If a child's first language is not the dominant language of the community, then learning and incorporating words of welcome from the languages of each community member can be a valuable inclusive strategy. In the same way as language, respecting the different ways of communicating and showing equal valuing of diverse communication methods is essential.

Marco is three years old, small for his age, and full of energy. He is very affectionate and communicates through smiles, hugs and touching. He loves to sing and his current favourite song is 'Baa, baa black sheep'. He is learning to communicate through Key Word Signs and visual choice boards, so he brings a small folder of visuals, organised by pages into categories such as favourite songs, toys and food. This has been set up by his family, with guidance from his speech and language therapist. On arrival at the early years setting, he thrusts the folder towards educator Marie, who opens it at the song page. Marco grabs the sheep visual (for 'Baa, baa black sheep') and holds it up with a huge smile. Marie smiles, signs 'sing' with one hand, and begins to sing... the wrong song. Marco frowns and shakes his head vehemently. 'Not that song?' says Amanda, also signing 'no'. She starts a new song.... also the wrong one. Marco frowns, then smiles, entering into the joke. The game continues with one more wrong song, and finally the right song. Marco bounces up and down, smiling, and signs 'more' with his hand. 'Baa, baa black sheep' is sung several more times. As a few more children arrive for the day,

> Amanda brings them into the impromptu song circle, and together they explore some more of Marco's favourite songs from his folder of visuals, playing the 'wrong song, right song' game with much laughter (Amanda, anecdotal observation).

The case study above is an example of how simple inclusive actions can sometimes be – sharing songs, using multimodal communication, and laughing together. The relationship-building that the educators had done with Marco and his family helped Amanda to develop the inclusive pedagogy of this early years' setting. She used music as inclusion-in-action, supporting Marco's sense of belonging while also enriching the lives and learning of all the children. This was facilitated through using a small folder with cardboard pages and stick-on pictures symbolising popular nursery songs, the knowledge of one Key Word Sign, and some conversations and collaborations with Marco's family to learn about his favourite songs and their approach to using the communication folder and signs (developed by a speech and language professional working with Marco's family). The children developed their literacy skills by learning to read and expressions of preferences through visual tools and signs were valued, recognised, encouraged and responded to. The children were supported to develop their understanding of diverse ways of communicating. Over time, several children built friendships with Marco by using the visuals folder and other visuals in the environment to play with him throughout the day. Significantly, the singing interactions helped to establish feelings of belonging for Marco and all the children right from the moment they arrived at the setting.

Below is a case study, in which the visual arts are used with the aim of making children feel welcomed at the start of the day, and supporting them in getting to know each other. The resources used are responsive to the linguistic backgrounds and preferences of every child.

> At the early learning centre, next to the table where parents sign their children in and out each day, there is an easel and a long, low table with a large paper roll holder on the end. On the table there are tubs of coloured crayons and pencils and a basket containing each child's photo and name on individual, laminated cards. The children's names are printed in English, in braille, and in their first language if it uses different written symbols (such as Thai, Arabic or Mandarin). A fresh length of paper from the roll stretches most of the way along the table, anchored underneath by double-sided tape. On the nearby easel there are Velcro dots so that each child can find their photo/name card and attach it to the easel to show that they have arrived. The children and their adult spend a moment or two at the easel, with the children deciding where to place their card, and often looking at all the photos to see who is there. If they choose to, and many do, they can do some mark-making on the long paper, on which an educator has also written the day and the date. Sometimes children and their adult spend a few moments together working on the paper and looking at what others have done. This paper remains out until the space is needed for other things later in the day, and the easel remains out all day, so that children can return their photo to the basket when they go home.

As the two case studies above show, interactions at the start of each day in an early years' setting may have an important role to play in relationship-building. However secure, trusting, positive relationships depend on interactions throughout the day. Each child's sense of belonging is affected not only by their own interactions but also by their observations of other interactions in the early years' settings. Early year practitioners can enact and show their respect for, and responsiveness to diverse ways of being and doing through their interactions with every child, acting as role models for inclusivity.

To think about...

We all find some people easier to interact with and understand than others in our lives. Take a moment to identify some people close to you that you find easier to interact with, as well as some you find more demanding to be with:

- What do you notice?
- Are these people different/similar to you and in what aspects?

COMMUNICATING WITH CHILDREN AND FAMILIES

We communicate with each other in many ways, both formal and informal, verbal and non-verbal, spoken, written and visual. In early years' settings, communication happens between children, practitioners and families. Communication both about and through arts activities can help to develop a warm and respectful community and support children and their family members to feel welcomed and valued in the early years' setting. The sharing of stories of children's art-making or explorations at home, in the community and in the early years' setting is a way to celebrate children's creativity, and through that, honour their ways of being and doing. Arts activities such as the sign-in and mark-making table in the case study above can provide moments for these kinds of spontaneous communication between practitioners, family members and children.

Using children's preferred modes of communication with each child as they arrive and through the day, as well as using a variety of modes regardless of whether they are used by anyone currently attending the setting or not, provides opportunities for all children to develop their communication skills in multiple modes, as part of early literacy learning. Becoming confident in multiple modes of communication can also facilitate connections between peers and peer-to-peer learning, positioning children as experts in a variety of forms of communication. The case study below is an example of this.

Several educators at the early years centre have been learning Deaf Culture and Auslan (Australian Sign Language) from a Deaf Auslan teacher and have been sharing their learning with colleagues and with the older children at the centre. The children all have a small vocabulary of signs, and a few are so keen that they keep asking to learn more and more signs. They have also begun to develop their own signs and have asked to use the Centre's camera to make short instructional videos, similar to those in the Auslan online dictionary their educators have shown them on the iPad. One day while drawing together and telling an elaborate spoken story about the adventures unfolding on their page, Li Ying and Aisha asked if they could make a video of their story. Their drawing was placed on an easel and the two children stood on either side. Li Ying spoke and Aisha signed the story for the video, translating Li Ying's words in a mixture of Auslan, mime gestures and their own visual representations.

Realising the potential of the arts as facilitators of inclusive communication involves not just communication through the arts, in the ways that have been explored in earlier chapters, but also communication with children about their art-making. Practitioners' interactions with children during their creative processes, and their responses to the art-making children may choose to share, can influence how the children feel about their work and themselves. Below are some examples of communication moments and possible ways of responding that are aimed at showing our respect and valuing of the children as artists (or musicians, dancers, storytellers and so on). These types of adult responses also aim to position children as experts, while letting them know that the adults are there to support them if the child wishes.

- During visual arts play – narrate and converse in ways that show you are attending and interested in what they are doing - 'I can see you're using green......' or 'Tell me about this ....'
- Narrate or provide encouraging comments about processes or outcomes that show multi-sensory ways of attending/noticing – 'That feels smooth' or 'Can we listen to what these sound like if we tap them?'
- Where you can see possibilities to support children to achieve something they seem to be aiming for – 'I wonder if you might like to try ...?' or 'I wonder what would happen if ....?'. This could apply to visual arts, music, dance or dramatic play.
- Look for opportunities to offer possible help through thoughtful provisioning of the environment. For example, place some helpful tools or supplementary materials where the child can see/hear/grasp them if they wish; or mirror the children's music-making or movements to music.
- Where other children are nearby, draw them into your noticing and communication – 'I can see/hear.... in the magic garden Carlo is making here; I wonder what you can see/hear?' This can help children get to know each other's particular interests and skills, celebrate peers' processes, and foster opportunities for peer-to-peer learning.

ACCESSIBLE MATERIALS AND RESOURCES FOR INCLUSIVE ARTS

Ensuring that materials and resources are accessible and interesting for every child comes from pedagogical thinking and sensitivity that arises from professional expertise and the development of close relationships between practitioners and children in an early years' setting. When we get to know children and families, we learn about their interests, preferences, backgrounds, abilities and needs, and can use this knowledge to inform our pedagogical decision-making. The principles of Universal Design for Learning may assist in supporting this aspect of inclusion (see Chapter 10). Providing materials and resources that are accessible and engaging for all children also supports them in using their agency – in particular the 'possibility to do something' that is mentioned in Chapter 1 of this book, and below.

Beyond accessibility, practitioners' relationships with children also enable them to provide materials and resources for the arts that are reflective of, and responsive to, children's diverse identities. In Chapter 8, we explored the importance of positive representations of all our diversities in picture books and introduced the idea that children may experience picture books as 'mirrors', 'windows' or 'sliding doors' (Bishop, 1990). Spending time exploring picture books together can be a wonderful way to get to know and build relationships with children. A book in which children can identify with an aspect of themselves and their life – a 'mirror' for them – might also be a window or sliding door for an early years' practitioner to enter the child's world and through this foster a secure and trusting relationship. In Chapter 8, we shared tips to use for auditing your early childhood book collections and to guide you in building a library of books that are inclusive of diverse life contexts and ways of being. The sharing of books that are meaningful to particular children with other children, through shared reading in groups, can contribute to showing that each child's interests are valued, and may lead to connections between children – adding more threads in the weaving of inclusion in an early years' setting. The use of the framework or loom of Universal Design for Learning will also be part of this book sharing.

The case study below is inspired by the creative approach of one early years' practitioner who worked with young children to develop more inclusive approaches to books and stories in his setting.

When Sami started his first job as a newly qualified early childhood teacher, he was especially keen to share his passion for children's literature with children. However, he quickly discovered that the strategies he used for shared read-alouds with an early years class (partly inspired by memories of his own early schooling) were not successful in engaging the interest of many children in the group. As Sami was eager to build positive relationships with every child, he observed the children carefully during the group reading sessions, documented his observations with a critical reflection lens, and discussed the situation with his more experienced colleagues. "Is it my reading style? Is it the books I'm choosing?" he asked them. One educator suggested that he just needed to be stricter about 'proper' behaviour during 'story time'. "But I want the children to love books and being read to," he countered. Another colleague encouraged Sami to research Universal Design for Learning. This was an inspiring revelation for him. A few weeks later, the approach to shared reading in Sami's early years setting was transformed.

Firstly, Sami enlisted the children's and families' help to revitalise the 'reading corner'. He asked them to tell him about or bring in favourite books and stories from home, so that he could learn more about the children's interests and preferences. Then he added some cosy floor cushions, a small sofa, some sheer fabrics and fairy lights suspended from the ceiling to the area, and rearranged the nearby furniture slightly to make the reading area more of a quiet area that felt separate from the busier play areas. Next, Sami chose books from the centre's collection that related to children's preferences, backgrounds and ways of being, and displayed them in a neat, accessible way. He also obtained funding to purchase more books and was able to add some multilingual and braille books to the setting's collection. Finally, Sami added some small baskets containing puppets and other items related to the books on display

Sami began to regularly sit in the reading corner, to read with children individually or in small groups, adding in use of the puppets or related items, and communicating with the children about the books. Sami also worked on including gesture, mime, Auslan signs and sound effects in his 'reading', and gave the children 'spaces' to join in with him. Children were free to come and go, and over the weeks and months, the reading corner became more and more popular - some children just spent time there alone browsing the books, others came to listen to read-alouds, and some 'read' to their friends or used the puppets and toys to create their own versions of the stories. Through the time spent with the children, interacting responsively with them, Sami built close, trusting relationships with the children, and was able to use these to foster a sense of belonging.

The approach Sami used to make books and stories more inclusive of, and accessible to, all children can be adapted to other aspects of environments, pedagogy and curriculum. To summarise, Sami:

- Observed children to learn about their ways of being and doing – their interests, preferences and relationships in the early years' setting
- Reached out to families to learn more about the children's lives outside the setting
- Asked self-reflective questions, focusing on 'What am I doing? Why and for whom? What could I do differently?' – seeking to understand and accept the children as they are and reflect on his own thoughts and actions, rather than seeing the children as the problem
- Learnt about Universal Design for Learning and used its principles in the provision of resources and his modes of interaction (representation), to allow children opportunities for multiple ways of engaging and expressing themselves
- Spent time interacting responsively with children, learning from and with them

EXPRESSING AND EXPLORING WHO WE ARE

When the aim of inclusion drives practice, then every art form can be facilitated in ways that invite meaningful participation by all children. Focusing on children's agency in our pedagogical thinking directs us to look for ways to create opportunities for children to experience, implement and evolve their agency. In the arts and the curriculum more broadly, materials, resources and means of communication can be developed that respond to the preferences and abilities of each child, allowing children to choose, decide and contribute, and to be creative in their own ways.

Agency, as explored in Chapter 1, is about making decisions and choices and taking action (Sairanen & Kumpulainen, 2014). Facilitating opportunities for children to implement their agency involves early years' educators in reflecting on both material and relational aspects of their pedagogy. Where environments and materials are responsive to children's physical, emotional, and sensory well-being, and their preferred ways of being and doing, then possibilities for experiencing and evolving agency are established. This material aspect, however, relies on educators' attunement and responsiveness to the children in their early years' setting – things which lie in the relationships that are foundational to the weaving of inclusion into early years' settings.

ANTI-BIAS ARTS PEDAGOGY AND PRACTICE

Educators engage children in learning that promotes confidence, creativity and enables active citizenship. They celebrate diversity with children and their families, and the opportunities diversity brings to know more about the world. (AGDE, 2022, p. 6)

This quote is part of the vision statement in the recently updated Australian early childhood curriculum, the Early Years Learning Framework (EYLF) version 2.0 (AGDE, 2022). It is significant that creativity is mentioned, as while creativity is part of children's playful approach to exploring and learning about their world, it can of course also be fostered through the arts. Important too are the acknowledgement of 'active citizenship', and the highlighting of the value of celebrating diversity. The inclusive vision of the EYLF, as expressed in this quote, can be supported by using the anti-bias goals as a guide to inclusive pedagogy. These goals, set out in Chapter 2 of this book, support a strong sense of identity for every child, an appreciation of the diversity of every member of the early years' community, recognition of unfairness when it arises and the need to towards socially just solutions for everyone.

CREATING SAFER SPACES

The role that arts can play in the creation of caring, safe, inclusive spaces in early years' settings has been highlighted in many chapters of this book. In Chapter 3, for example, we met Matti, the practitioner who used a richly varied collection of teddy bears to welcome a new group of children to the early years' setting. By celebrating the unique qualities and 'personalities' of each bear in creative play activities and routines, he aimed to help the children settle in by providing a model of inclusion aimed at building a welcoming culture and empowering all the children to feel safe to be themselves. Feeling safe is a fundamental human need (Maslow, 1943) and therefore advancing children's emotional well-being and sense of belonging should be the pedagogical top priority in early years' settings.

Pedagogical sensitivity is an essential companion in early years' practice (see Chapter 11). Being mindful of experiences that children carry with them, or that they encounter in their daily routines, requires acknowledging that experiences in any setting, including early years' education, can be problematic, difficult, even traumatic for some children. Traumatic experiences that affect the whole being may be caused by physical threats or violence, abuse, bullying and importantly in early years' settings, exclusion. Significantly, children from marginalised or minority backgrounds, including children and families experiencing disability, are more likely to have faced trauma in their lives than others (Shaw, 2023; Thomas-Skaf & Jenney, 2021). The key principles of trauma-informed practice, according to Cavanaugh (2016), are safety and consistency, positive interactions, culturally responsive practice and peer support, all within a strengths-based approach to pedagogy and practice. Similarly, the toolkit developed by the Scottish Government (NHS, 2021) outlines safety, trustworthiness, choice, collaboration and empowerment as key principles. Increasingly, the need to focus more explicitly on children's safety and well-being is being recognised in education (AGDE, 2022; Brogaard-Clausen et al., 2022; MoE, 2017).

Arts activities hold the potential for creating safer spaces in early years' settings. The sonic and kinaesthetic qualities of music, dance and visual art-making can be relaxing and calming, while the imaginative worlds of drama, storying and picture books provide spaces to explore feelings and difficult life experiences, and to express thoughts in multimodal ways. In earlier chapters, there are many examples of how the arts can provide opportunities for enacting such principles. We have explored the ways in which the arts allow children to connect with others in positive ways and to use their agency and power as dramatists, dancers, artists, musicians or storytellers. For example, in Chapter 3, we met Susie, whose mother soothed her upset with a special song, and Tom, who used drawing to express his frustration with his feelings of powerlessness. In Chapter 4, we met educator Cara, whose sensitive pedagogical approach gave Vili time and choices and elicited peer support so that he eventually felt safe to join in with the group for music time. In Chapter 7, there is a powerful example of Janie's creation of a story about her father who died in the 11 September 2001 terrorist attack in New York.

Arts activities and examples provide many possibilities for connecting with others, enjoying moments alone, shaping mood and exploring emotions. Using the arts in ways that are sensitive and responsive to children's emotions can shift our thinking away from simply reacting to what we might see as problematic behaviours and instead towards seeking to understand what children are experiencing, how they might be feeling, and how we can support their emotional well-being.

> **To think about...**
>
> - Take a moment to think about your daily practice, how have you used/could you use arts activities to create emotionally safer spaces for children?
> - How do the principles of trauma-informed practice resonate with you?

CONCLUSION

This chapter has revisited some of the 'big ideas' from throughout the book and drawn them together through some examples of inclusive arts practice in the case studies. These examples, inspired by our experience as early years' professionals and researchers, have shown how inclusive arts practices can be part of everyday life in early years' settings. They can help to build an environment where children feel and are actively welcomed, valued and safe to use their curiosity and creative capacities to play and flourish.

> **To think about...**
>
> - What will your next steps on your arts and inclusion journey be?
> - What listening, interacting, doing and reflecting might those steps involve?

REFERENCES

Australian Government Department of Education [AGDE] (2022). *Belonging, being and becoming: The early years learning framework for Australia (v 2.0)*. Commonwealth of Australia.

Bishop, R. S. (1990). Mirrors, windows, and sliding glass doors. *Perspectives, 6*(3), ix–xi.

Brogaard-Clausen, S., Guimaraes, S., Rubiano, C., & Tang, F. (2022). International perspectives on wellbeing and democratic living in early childhood curricula. *Early Years*, 1–15. https://doi.org/10.1080/09575146.2021.2010663

Cavanaugh, B. (2016). Trauma-informed classrooms and schools. *Beyond Behavior, 25*(2), 41–46.

Maslow, A. H. (1943). A theory of human motivation. *Psychological Review, 50*(4), 370–396.

Ministry of Education. (2017). *Te whāriki: He whāriki mātauranga mō ngā mokopuna o. Aotearoa early childhood curriculum*. https://www.education.govt.nz/assets/Documents/Early-Childhood/Te-Whariki-Early-Childhood-Curriculum-ENG-Web.pdf

NHS Scotland. (2021). *Trauma-informed practice: A toolkit for Scotland*. Scottish Government. https://www.gov.scot/publications/trauma-informed-practice-toolkit-scotland/Refstyled

Sairanen, H., & Kumpulainen, K. (2014). A visual narrative inquiry into children's sense of agency in preschool and first grade. *International Journal of Educational Psychology, 3*(2), 141–174.

Shaw, N. (2023). Social and emotional well-being in a turbulent world. In K. Cologne & Z. Mevawalla (Eds.), *Inclusive education in the early years: Right from the start* (2nd ed., pp. 307–327). Oxford University Press.

Thomas-Skaf, B. A., & Jenney, A. (2021). Bringing social justice into focus: 'Trauma-informed' work with children with disabilities. *Child Care in Practice, 27*(4), 316–332.

CONCLUSION TO THE BOOK

Amanda Niland

Working with young children as they travel along their paths of discovery and learning in the early years of life – respecting and valuing who they are now and who they may become – is arguably the most important work there is in the human world. We have written this book in the hope that it may support you in that work and open up many possibilities for developing inclusive practice. Inclusion is not something to be added into your early years programme; it is an overall approach – a way of developing a programme and curriculum and putting it into practice. It guides every aspect of practice and the thinking that underpins it.

For the purposes of this book, our focus has been on the specific aspects of early years practice that involve working directly with children in the planning and implementation of inclusive curriculum in and through creativity and the arts. We recognise that inclusion also encompasses broader aspects of management, leadership and policy, and these are important areas of focus within other books.

THE INCLUSIVE POTENTIAL OF THE ARTS

For this book, we chose to explore the journey of inclusion in the early years through the rich world of the creative arts because for all three of us, the arts have been central to our work as early years professionals and researchers, as well as to our own lives. In the uncertain times of the current world, the arts can offer children safe spaces to play, explore, create and express their ways of being. The arts also offer diverse ways to communicate, giving possibilities for all to be heard. Being open to take notice of and be responsive to those diverse perspectives fosters understanding of different ways of being. The arts can enable us to build connections with others through the opportunities they give for communicating in a range of modes; these connections help to foster a sense of belonging. The arts therefore provide unique and important possibilities for inclusion. Diversity is inherent in the arts, as our artistry is unique to each of us. Therefore, when the materials, resources and experiences of arts are made accessible for all, and attitudes that privilege narrow understandings of 'talent' are challenged and set aside, then the arts can become forms of inclusion-in-action in early years settings and beyond.

The aim of this book has been to show how arts activities can provide a framework for inclusive practice in early years settings. In each of the chapters, we have explored key aspects of inclusion and the various forms of arts. There are discussions of findings from research, guiding principles, case study examples, strategies for practice and questions for thinking about and discussing with colleagues.

EMBARKING ON THE JOURNEY OF INCLUSION

We offer you this book therefore as a 'map' to facilitate your inclusion journey; but it is a map that forms an outline waiting for you and the children in your early years setting to fill in the details of your routes and modes of 'travel'. The question of where to start naturally arises. Often in educational curriculum planning, starting with the setting of outcomes, objectives or goals is recommended. We suggest a different, more open-ended approach, one that recognises the importance of allowing time to build relationships and respond with sensitivity – essential building blocks for inclusion. Breaking your journey down into smaller steps or stages can be very valuable. You could think of these as 'signposts' on your inclusion map, or as a series of destinations along the way.

Decisions about the possible signposts or destinations will be underpinned of course by the principles that guide your practice, and that have been explored in this book – principles of inclusion, anti-bias and responsive pedagogy. Most of all, however, they will be informed by your observations of, and interactions with children and your understanding of their ways of being and doing, and their family and life backgrounds. And as every person and every early years setting is different, and creative artistry is unique to each person, so every route on an inclusion journey will be different. Reflection, including with colleagues, the children themselves and families, will also be part of your map-making processes, as you reach each of the signposts or destination points on your evolving map.

Below are some key questions that you can use as you begin to map out your inclusion journey.

- What do I/we want to achieve?
- Why is this important? How will working towards these achievements support progress in creating inclusion through the arts for these children in this setting?
- What strategies, resources, art forms and arts activities could we use?
- How will we know that we are making progress? What will progress look like?
- At what points might we pause and reflect, before embarking on the next stage of our inclusion journey?

We wish you all the very best on your journeys of inclusion, as you work to create caring and compassion-infused early years communities. We hope you find this book helpful as you bring creativity, imagination and the arts into your practice and support children to develop, learn and flourish together. While keeping the ultimate aim of inclusion in mind, we encourage you to consider the message of an ancient Chinese proverb – that every journey begins with just one step. And as all of us who work with young children know, each moment matters to them, and small steps can lead to huge differences.

Index